The Before and After Dinner Cookbook

The Before and After Dinner Cookbook

Charlotte McNamara &
Lenore Howell

Illustrations by James Marthai

New York *1977* Atheneum

For M A R I E and T O M and N E V I N

Library of Congress Cataloging in Publication Data

McNamara, Charlotte.
  The before and after dinner cookbook.

  Includes index.
  1. Cookery (Appetizers) 2. Snack foods.
I. Howell, Lenore, joint author. II. Title
TX740.M16 1977   641.8   77–5374
ISBN 0–689–10824–9

Copyright © 1977 by Charlotte McNamara and Lenore Howell
All rights reserved
Published simultaneously in Canada by
McClelland and Stewart Ltd.

Manufactured in the United States of America by
American Book–Stratford Press,
Saddle Brook, New Jersey
Designed by Kathleen Carey
First Edition.

Introduction

There are poles in eating, as in all aspects of life. At one end is the school of "stove to stomach to silence," or the eat-to-live group. We encourage the other—the "pan to palate to pleasure" approach, the sweet essence of dining. Byron said it well: "That all-softening, overpowering knell,/The tocsin of the soul—the dinner bell."

For the cook we see two major pleasures. The first lies in the action itself. The creative hours spent in composing with the infinite colors, aromas, textures, and flavors of foodstuffs can provide pure personal enjoyment for all the senses. But perhaps the greater reward for most of us lies in the appreciation, spoken or implied, of those who share what we have created. A favorite friend invariably falls into a satisfied snooze (stupor?) for a few moments after one of our dinners. It is a compliment, albeit not generally a socially recognized one! A sister, an excellent and happy cook, some years ago had to enforce a rule that her three impatient bite-sized gourmands not lift the first forkful until she was seated, lest they be ready for a second serving before her first taste. They have since become gourmets, of course.

To increase your pleasure in the kitchen, and the articulate appreciation of friends at your table, we present our collection of recipes.

Our purpose is to tantalize you with two new directions in eating.

First, many modern cooks have forgotten the first course. We hereby reintroduce it with emphasis, and have devoted half our book to this happy purpose. A leisurely meal separated into its appropriate parts is not only relaxing, but also encourages the lost art of conversation. Such a meal certainly gives the digestive processes a fairer chance, and does battle with the modern "eat-and-run" syndrome.

Second, we are bringing back the late-evening sharing of food, with special emphasis on the unusual or long-forgotten. These are not desserts; each is a substantial dish to provide a taste sensation with which to end the evening in the company of friends or family.

"Before Dinner" means first courses or appetizer courses, served before a main course. The entire world enjoys them, as *acepipe, antipasto, deem sum, hors d'oeuvre, pupus, tapas,* and *zakuska.* They are intended only to whet the appetite, not to satisfy it. They are not the meal—only the fore-runner—but they are also tantalizing comment-provokers. Many are so enticing that you will be tempted to serve more than the recommended quantity. We ask that you resist the temptation. There should be anticipation for what is to follow—like the opening paragraphs of a good mystery.

In this era of vanishing household help, we have made it easier for you to serve a first course by providing many that may be eaten in the living room, on the patio, or wherever cocktails have been served. They may be presented on individual dishes, or, for the eye's delight as well, on a large platter on a side table or coffee table. Soups, mousses, *pâtés* are best presented this way, of course. Many can be eaten while standing (soups in mugs, for example), some require sitting, but most do not require that one be seated at the dining table. However, for most you will need at least a fork or spoon.

"After Dinner" contains recipes for eating late in the evening, after whatever activities you and your friends or family have enjoyed, when you are at least a little hungry again. They are not desserts, served immediately after a main course, nor are many of them sweets. Some are substantial, some are "snacks," all are intriguing. We have in our own varied lifetimes become quite jaded with the uninspired offerings of overdone scrambled eggs and bacon, routine cheese and crackers, or even Aunt Emma's heaped-with-whipped-cream prune cake as an evening-ender after cards, the theater, or bowling. Why not end the day with a gastronomic memory-maker, rather than just a vehicle to prolong the good-nights and quiet the hunger pangs. We have gathered the means to do this over many years, and share them now with you.

About the recipes, there is something for everyone, the beginning cook, the creative cook, the dieter, the lean. Some are simple, quick and easy to prepare, others are more complicated. There are many variations on classic recipes that we believe deserve revival and promotion. Some favorites have come from friends, duly noted in their titles. There are a number of exotic recipes, enjoyed on our world-wide travels and re-created at home. Each and every one of them has been personally tested in our kitchens in Mexico, not only once but often several times.

The recipes are written in an easy-to-follow style. At the beginning of each, we have included nice-to-know facts in the upper left, such as the need for special equipment, whether the dish can be frozen, and how far ahead it can be prepared. At the right is, where appropriate, a brief description of the recipe or its origin. There is a complete yet simple description of each ingredient and the amount, as well as the form in which it is used (cooked, chopped fine, fresh, and so on). The text for putting together the ingredients is full and clear; we want you to know how your creation should look or taste or feel as you progress.

The modern cook likes the convenience of preparing ahead, and we have kept this in mind throughout the book. Most dishes can be prepared well in advance; very few require last-minute preparation, except for the assembling of already prepared ingredients or parts. Our caution to "assemble and prepare all ingredients" at the outset is an important one; nothing is quite so disheartening as to have scanned a recipe only briefly, then find later, when you are in the middle of preparing it, that there is no mustard in the house and the shrimp should have been cooked, peeled, and marinated the day before!

At the end of each first-course recipe, there are two suggestions for a possible main course to be served. These have been selected for compatibility in flavor, color, and texture. They can be found in any complete standard cookbook. We have also often suggested recipes that are included here in this book.

This leads us to a final comment. Almost all of the recipes can play several roles, many of them make superb main courses for a breakfast, luncheon, buffet, dinner, or supper, or as cocktail-party fare. Some first courses can be used as evening snacks, and vice versa. For your convenience we have provided lists of those recipes that are appropriate for different uses. One warning: if a first-course recipe or a snack recipe is to be used as a main course, adjust the number of servings. For example, a first-course recipe that makes eight servings will serve from four to six as a main course. Your own good judgment is the best rule.

We hope that each recipe will first be used as we have intended: a "Before" as a distinct first course, to be enjoyed for its own special tastes and to be recalled as a memorable introduction to the meal; or an "After" near the close of the evening, a special enjoyment as a finale.

And now you are on your own. We wish we could be with you!

A Special Note

I call myself a "creative cook." Actually, what this means is that I don't pay exact attention to most recipes, preferring to make "minor" changes here and there. Strangely enough, they turn out reasonably well, for the most part. Some cooks, new ones especially, are not so lucky.

One day, after we had edited too many recipes, I said groggily and, I suspect, with some vexation, "Charlotte, is it *really* necessary to: 'One, put the skillet on the stove over high heat; two, put the butter in the skillet; and three, when the butter stops sizzling, put in the fine-chopped onions and lower the heat to moderate'?"

"Yes," she said, "it is."

"Why can't one put the butter and onions in the skillet and *then* put the skillet on the heat?" I challenged.

"Because it is not good technique," she said firmly.

"But *why?*" I insisted.

"The proper technique improves the flavor of the onions," she said, "and most of my twenty-four hundred cookbook authors agree with me."

That was that. Charlotte has a lifetime collection of over twenty-four hundred cookbooks, and certainly knows a good technique when she sees one.

This book is loaded with good techniques. Sometimes we even tell you why. For example, water is bad for mushrooms, so we ask that you wipe them clean (they are seldom dirty) with a damp paper towel. We hope that you will use all the techniques. I do now, to my advantage.

LENORE HOWELL
Ajijic, Jalisco
Mexico

CONTENTS

Before Dinner: First Courses

After Dinner: Evening Snacks

Before Dinner: First Courses

Cold

Soups

JELLIED CONSOMME FROM AN UNKNOWN EMBASSY

8 SERVINGS

The consommé must be prepared and refrigerated at least 6 hours in advance, but it can be done up to a day ahead.

Fold in the remaining ingredients just before serving.

Serve very cold.

CANNED CONDENSED
  BEEF BROTH 2 *cans*
  (*10½ ounces each*),
  undiluted
DRY RED WINE *¼ cup*
UNFLAVORED GELATIN
  1 tablespoon (1 enve-
  lope), plus ¼ teaspoon
HEAVY CREAM *½ cup*

Annabelle Mitchell made this delicious concoction from a recipe that came via the U.S. Embassy in London from an unknown Embassy on the Continent. Since the recipe itself was Top Secret, we were forced to decode it by taste, and this is how the message came through.

Assemble and prepare all ingredients.

1. In a mixing bowl, combine the beef broth and the wine. Spoon about 1 cup of it into a small saucepan, sprinkle with gelatin, and let it soften for 5 minutes.

2. Melt the softened gelatin over low heat, stirring vigorously.

3. Combine the melted gelatin with the remaining beef-broth-and-wine mixture and stir well. Refrigerate for at least 6 hours, until firm, or for up to 24 hours.

JUST BEFORE SERVING: 1. Whip the cream until it forms soft peaks.

HARD-COOKED EGG
1, chopped fine
CHIVES *To make 3 table-*
spoons when snipped

The Garnish
BLACK CAVIAR *1 jar (3¾-*
ounce size)

2. Break up the consommé with a fork and carefully mix in the chopped egg and chives. Then fold the whipped cream into it, lightly but thoroughly. There should be small, dark lumps of consommé showing, to make a brown-and-white contrast. Serve at once.

TO SERVE: Seat your guests at the table first—this delicate consommé doesn't wait well. Spoon into 8 small, chilled bowls—crystal if you have them. Top each serving with a tablespoon of caviar.

SUGGESTED MAIN COURSE:
Roast Leg of Pork, Glazed with
Orange Juice
OR *Baked Cornish Game Hens*

GAZPACHO

6 SERVINGS

A blender is a must.

May be made up to a day ahead and refrigerated.

Serve well chilled.

—————

TOMATOES *4 large, quar-*
tered
GREEN BELL PEPPER
½ large, seeded and
sliced

Spanish gazpacho *is one of the best of the cold soups. It has become popular all over the world, especially in the calorie-conscious United States. It's a simple-ingredient, easy-to-make example of culinary art. You may also serve it as a near-midnight snack, as they do in Seville. Our version is light and full of flavor.*

Assemble and prepare all ingredients.
1. Put half the tomatoes, green pepper, onion, cucumber, garlic, and olive oil into a blender and blend for several seconds at high speed. Empty into a bowl.

ONION *1 medium, peeled and sliced*
GARLIC *2 cloves, peeled*
OLIVE OIL *6 tablespoons*
TABASCO SAUCE *¼ teaspoon*
SALT *1 teaspoon*
WINE VINEGAR *2 tablespoons*
TOMATO JUICE *1 cup*

The Garnish
CUCUMBER *1, peeled and diced*
GREEN BELL PEPPER *1 seeded and diced*
ONION *1 medium, peeled and chopped fine*
SMALL CROUTONS *About 2 cups*

The Accompaniment
CHEESE FLOWERS, *page 308*
OR POPPY SEED CRACKETS, *page 315*

6 SERVINGS

A blender is a must.

Make no more than 3 hours ahead and refrigerate.

2. Repeat with the rest of the vegetables and oil. Add the Tabasco sauce, salt, wine vinegar, and tomato juice, and mix well.

3. Refrigerate for at least 2 hours.

TO SERVE: Divide among 6 soup plates. Put an ice cube in each. Pass the garnishes and crackers, each in a separate bowl.

SUGGESTED MAIN COURSE:
Tamale Pie
OR *Paella*

CHILLED CREAM OF AVOCADO SOUP

Assemble and prepare all ingredients.

1. Peel and seed the avocados. Cut the meat into chunks and sprinkle with the lemon juice.

2. Taking a small amount at a time, purée the avocado in a blender, adding

Serve cold in chilled soup
cups: glass cups or
small glass bowls are
ideal.

AVOCADOS *3 medium*
   (*about 10 to 12 ounces
   each*)
LEMON JUICE *2 table-
   spoons*
CANNED CONDENSED
   CHICKEN BROTH *2 cans*
   (*10¾ ounces each*),
   undiluted
CHILI POWDER *1 teaspoon*
GROUND CORIANDER
   ½ teaspoon
HEAVY CREAM *1½ cups*
SALT
WHITE PEPPER, GROUND
   FRESH

The Garnish
BLACK CAVIAR *1 jar* (*3¾-
   ounce size*)

The Accompaniment
POPPY SEED CRACKETS,
   page 315
OR TINY CHEESE PUFFS,
   page 305

some of the chicken broth, as necessary,
until it is very smooth. Pour into a bowl
as it is puréed. Add the chili powder, coriander, and any remaining lemon juice
with the last batch of avocado.

3. Put in the top section of a double
boiler along with any remaining chicken
broth, and stir well. Heat over simmering
water for 10 minutes.

4. Cool and add the cream, mixing
thoroughly. Salt very lightly—the caviar
topping will be salty. Add pepper to taste.
Cover tightly and chill until ready to
serve.

TO SERVE: Divide the soup among 6
chilled cups or bowls. Float a teaspoon or
more of caviar on each serving. Pass the
crackers or puffs.

SUGGESTED MAIN COURSE:
   Veal Birds
   OR *Lake Chapala Fish Market Pâté,
   page 137*

IN-THE-PINK COLD BORSCH

Borsch, borscht, borshct, borsht, borstch, or borshch. There are 6 ways to spell it and 100 times 6 ways to make it. The only thing they have in common is beets. This version is creamy and tangy with yogurt. It is colorful when poured from a pitcher into crystal glasses as a first course in the living room.

8 TO 10 SERVINGS

A blender is a must.

Must be made a day ahead.

Don't forget to chill the cups, bowls, or glasses.

Serve cold.

BEETS 4 or 5 *medium, to make 4 cups when cooked, and cut in small chunks: see text for cooking directions*

CONDENSED BEEF BROTH (NOT CONSOMME) 2 *cans (10½ ounces each), plus enough water to make 4 cups of liquid*

ONION ½ *medium, peeled and cut in small chunks*

PLAIN YOGURT 2 *cups*

DRIED DILL WEED 1 *teaspoon, plus enough more for garnish: if available, use fresh dill for garnishing*

RED WINE VINEGAR 1 *to* 1½ *tablespoons*

Assemble and prepare all ingredients.

1. Scrub the beets thoroughly. Cut off the tops and discard, but leave about 2 inches of the stem above the crown. Do not remove the root or skin lest the beets "bleed" while cooking.

2. Bring a large saucepan of water to a boil. Add the whole beets, cover, and cook rapidly until tender. Depending upon the quality and variety, this will take from 30 to 60 minutes, or until they can be pierced with a thin skewer.

3. Drain, then, holding them under running water, rub off the skins, cut off the tops and roots, and discard.

4. Cut the beets in small chunks and measure about 4 cups. Combine about a third of the beets and a third each of the beef broth, onion, and yogurt in a blender. Whirl at the highest speed for about 20 seconds, or until the mixture is smooth and there are no bits of beet or onion visible. Transfer to a bowl. Repeat until all is blended. Add the dill weed with the last

SALT

BLACK PEPPER, GROUND
   FRESH

ADDITIONAL BEEF BROTH
   FOR THINNING, IF
   NECESSARY

The Garnish

COMMERCIAL SOUR
   CREAM

DILL WEED, PREFERABLY
   FRESH

The Accompaniment

FINGERS OF TOASTED AND
   BUTTERED BLACK
   BREAD

OR BREAD STICKS AND
   SWEET BUTTER

third. Mix well. Then add 1 tablespoon of vinegar, salt, and a few grinds of the pepper mill. Stir and taste. Add more vinegar if necessary. Borsch should be very faintly tart and sharp. Cover and refrigerate 24 hours.

TO SERVE: Stir the Borsch well. If it seems thick, add a little more beef broth. It should be very creamy—about the consistency of a bisque. Divide among well-chilled cups, small bowls, or wide-topped crystal glasses. (Manhattan glasses are perfect.) Top each portion with a generous tablespoon of sour cream and a small sprinkling of dill. Serve with fingers of toasted and buttered black bread, or bread sticks and sweet butter.

SUGGESTED MAIN COURSE:
   *Cold Meat with Anchovy Sauce,
   page 142*
   OR *Scandinavian Fish Pudding with
   Shrimp Sauce, page 96*

Seafood

BRANDADE OF SALTED COD

10 TO 12 SERVINGS

A blender is required.

The fish must be soaked overnight.

The finished dish may be tightly covered and refrigerated for up to 5 days before serving.

Serve well chilled from a platter or put into individual ½-cup ramekins.

SALTED BONELESS, SKIN-
LESS COD *1 pound*
MILK *About 1½ cups, or enough to cover the cod*
OLIVE OIL *1 cup, plus a little more if necessary*

A smooth, almost velvet purée of cod blended with cream, olive oil, garlic, and seasonings to make a thick mayonnaise. Hauntingly delicious. This was inspired by a smoked trout brandade we enjoyed at Robert Carrier's restaurant in London.

Assemble and prepare all ingredients.

1. Put the cod in a medium bowl, cover it with milk, and soak overnight.

2. The next day drain the cod, discard the milk, and break the fish in small chunks. Put it into a medium saucepan, add cold water to cover, and bring to a boil over moderate heat. Lower the heat and let it simmer for 20 minutes, or until it is very tender and the fish can be easily flaked. Drain.

3. While the cod is simmering, put 1 cup of oil into a small saucepan and the 2½ cups of the cream into another. Place each over low heat until they are warm, but do not let either liquid boil or smoke.

HEAVY CREAM *2½ cups,*
plus a little more if
necessary
GARLIC *1 clove, peeled and*
minced almost to a
paste with a little salt
LEMON JUICE *1 table-*
spoon
NUTMEG, GRATED FRESH
⅛ teaspoon
WHITE PEPPER, GROUND
FRESH *5 or 6 grinds*
OR CAYENNE PEPPER *⅛*
teaspoon
SALT

The Garnish
FRESH MUSHROOMS *To*
make ⅓ cup when
chopped fine and sautéed
(about ¼ pound, un-
cooked)
OR PARSLEY *To make ⅓*
cup when chopped fine

The Accompaniment
PLAIN CRACKERS, MELBA
TOAST, LIGHTLY FRIED
BREAD TRIANGLES, OR
POPPY SEED CRACKETS,
page 315

4. Shred the drained cod as fine as you can, using 2 forks or your fingers. Remove any bones or skin. Divide it into 3 parts.

5. Put a third into the blender set at medium speed, slowly add about a third of the warmed oil, and blend to a thick paste. Transfer from the blender to a bowl and repeat with the rest of the fish and oil, blending a third at a time. Mix the 3 parts well.

6. Taking about a third of the fish-and-oil mixture, return it to the blender set at medium-high speed and add a third of the warm cream, *a tablespoon at a time.* Remove from the blender into a large bowl and repeat with the rest of the fish mixture, a third at a time, always adding the cream by tablespoonfuls.

7. Now combine the mixture in the bowl. It should be like a thick purée. Add the garlic, lemon juice, nutmeg, and pepper or cayenne. Mix well and taste. Surprisingly, it may need a little salt. If too stiff, blend in a little more oil and cream.

8. Chill, well covered, for several hours before serving, or refrigerate for up to 5 days.

TO SERVE: Mound on a chilled platter, and sprinkle with the mushrooms or parsley. Surround with the accompaniment of your choice and serve on small chilled plates at the table. This is most impressive served in individual, chilled

½-cup ramekins, individually garnished. Pass the accompaniments separately.

SUGGESTED MAIN COURSE:
   Roast Beef
   OR *Herbed Lamb Chops*

CAVIAR PIE

10 TO 12 SERVINGS

You will need an 8-inch pie pan.

The cream-cheese-and-gelatin mixture must be made and put into a pie pan at least 3 hours, or up to a day, ahead.

The pie may be finished and garnished about 1 hour before serving.

Serve cold.

———

OIL FOR PAN
MILK ¾ *cup, plus* ¼ *cup for softening the gelatin*
UNFLAVORED GELATIN 1 *tablespoon* (1 *envelope*)
CREAM CHEESE 1 *package* (6- *to* 7-*ounce size*), *cut in chunks*

Caviar purists will say that we are gilding the lily, but the pie is so festive and decorative that raves will drown out protests. Contributed by Sylvia Bauman and we are glad.

Assemble and prepare all ingredients.

1. Lightly oil the pie pan and set aside.
2. Put the ¼ cup of milk into a small bowl. Sprinkle with the gelatin and let it stand for 5 minutes.
3. Put the ¾ cup of milk into a heavy-bottomed saucepan. Add the softened gelatin and stir constantly over low heat until the gelatin is completely dissolved. Allow plenty of time for this and do not let the milk simmer or boil.
4. Remove from the heat and let it cool.
5. Put the cream cheese into a bowl and add the cooled milk-and-gelatin mixture. Beat until it is the consistency of heavy cream.
6. Pour the mixture into the prepared pan and refrigerate until set, for at least 3 hours or up to a day ahead.

BLACK CAVIAR *At least a 4-ounce jar, more if you like*

HARD-COOKED EGGS *3 large, peeled*

SCALLIONS *To make ⅔ cup when chopped fine (6 to 9), include some of the pale-green stems*

WHITE PEPPER, GROUND FRESH

The Garnish
PARSLEY SPRIGS

The Accompaniment
HOT FRESH TOAST FINGERS

ABOUT 1 HOUR AHEAD: 1. Unmold the pie by running the tip of a small, thin knife about ¼ inch down from the edge. Dip the pan, not quite to the top, in warm water and invert onto a serving plate.

2. Spread the top evenly with the caviar as thick as you like.

3. Press the yolks and whites of the eggs separately through a fine-meshed sieve.

4. Circle bands of the sieved yolks, the whites, and the scallions alternately on top of the caviar.

5. If there is any left over, press on the sides to frost like a cake. Sprinkle the top with a few grinds of white pepper. Refrigerate, lightly covered, until ready to serve.

TO SERVE: Garnish the plate with parsley sprigs and bring to the table along with small individual dishes. Cut into wedges and serve. Pass the warm toast fingers separately.

SUGGESTED MAIN COURSE:
Roast Leg of Lamb
OR *Braised Beef*

COLD POACHED FISH WITH AIOLI SAUCE

6 TO 8 SERVINGS, DEPENDING ON THE SIZE OF THE FISH

A fish poacher or a very large, deep roasting pan

One of the most impressive and delicious-first courses we know, and too much overlooked by cooks. Also good hot or cold as a main course.

with a cover is necessary: it must be an inch larger than the fish, all around.

You will also need a large piece of cheesecloth.

The fish may be poached the day before and refrigerated.

The Aïoli Sauce may be made 1 or 2 days ahead.

——————

WATER 2 *quarts*

WHITE WINE *1 cup*

WHITE VINEGAR *¼ cup*

SALT *½ teaspoon*

ONION *1 large, peeled and cut in chunks*

CARROT *1 medium, peeled and cut in medium dice*

PARSLEY *3 sprigs*

CELERY *1 stalk with leaves, cut in chunks*

WHOLE FRESH FISH (RED SNAPPER, SEA BASS, OR SALMON) *1, (4 to 6 pounds)*

BOILING WATER, IF NECESSARY

AIOLI SAUCE *1 recipe* *page 295*

Assemble and prepare all ingredients.

1. In a 1½- or 2-quart saucepan, combine the water, wine, vinegar, salt, onion, carrot, parsley, and celery. Cover and simmer gently ½ hour.

2. Wrap the fish in a double layer of cheesecloth, leaving 4 inches at the head and tail to use as handles.

3. Bring the court bouillon to a boil. Lower the fish into the liquid, leaving the cheesecloth ends outside the pan. If the fish is not covered with liquid, add boiling water to cover.

4. Simmer (do not boil) until the fish feels tender when pierced with a fork, about 7 minutes per pound for a large fish.

5. Gently lift out the fish by the cheesecloth handles, put it on a large serving platter, and, rolling it over, carefully remove the cheesecloth. If the skin didn't come off with the cheesecloth, remove the skin between the head and the tail on both sides.

6. Cover, cool, and refrigerate until serving time.

TO SERVE: Decorate the fish with lemon slices and parsley sprigs. Serve the Aïoli Sauce in a bowl. You may allow guests to serve themselves or serve the fish yourself, at the table.

NOTE: If you simply can't tolerate garlic, substitute Mustard Mayonnaise, page 140, or Creamy Dill Dressing, page 297, for the Aïoli Sauce.

The Garnish
LEMON SLICES
PARSLEY SPRIGS

SUGGESTED MAIN COURSE:
Standing Rib Roast
OR *Rolled Veal Roast*

CEVICHE

8 SERVINGS

Prepare and refrigerate at
 least 5 hours in advance,
 but may be made 1 or 2
 days ahead.

Serve cold.

———————

UNCOOKED FRESH FISH
 FILLETS (NOT FROZEN)
 *1 pound of any firm
 white fish, such as sea
 bass, haddock, sole, or
 flounder, cut in strips
 about ¼ by ¼ by ¾
 inch*
FRESH LEMON OR LIME
 JUICE *⅔ cup*
ONION *To make ⅓ cup
 when chopped fine*
CANNED CALIFORNIA
 GREEN CHILI *1 medium,
 chopped fine: it should
 be mildly hot—if not,
 add a drop or two of
 Tabasco sauce to the
 Ceviche*
CANNED PIMIENTOS *1,*

In Mexico ceviche *is served in markets, at
little street stands, in restaurants, snack
bars, and homes. It is often a midafternoon
snack. This recipe comes from Acapulco
and is one of our most popular appetizers.*

Assemble and prepare the fish and lemon
or lime juice.

1. Put the uncooked fish strips into a
1½-quart glass, ceramic, or stainless-steel
bowl (not aluminum). Mix with the
lemon or lime juice until each piece is
coated.

2. Cover and refrigerate for at least 3
hours, stirring well with a fork every half
hour or so. The lemon juice in effect
"cooks" the fish.

3. After 3 hours in the marinade, each
piece should look white and firm. If it is
not, stir again and put it back in the refrigerator for an hour or more.

In the meantime assemble and prepare
the other ingredients.

4. When the fish is ready, add the onion, chili, Tabasco sauce, if necessary, pimiento, tomatoes, bell pepper, oregano,
and salt. Mix well, cover, and refrigerate
for another 2 hours.

chopped fine, plus
enough extra to make
eight ¼-inch-wide strips
for garnishing: cut each
strip in half
FRESH TOMATOES 2
medium, peeled, seeded,
and cut in ¼-inch cubes
GREEN OR RED BELL
PEPPER *1 small: remove*
and discard core, seeds,
and veins, and chop fine
DRIED OREGANO LEAVES
¼ teaspoon, crumbled
SALT *½ teaspoon or more*

The Garnish
LETTUCE LEAVES
(OPTIONAL) 8
AVOCADO *½ medium,*
peeled, pitted, and cut
in 8 slices lengthwise,
then each slice cut in
half
RESERVED PIMIENTO
STRIPS
PARSLEY OR FRESH
CORIANDER *Chopped*
fine

The Accompaniment
ROQUEFORT SHORT-
BREAD (OPTIONAL)
page 310

TO SERVE: Put into small bowls or large scallop shells lined with a crisp lettuce leaf, if you wish. Garnish each serving with 2 slices of avocado, 2 strips of pimiento, and a sprinkle of chopped parsley or coriander. If you choose, accompany with Roquefort Shortbread.

NOTE: In Mexico fresh chopped *cilantro*, or coriander, is added or used as a garnish; it is often called "Chinese parsley" in the United States. It adds a distinctive, pleasant flavor, but it isn't necessary. If it is available to you, add a teaspoon of it, chopped fine, to the Ceviche, and use it instead of the parsley as a garnish.

SUGGESTED MAIN COURSE:
Moctezuma's Pie, page 208
OR *Enchiladas*

YO'S DANISH APPETIZER

6 SERVINGS

The herring and the onions
    may be sliced several
    hours ahead, tightly
    covered with plastic
    wrap and refrigerated.

Assemble just before
    serving.

Serve at room temperature.

———————

PACKAGED, SMOKED,
    SKINLESS HERRING
    (NOT IN A JAR) 4
    ounces or more
RED OR WHITE ONIONS
    *1 or 2 large, peeled and
    cut crosswise in 6 rounds
    ¼ inch thick or less:
    keep the rounds intact*
DARK, MOIST EUROPEAN
    PEASANT-STYLE BREAD,
    OR PUMPERNICKEL
    BREAD 6 *very thin slices,
    about 3½ to 4 inches
    square: the packaged,
    precut kind is best*
SWEET BUTTER *Softened*
LARGE FRESH EGGS 6
BLACK PEPPER, GROUND
    FRESH

*Yo Sheppard has great talent in many di-
rections—she is mainly a noted sculptor,
and entertains family and friends with food
that is more than ordinary nourishment.
This is one of her favorites, and ours too.*

Assemble and prepare all the ingredients
except the eggs.

1. Using a small, very sharp knife, slice
the herring crosswise, paper-thin, on a long
diagonal. Wrap very tightly so that it will
not dry out. Refrigerate or reserve at room
temperature.

2. Wrap the onion rounds separately
and refrigerate or reserve at room temperature.

JUST BEFORE SERVING: 1. Spread each
slice of bread with a thin layer of softened
butter, covering the entire surface.

2. Place part of the sliced herring on
each piece of bread, in a single layer, to
cover it.

PARSLEY *To make 1 table-*
spoon when minced
COARSE SALT (OPTIONAL)

The Garnish
CRISP, RED RADISHES *12,*
trimmed, washed, and
dried

3. Remove and discard 2 or 3 of the center rings of each onion round, until a hole about 1¼ inches in diameter is left open. Center 1 onion ring on each herring-covered slice.

4. Break 1 egg carefully, and put the *yolk only* into the center of an onion ring. Reserve the white for another use. Repeat with each egg until all the rings are filled.

5. Sprinkle the top of each yolk with a few grinds of the pepper mill and some minced parsley.

TO SERVE: Put on individual small plates and garnish each serving with 2 radishes. Pass the coarse salt for those who wish it. Remember the herring may be salty!

SUGGESTED MAIN COURSE:
  Rack of Lamb
  OR *Veal Cordon Bleu*

NOTE: If used as an evening snack, serve with white wine or Danish beer.

ZAKUSKA OF HERRING AND BEETS

12 SERVINGS (ABOUT
  ⅓ CUP EACH)

All the ingredients except
  the apples and sour
  cream may be prepared
  and mixed a day ahead.

Prepare the apples at least
  1 hour before serving.

Another surprisingly good combination of textures and flavors. Zakuska is the Russian word for appetizer.

Assemble and prepare all ingredients.

1. In a medium bowl, mix the diced beets, herring, dill pickles, minced onion, reserved pickling liquid, reserved onion from the herring, and dill. At this point

Add apples and sour cream about 1 hour before serving.

Serve chilled, on chilled plates.

———————

COOKED BEETS *To make 1 cup when cut into ¼-inch dice (2 medium)*

SPICED PICKLED HERRING OR HERRING IN WINE SAUCE *2 jars (6 ounces each): drain and reserve the liquid, discard any bits of spice and bone but reserve the onions; cut the herring in ¼-inch dice*

DILL PICKLES *To make ½ cup when peeled and chopped fine*

ONION *To make 1 table-spoon when minced*

RESERVED PICKLING LIQUID *3 teaspoons*

RESERVED ONION FROM HERRING *Chopped coarse*

DILL WEED *1 teaspoon if dried, or, if fresh, 1 table-spoon plus a little extra for garnishing*

CRISP GREEN APPLES *To make 1 cup when cored, peeled, and cut in ¼-*

the mixture may be refrigerated up to a day ahead. Refrigerate the marinated sliced beets for the garnish also.

2. About an hour before serving, thoroughly drain the apples, and add them to the beet mixture along with the sour cream. Mix again and add salt and pepper to taste. Refrigerate.

TO SERVE: Flatten 1 or 2 lettuce leaves on each small plate. Take about ⅓ cup of the herring mixture and mound in the center of each. Tuck 3 marinated beet slices, evenly spaced and partially under each mound. Top with a sprinkle of dill and serve.

SUGGESTED MAIN COURSE: *Meat Balls Stroganoff* OR *Shish Kabob*

inch dice
SOAKED IN:
LEMON JUICE *Juice of 1*
MIXED WITH:
WATER *2 cups*
COMMERCIAL SOUR
   CREAM *1 cup, at room
   temperature*
SALT
BLACK PEPPER, GROUND
   FRESH

The Garnish
LETTUCE LEAVES
SLICED BEETS *1 can (16-
   ounce size), drained and*
   MARINATED IN:
SALAD OIL AND VINEGAR
   *3 tablespoons of each,
   mixed*
DILL

SYLVIA'S ARTICHOKES AND SHRIMP

6 SERVINGS

May be made up to a day
   ahead, but must mari-
   nate for at least 2 hours.

Serve chilled.

_____

FROZEN ARTICHOKE
   HEARTS *1 package (9-
   ounce size)*
SALTED WATER *For sim-*

*Sylvia Bauman, an elegant Palm Springs
hostess, says she sometimes serves this as
an hors d'oeuvre.*

Assemble and prepare all ingredients.
   1. Cook the artichoke hearts according
to package directions. Drain and chill
them.
   2. Heat a saucepan of well-salted water
to a boil, add the shrimp, and when the
water returns to a simmer, let them cook
for another 5 minutes. Remove from the

mering shrimp

UNCOOKED SHRIMP *30 medium (about 1 pound)*

EGG YOLK *1*

OLIVE OIL *½ cup*
   MIXED WITH:

SALAD OIL *¼ cup*

RED WINE VINEGAR *¼ cup*

DIJON MUSTARD *2 table-spoons*

PARSLEY *To make 2 table-spoons when minced*

CHIVES *To make 2 table-spoons when minced*

SHALLOTS OR SCALLIONS *To make 1 tablespoon when minced*

SALT

BLACK PEPPER, GROUND FRESH (OPTIONAL)

The Accompaniment
BUTTERY COMMERCIAL CRACKERS

OR MARINATED SODA CRACKERS, *page 311*

6 SERVINGS

You will need 6 scallop shells, at least ½-cup

heat and let the shrimp remain in their cooking liquid for 10 minutes. Drain. When they are cool enough to handle, peel and discard the shells. It is not necessary to devein the shrimp unless you wish to. Chill and reserve.

3. Put the egg yolk into a medium bowl, add the mixed olive and salad oil, the vinegar, and mustard and beat well.

4. Add the parsley, chives, and shallots and mix thoroughly. Add salt to taste and a few grindings of the pepper mill.

5. Add the reserved artichoke hearts and shrimp, mixing gently. Marinate in the refrigerator for at least 2 hours, or up to 1 day, turning occasionally.

TO SERVE: Using a slotted spoon, divide the mixture among 6 small chilled bowls or scallop shells. Spoon a little of the marinade over each serving to moisten, but don't float the solids in marinade. Pass the crackers separately.

NOTE: You will have a little extra marinade; save it. It is delicious tossed with a plain green salad.

SUGGESTED MAIN COURSE:
   Broiled Steak
   OR *Curried Lamb*

SHRIMP ON A VELVET CLOUD

A heavenly combination—smooth and melting on the tongue.

Assemble and prepare all ingredients.

size (5 to 5½ inches at the widest point), or 6 ramekins, ½-cup size.

May be made up to a day ahead, but must be completed at least 4 hours in advance.

Serve cold.

———————

TINY, WHOLE COOKED SHRIMP OR SMALL UN-COOKED FRESH SHRIMP *½ pound when cooked and shelled: if using small uncooked shrimp, buy a pound, they will lose half their weight when cooked; reserve 12 for garnish*

CANNED CONDENSED CHICKEN BROTH *1 can (10¾-ounce size), un-diluted*

UNFLAVORED GELATIN *1¼ teaspoons*

CREAM CHEESE *1 large package (8-ounce size), softened to room temperature*

CURRY POWDER, THE BEST QUALITY AVAILABLE *1 teaspoon or more, to taste*

1. If the shrimp are uncooked, prepare them by simmering in enough water to cover for 5 minutes. Remove from the heat and let them remain in their cooking liquid for 10 minutes. Drain and shell.

2. Remove *all* the fat that will be floating on top of the chicken broth. This is best done by removing the large blobs with a spoon and then lightly brushing the top of the liquid with a torn edge of paper toweling.

3. Sprinkle the gelatin on ½ cup of the broth in a small saucepan. Let stand for 5 minutes to soften.

4. Over medium heat stir constantly until the gelatin is dissolved. Remove from the heat and add to the rest of the broth. Stir and cool.

5. Put the cream cheese into a bowl, add the curry powder, and mash it with a spoon or rubber spatula until smooth and well mixed. Taste and add a little more curry powder if you wish, but don't let the curry taste overpower the delicate flavor of the shrimp and avocado.

6. Measure out a *scant* ⅔ cup of the cooled chicken-broth–gelatin mixture and gradually add it to the cream cheese, blending well. The mixture should be perfectly smooth and quite liquid. Reserve the balance of the broth at room temperature.

7. Add the shrimp to the cream cheese mixture, reserving 12 whole ones for garnish. If you are using small rather than tiny shrimp, cut all but 12 in half or thirds, to about the size of tiny shrimp. Mix well.

FIRM, RIPE AVOCADOS
  2 small (about 4 inches long): ½ cup pitted, peeled, and diced for the aspic; the balance cut and peeled later into 6 crescents for the garnish.

The Garnish
AVOCADO CRESCENTS 6
RESERVED WHOLE SHRIMP
  12

8. Add the diced avocado and mix it carefully.

9. Divide among 6 scallop shells or ramekins. Smooth the top. Place them on a tray or jelly-roll pan. If using scallop shells, prop them against the sides of the pan so that they will stand as evenly as possible. Refrigerate for about 2 hours or until slightly firm.

10. Remove from the refrigerator. Peel and cut the remaining avocado crosswise in 3 rings about ¼ inch thick. Cut the rings in half to form crescents.

11. Place 1 crescent in the center of each shell and garnish with 2 whole shrimp, hooking them on one side of the crescent.

12. Gently spoon part of the reserved chicken-gelatin broth over each, being careful to coat the avocado entirely so that it will not turn dark. Revolve the dishes slightly so that the aspic spreads evenly and covers all. (If the reserved aspic has gelled, warm it slightly, stirring well, until it is a smooth liquid.)

13. Refrigerate for at least 1 hour or until set. Cover until ready to serve. Serve cold.

SUGGESTED MAIN COURSE:
  Wiener Schnitzel
  OR *Steak Diane*

SHRIMP IN MARINADE, VERACRUZ STYLE
(Camarones en Escabeche, Veracruzano)

8 SERVINGS

Must be made 24 hours in advance.

Serve very cold.

_____

UNCOOKED MEDIUM
  SHRIMP, FRESH OR
  FROZEN _1¼ pounds_
WATER _4 cups_
SALT _1½ teaspoons_
MILD OLIVE AND SALAD
  OIL _¼ cup of each,
  mixed_
SMALL RED ONIONS OR
  MILD SWEET WHITE
  ONIONS _To make 1 cup
  when peeled, sliced, cut
  in ⅛-inch rings, each
  ring cut in half and
  separated_
GARLIC _3 cloves, peeled
  and minced almost to a
  paste with a little salt_
CANNED CALIFORNIA
  GREEN CHILIES _To
  make ¼ cup when
  chopped fine: first rinse
  and remove the veins
  and seeds, plus enough_

_Our witty profesora and tiny dear friend,
la Señorita Guadalupe Santana Camberos,
of Chapala, Mexico, gave us this recipe.
It is adapted from a prizewinner in a Mexico City recipe contest for doctors' wives.
We've never tasted better marinated
shrimp._

Assemble and prepare all ingredients.

1. Wash and drain the shrimp. Bring
the water to a boil in a 1½-quart saucepan
and add the salt. Add the shrimp, and
when the water returns to a boil, lower the
heat and simmer, uncovered, for 5 minutes. Remove from the heat and let the
shrimp remain in the cooking water for 10
minutes. They should be slightly firm to
the bite. Drain and set aside until cool
enough to handle.

2. Peel the shrimp and discard the
shells. It is not necessary to remove the
vein unless you prefer. Put the shrimp into
a large bowl made of stainless steel, glass,
or ceramic (not aluminum) and set aside.

3. Put the mixed oils into a medium
skillet—any type other than aluminum.
When the oil is very hot, add the onions.
On medium-low heat, sauté until soft but
still a little crisp, stirring frequently.

4. Add the garlic and sauté together
with the onions for 1 minute more.

extra to make eight
⅛-inch strips for
garnishing

CANNED PIMIENTOS
To make ½ cup when
chopped fine, plus
enough extra to make
eight ⅛-inch strips for
garnishing

**WHOLE BLACK PEPPER-
CORNS** About 15

DRIED OREGANO LEAVES
½ teaspoon, crumbled

BAY LEAF 1 large,
crumbled

GROUND THYME ⅛ tea-
spoon

**DRIED MARJORAM
LEAVES** ⅛ teaspoon,
crumbled

**DRIED HOT RED PEPPER
FLAKES** ¼ teaspoon

WHITE WINE VINEGAR
½ cup or a little more,
to taste

**STRAINED FRESH ORANGE
JUICE** ½ cup

**YOLKS OF LARGE HARD-
COOKED EGGS** 4
MASHED WITH:

PREPARED MUSTARD
2 teaspoons

**WHITES OF LARGE HARD-
COOKED EGGS** 4,
chopped fine

SALT

5. Add the ¼ cup of chopped chilies, the ½ cup of chopped pimientos, the peppercorns, oregano, bay leaf, thyme, marjoram, and hot pepper flakes and cook for a minute or two, stirring constantly until all is well mixed.

6. Add the vinegar, only ½ cup at first. You may add more later if the flavor is not tart enough. Then add the orange juice and bring the mixture almost to a boil.

7. Remove from the heat, gently stir in the egg-yolk-and-mustard mixture, and then the chopped egg whites. Add salt and pepper to taste. Let cool to room temperature.

8. Pour the cooled marinade over the reserved shrimp and toss until the shrimp are well coated. Cover tightly and refrigerate for at least 24 hours. Stir from time to time.

9. A few hours before serving, taste for seasoning and add a little more vinegar if necessary. The marinade should have a slightly sharp taste.

TO SERVE: Shape several lettuce leaves into cups on individual, small chilled plates. Using a slotted spoon, put a portion of the shrimp on each. Garnish each serving with 1 strip of the green chili and 1 strip of the red pimiento placed at right angles to each other to form a cross. Place a few olives around the perimeter. Serve very cold.

BLACK PEPPER, GROUND
FRESH

The Garnish
LETTUCE LEAVES
RESERVED PIMIENTO
STRIPS
RESERVED GREEN CHILI
STRIPS
STUFFED GREEN OLIVES
OR PITTED RIPE OLIVES

SUGGESTED MAIN COURSE:
Veal Scaloppine
OR *Chicken Breasts Supreme*

MARINATED SMOKED SALMON

8 SERVINGS

Must marinate overnight
or for up to 24 hours.

May be completed several
hours in advance.

Serve chilled.

———————

SMOKED SALMON 24 *thin
slices, long enough to
fold or roll*
DILL WEED *About 1½
tablespoons if dried,* or,
*if fresh, to make 2 table-
spoons when minced*
BLACK PEPPER, GROUND
FRESH
DRY WHITE WINE *1 cup*
OLIVE OIL *½ cup*

Assemble and prepare all ingredients.
  1. In a shallow dish, place a single
layer of salmon, a sprinkle of dill, and a
few grinds of the pepper mill.
  2. Repeat, layering more salmon, dill,
and pepper, until all is used.
  3. Pour the wine and the olive oil over
all. Let marinate overnight or for up to 24
hours.

UP TO SEVERAL HOURS BEFORE SERVING:
  1. Drain the salmon and save any remaining marinade for another use—it's delicious on a salad or cold vegetables.
  2. Spread each slice of salmon generously with the sour cream and fold or roll
them up. Refrigerate until ready to serve.

TO SERVE: Place 3 salmon rolls or folds
on each of 8 small chilled plates, along
with 2 lemon wedges. Spread the bread

COMMERCIAL SOUR
    CREAM, *about 1 cup*

The Garnish
LEMON WEDGES *16*

The Accompaniment
RYE OR BLACK BREAD
    *8 slices, toasted and cut
    in fingers or triangles*
SOFT BUTTER
OR POPPY SEED CRACKERS,
    page 315

with the softened butter, and put it in a basket lined with a gay napkin to pass separately. Or serve with Poppy Seed Crackets.

SUGGESTED MAIN COURSE:
    Beef Bourguignon
    OR *Veal Cordon Bleu*

SERVES 12 TO 14

12 to 14 molds of ½-cup
    capacity are required—
    metal is best.

You will also need a pan
    of ice.

Prepare and drain the
    cucumbers at least 40
    minutes ahead of
    assembling and
    preparing the rest of the
    ingredients.

May be prepared and
    refrigerated a day in
    advance, but must be

COLD SWEDISH SALMON MOUSSE

TO PREPARE THE DICED CUCUMBERS: Sprinkle them lightly with salt and let them drain in a colander for at least 40 minutes. Reserve.

THE MOUSSE: Assemble and prepare all ingredients.

1. Coat the molds lightly with oil and drain them upside down on paper toweling. Set aside.

2. Sprinkle the gelatin over the wine and let it stand 5 minutes to soften. Heat the broth to just under a simmer (be sure you have removed all the fat first). Add the softened gelatin and wine and stir over low heat until the gelatin is dissolved. Remove from the heat and add the lemon juice and salt.

completed at least 2 hours before serving.

———————

CUCUMBERS *To make 1 cup when cut in ¼-inch dice: first peel and cut them in half lengthwise, then, using a spoon, scoop out and discard the seeds and pulp, and dice the remaining shell*
SALT

The Mousse
FLAVORLESS VEGETABLE OIL *For the molds*
UNFLAVORED GELATIN *1 tablespoon (1 envelope)*
DRY WHITE WINE *½ cup*
CANNED CHICKEN BROTH (NOT CONCENTRATED) *1 cup, thoroughly degreased: best done by removing the larger blobs of fat with a spoon and then blotting the top with a torn edge of paper toweling*
FRESH LEMON OR LIME JUICE *1 tablespoon*
SALT *1 teaspoon*
RESERVED PREPARED CUCUMBERS
CAPERS *¼ cup when*

3. Transfer the gelatin mixture to a bowl, preferably of stainless steel, glass, or ceramic, and refrigerate it, stirring occasionally, until it chills and starts to thicken to about the consistency of an unbeaten egg white. Watch it carefully. Once it cools, it thickens quickly. If the mixture should accidentally become too thick, put it back on the stove, heat it just enough to melt it completely, and refrigerate it over again.

4. Place the bowl of thickened gelatin mixture into a larger bowl or pan half filled with ice. Using an electric or rotary beater, beat the mixture until it is the consistency of whipped cream.

5. Gently fold in the drained, prepared cucumbers, the capers, parsley, shallots or scallions, chives, paprika, tomato paste, Tabasco sauce, and mayonnaise. Taste for seasoning, adding salt and pepper if necessary.

6. When well mixed gently fold in the salmon. Lightly whip the cream and fold in only until no white streaks remain.

7. Spoon the mixture into the prepared individual molds. Place on a tray and refrigerate. When the tops are slightly firm (about ½ hour), cover with plastic wrap or aluminum foil and continue to refrigerate for at least 2 hours or until set, or for up to a day.

JUST BEFORE SERVING: Unmold by using the tip of a small, thin, sharp knife. Loosen the edge of each mousse to about ¼ inch

drained: press the capers gently against the bottom of a sieve, so that the preserving liquid is extracted

PARSLEY *To make 1 table-spoon when minced*

SHALLOTS OR SCALLIONS (WHITE PART ONLY) *To make 1 tablespoon when minced*

CHIVES *To make 1 table-spoon when cut fine*

PAPRIKA *1 teaspoon*

TOMATO PASTE *2 tea-spoons*

TABASCO SAUCE *⅛ tea-spoon*

MAYONNAISE, PREFER-ABLY HOMEMADE, *(page 296)* *½ cup*

SALT

WHITE PEPPER, GROUND FRESH

FRESH-POACHED OR CANNED SALMON (1-POUND CAN OF THE BEST QUALITY) *To make about 2 cups when drained and flaked: remove and discard the skin, bones, and most of the dark meat*

HEAVY CREAM *½ cup*

The Garnish
WATERCRESS OR PARSLEY

deep. Dip the bottom and sides of a mold for a second or two in warm but not hot water. Center a small, individual serving plate upside down over the mold. Invert plate and mold, holding them firmly together and giving them a sharp, downward shake. If the mousse won't come out, dip in warm water and invert again. Repeat for each mold. If necessary, blot up any damp spots with a torn edge of paper toweling.

TO SERVE: Tuck a few sprigs of watercress or parsley partially under each mousse. Place 3 or 4 olives on 1 side of each plate. Pass the Poppy Seed Crackets.

SUGGESTED MAIN COURSE:
London Broil
OR *Roast Turkey*

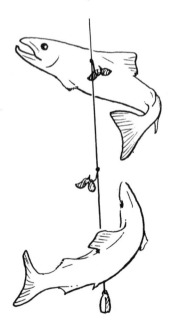

PIMIENTO-STUFFED
GREEN OLIVES OR
PITTED BLACK OLIVES

The Accompaniment
POPPY SEED CRACKETS,
  page 315

8 SERVINGS

Prepare and marinate for
  at least 3 hours or up to
  2 days ahead.

Make the dill sauce at
  least 1 day or up to 3
  days ahead.

Serve well chilled.

———————

The Oysters
SHUCKED OYSTERS,
  PREFERABLY SMALL
  4 cups when drained:
  reserve the liquor and
  cut the larger oysters
  into bite-sized pieces
RESERVED OYSTER LIQUOR
WATER *If necessary*
GARLIC 2 *large cloves,*
  peeled and chopped

MARINATED OYSTERS WITH DILL SAUCE

THE OYSTERS: Assemble and prepare all ingredients.

1. In a 1½-quart saucepan, poach the oysters in their liquor until the edges of the oysters just start to curl. Do not let them boil.

2. Strain and reserve the liquor. Cool the oysters in the freezer for 20 to 30 minutes. Remove and set aside.

3. In the meantime measure the remaining oyster liquor. If necessary, add enough water to make 1 cup.

4. Tie the garlic, bay leaves, peppercorns, and mace in a square of doubled cheesecloth, making a *bouquet garni.*

5. Put the oyster liquor into a saucepan, add the *bouquet garni,* the vinegar, onion, lemon, and salt, and simmer, covered, for 10 minutes. Remove from the heat and cool.

6. Add the reserved, cooled oysters, *jalapeños,* and oil. Mix well, cover, and refrigerate for at least 3 hours, or up to 2

BAY LEAVES 2, *well
crumbled*
WHOLE PEPPERCORNS
½ teaspoon
GROUND MACE *Pinch*
TARRAGON VINEGAR
½ cup
ONION *1 medium, peeled
and sliced into very thin
rings, each ring cut into
quarters*
LEMON *1, sliced very thin*
SALT *½ teaspoon*
JALAPENO PEPPERS,
CANNED OR FRESH
*To make ½ tablespoon
when minced: first split,
remove, and discard
seeds and inside veins
(5 dashes of Tabasco
sauce may be substituted)*
SALAD OIL *½ cup*

The Dill Sauce
COMMERCIAL SOUR
CREAM *1 cup*
MAYONNAISE, PREFER-
ABLY HOMEMADE,
(*page 296*) *2 table-
spoons*
DILL WEED *½ teaspoon, if
dried,* or, *if fresh, to
make 1½ teaspoons
when minced*
SEASONED SALT *1½ tea-
spoons*

days. Stir occasionally. Remove the *bouquet garni* just before serving.

THE DILL SAUCE: 1. Thoroughly mix together the sour cream, mayonnaise, dill
weed, and seasoned salt. Refrigerate, covered, for at least 1 day or for up to 3 days.

TO SERVE: Line 8 scallop shells, sherbet
glasses, or small plates with lettuce leaves
or watercress. Drain the oysters and divide
them evenly among the dishes, putting a
slice or two of the onion and a slice of the
lemon on each serving, along with whatever amount of other seasonings clings to
the oysters. Top each serving with a generous dollop of dill sauce. Serve well
chilled and pass the hot Melba toast or
crackers separately.

NOTE: If using as part of a Tray of Hors
d'Oeuvre, page 285, serve the dill sauce
separately.

SUGGESTED MAIN COURSE:
Herbed Meat Loaf
OR *Sautéed Chicken*

The Garnish
LETTUCE LEAVES OR
WATERCRESS

The Accompaniment
HOT MELBA TOAST
OR MARINATED SODA
CRACKERS, *page 311*

TARAMASALATA

8 SERVINGS (ABOUT
 1 CUP EACH)

You will need a blender.

At its best made a day
 ahead.

Chill for at least 1 hour
 before serving.

COD ROE *½ of an 8-ounce*
 jar or 7-ounce can
ONION *1 medium, peeled*
 and chopped coarse
OLIVE OIL *1 cup*
FRENCH BREAD *6 slices,*
 cut ½ to ¾ inch thick,
 trimmed of crusts, wet
 with water and squeezed
 dry
LEMON JUICE *6 table-*
 spoons

A Greek appetizer, delicate in flavor and texture, and appealing in recollection. Excellent to serve in the living room or on the patio before the meal.

Assemble and prepare all ingredients.

1. In a blender blend half the cod roe and onion with about ¼ cup of the olive oil, until smooth.

2. Add 3 slices of bread, crumbled, 3 tablespoons of the lemon juice, and another ¼ cup olive oil, and blend again to a smooth paste. Transfer to a bowl.

3. Repeat steps 1 and 2 and blend until the mixture is a delicate cream color. Stir well, cover, and chill until ready to serve.

TO SERVE: You may either spread the Taramasalata on the toast points or thin slices of French bread and serve in the living room or patio; or, to serve at the table, divide it into mounds on 8 small plates. Sprinkle each serving with minced parsley

The Garnish (for table serving)   .
MINCED PARSLEY
BLACK OLIVES, PREFER-
    ABLY GREEK

The Accompaniment
FRESH-MADE TOAST
    POINTS
OR THIN SLICES OF
    FRENCH BREAD

and press an olive into the center. Pass the French bread or toast points separately.

SUGGESTED MAIN COURSE:
    Baked Ham
    OR *Moussaka*

Meat and Poultry

MARINATED KIELBASA
(Variations on a Polish theme)

6 SERVINGS

Either "theme" may be made the day before, but they must both marinate in the refrigerator for at least 3 hours, preferably 6.

We like theme number 1 at room temperature and theme number 2 chilled.

KIELBASA (POLISH SAUSAGE) *1 large (about 9 ounces), cooked, skinned, sliced thin, and cooled*

Theme Number 1
WINE VINEGAR ¼ *cup*

Either of the "themes" makes a hearty and very tasty first course. Choose one.

IF YOU CHOOSE THEME NUMBER 1: Assemble and prepare all ingredients.

1. In a small bowl, combine the vinegar and monosodium glutamate. Stir vigorously with a wire whisk or fork while slowly adding the olive oil. Set aside.

2. In a separate bowl combine the cooked, sliced *kielbasa,* the scallions, parsley, tomatoes, and green pepper.

3. Combine gently but thoroughly with the oil-and-vinegar mixture. Add salt and pepper to taste, and marinate in the refrigerator for 3 to 6 hours, or up to a day ahead.

4. Remove from the refrigerator at least 1 hour before serving so that the oil will not be thick.

TO SERVE: Place a lettuce cup or leaf on

MONOSODIUM GLUTA-
MATE ¼ *teaspoon*
OLIVE OIL ½ *cup*
COOKED, SLICED KIELBASA
SCALLIONS 6, *chopped*
fine: include a little of
the green tops
PARSLEY, PREFERABLY
FLAT-LEAF *To make ¼*
cup when chopped fine
FIRM RIPE TOMATOES
2 medium: first peel
them, cut in quarters,
and gently squeeze and
shake to remove the
seeds and liquid, then
cut crosswise into fine
slices
GREEN BELL PEPPER
To make 2 tablespoons
when chopped fine: first
remove seeds and pits
SALT
BLACK PEPPER, GROUND
FRESH

The Garnish
LETTUCE CUPS OR
LEAVES 6

The Accompaniment
THIN-SLICED RYE BREAD
OR ANY FIRM DARK
BREAD (PREFERABLY
THE SMALLEST DI-
AMETER AVAILABLE)

each of 6 small plates and divide the marinated sausage among them. Pass the rye
bread and sweet butter separately.

IF YOU CHOOSE THEME NUMBER 2: Assemble all ingredients.

1. In a small bowl, combine all ingredients. Mix well and add salt and pepper to taste.

2. Marinate in the refrigerator for 3 to
6 hours, or up to a day ahead. Serve chilled.

TO SERVE: Place a lettuce cup or leaf on
each of 6 small plates and divide the marinated sausage among them. Pass the bread
and sweet butter separately.

SUGGESTED MAIN COURSE FOR EITHER
THEME:
   Stuffed Eggs in Soubise Sauce, page
      226
   OR *Roulade of Sole, page 101*

SWEET BUTTER *Cut in pats or rolled with a butter curler*

Theme Number 2
COMMERCIAL SOUR CREAM *¾ cup*
LIGHT CREAM (OPTIONAL) *2 tablespoons, but use it only if your sour cream is very thick*
DIJON MUSTARD *2 teaspoons*
PREPARED HORSERADISH *2 teaspoons*
COOKED, SLICED KIELBASA
SALT
WHITE PEPPER, GROUND FRESH

The Garnish and Accompaniment the same as theme number 1

STEAK TARTARE

12 SERVINGS (ABOUT ⅓ CUP EACH)

Buy the meat as close as possible to serving time, but definitely no more than 4 or 5 hours ahead (it darkens rapidly and looks best when red).

If you like steak tartare, you'll love this! It has many converts to the raw beef cult to its credit. Be an evangelist and add some more.

Assemble and prepare all ingredients.

1. Put all the ingredients into a large bowl, adding salt and pepper to taste. Mix lightly and thoroughly.

The seasonings and meat must be mixed 1 hour ahead and chilled.

RAW, LEAN TOP SIRLOIN
   OR TENDERLOIN BEEF
   STEAK (*Be sure it's
   trimmed of all fat*),
   *2 pounds, fresh-ground
   twice on the finest disk*
ANCHOVY PASTE *1 tube
   (2-ounce size)*
WORCESTERSHIRE SAUCE
   3 tablespoons
TABASCO SAUCE *Dash*
ONION *½ medium, grated
   to a pulp*
A.-I. SAUCE *2 tablespoons*
EGGS *2 whole*
FRESH LEMON *Juice of ½*
INDIA RELISH *3 table-
   spoons*
CAPERS *2 teaspoons,
   drained*
SALT
BLACK PEPPER, GROUND
   FRESH

The Garnish

LIGHT OR DARK RYE
   BREAD *12 to 18 thin
   slices: wrap tightly until
   ready to serve*
PARSLEY SPRIGS

2. Remove from the bowl. Press lightly together and wrap very tightly in plastic wrap or foil. Chill for an hour.

JUST BEFORE SERVING: 1. Cut the bread slices in half diagonally.

2. Lightly shape the seasoned meat into a large flattened mound, arrange on a large serving dish or tray, and decorate with parsley. Or form into 12 patties and place on individual plates. Garnish each with a small sprig of parsley placed in the center of the patty.

3. Surround with the bread triangles— 2 or 3 per person if served individually. Bring to the table and have the salt and pepper mill handy.

SUGGESTED MAIN COURSE:
   Cassoulet
   OR *Provincial Onion Soup, page 189*

Eggs

STUFFED EGGS ON PATE

8 SERVINGS

Assemble and prepare all ingredients.

The sauce must be made 2 hours in advance, but it may be made up to 2 days ahead.

The eggs may be made a day ahead, tightly covered, and refrigerated.

Fry the bread rounds and assemble just before serving.

Serve cold.

The Sauce
MAYONNAISE, PREFER-
ABLY HOMEMADE,
(*page 296*) *½ cup*

THE SAUCE: 1. Combine the mayonnaise, chili sauce or catsup, dry mustard, Worcestershire sauce, Tabasco sauce, vinegar, chopped capers, and tarragon. Add salt and pepper to taste. Refrigerate, covered, for at least 2 hours or up to 2 days, to let the flavors blend.

THE STUFFED EGGS: 1. Cut the eggs in half lengthwise. Carefully remove the yolks to a small bowl, keeping the whites intact. Set the whites aside.

2. Using a fork, mash the yolks. Add the olive oil, lemon juice, Worcestershire sauce, Tabasco sauce, and just enough mayonnaise to bind the mixture. Blend thoroughly until creamy. Add salt and pepper to taste.

3. Spoon the mixture equally into the hollow of the whites, mounding it a little.

CHILI SAUCE OR CATSUP
½ cup
DRY MUSTARD *¼ teaspoon*
WORCESTERSHIRE SAUCE
Dash
TABASCO SAUCE *2 or 3*
dashes
RED OR WHITE WINE
VINEGAR *½ teaspoon*
CAPERS *2 tablespoons,*
drained and chopped
fine, plus extra whole
capers for garnish
TARRAGON *¼ teaspoon,*
crumbled, if dried, or, if
fresh, to make ½ tea-
spoon when minced
SALT
BLACK PEPPER, GROUND
FRESH

The Stuffed Eggs
HARD-COOKED EGGS
4 large, cooled and
peeled
OLIVE OIL *1 teaspoon*
LEMON JUICE *½ teaspoon*
WORCESTERSHIRE SAUCE
Dash
TABASCO SAUCE *2 or 3*
dashes
MAYONNAISE *1 tablespoon*
or more
SALT
BLACK PEPPER, GROUND
FRESH
SALAD OIL

Cover and refrigerate up to a day ahead or until ready to serve.

TO ASSEMBLE AND SERVE: A few minutes before serving, heat enough salad oil in a heavy skillet to cover the bottom about ⅛ inch deep. When it is very hot and a haze is just visible, put in the bread rounds, 3 or 4 at a time, and fry quickly on both sides until a light golden-brown. It will take only a second or two. Do not let them get too dark. Drain on paper towels. Put a fried bread round on each of 8 small individual plates. Spread each round generously with *pâté*. Top this with a tomato slice. Place a half stuffed egg, *yolk side down,* on top of the tomato slice. Cover it with 1 or 2 tablespoons of the sauce, letting it run down over all. Garnish the top of the egg with 3 or 4 whole capers. Put 2 or 3 sprigs of watercress or parsley at the side and serve.

SUGGESTED MAIN COURSE:
Grilled Veal Chops
OR *Shish Kabob*

DAY-OLD FIRM WHITE
    BREAD *8 slices, ½ to*
    ¾ inch thick, cut in
    3-inch rounds
CANNED OR HOMEMADE
    CHICKEN LIVER PATE,
    LIVERWURST, OR
    BRAUNSCHWEIGER
    ¼ pound or a little more
FRESH TOMATO SLICES
    8 (2 or 3 large
    tomatoes): first peel
    the tomatoes, then cut
    them in half crosswise,
    gently squeeze and shake
    to extract the juice and
    seeds, cut in slices about
    ¼ inch thick, then trim
    to fit the bread rounds

The Garnish
CAPERS
WATERCRESS OR PARSLEY

CURRIED EGG MOUSSE WITH CURRIED TOAST

Eggs and curry—the perfect marriage.

10 SERVINGS

You will need 10 molds
    of ½-cup capacity, pref-
    erably made of metal,
    or a loaf pan, about
    4½ by 8½ inches, *or*
    a 1-quart ring mold.

THE MOUSSE: Assemble and prepare all ingredients.

1. Lightly oil the mold or molds and turn upside down on paper towels to drain. Set aside.

2. Sprinkle the gelatin over the water and let stand for 5 minutes to soften.

Complete at least 4
  hours or up to 1 day
  ahead.

The toast may be made
  early in the day, or just
  before serving.

Serve the mousse cold.

———————————

The Mousse

OIL FOR MOLDS

UNFLAVORED GELATIN
  1½ tablespoons (1 enve-
  lope, plus a very scant
  ½ tablespoon)

COLD WATER *¼ cup*

CANNED CHICKEN BROTH
  (NOT CONDENSED)
  2 cups, thoroughly
  skimmed of all fat: best
  done by removing the
  large blobs with a spoon
  and then skimming the
  top with a torn edge of
  paper toweling

ONION JUICE AND PULP
  To make 1 tablespoon:
  use a very fine grater

CURRY POWDER (THE
  BEST QUALITY AVAIL-
  ABLE) *2½ tablespoons,*
  mixed to a paste with a
  little water

MAYONNAISE, PREFER-

3. In the meantime bring the chicken broth to a rolling boil. Add the onion juice and pulp and the curry powder. Remove from the heat and add the softened gelatin. Return to low heat and stir until the gelatin is thoroughly dissolved.

4. Refrigerate the chicken-broth–gelatin mixture in a bowl, stirring occasionally, until it starts to thicken to about the consistency of an unbeaten egg white. If it should accidentally become too thick, put it back on the stove, heat just enough to melt it completely, and refrigerate again.

5. Remove from the refrigerator and mix in the mayonnaise until evenly distributed. Then fold in the sieved egg yolks and the chopped egg whites. Add salt to taste.

6. Whip the cream lightly, only enough to hold soft peaks, and fold it into the mixture. Spoon into the prepared molds, cover with foil or plastic wrap, and refrigerate for at least 4 hours until set, or up to a day ahead.

TO UNMOLD: Using the tip of a small, thin knife, loosen the edges of the mousse to a depth of about ¼ inch. Dip the bottom and sides of each mold for a second or two in warm, but not hot, water. If using individual molds, center a small individual serving plate upside down over each. Invert plate and mold, holding them firmly together and giving a sharp downward shake. If the mousse won't come out, dip in the warm water and invert again.

ABLY HOMEMADE,
(*page 296*) ⅓ *cup*
HARD-COOKED EGG YOLKS
7, *rubbed through a*
medium-mesh sieve
HARD-COOKED EGG
WHITES 7, *chopped*
medium-fine
SALT
HEAVY CREAM *I cup,*
chilled

The Curried Toast
BUTTER ⅓ *cup, softened*
to room temperature
CURRY POWDER (THE
BEST QUALITY AVAIL-
ABLE) 2 *teaspoons*
FIRM SLICED WHITE
BREAD 8 *slices, crusts*
removed

The Garnish
CANNED WHOLE
PIMIENTOS 3 *or 4, to*
make 20 strips when cut
⅛ *inch wide and about*
3 inches long
CURRIED TOAST
WATERCRESS OR PARSLEY
SPRIGS
INDIA RELISH

Repeat for each mold. If necessary, blot up any damp spots with a torn edge of paper toweling.

If using a loaf pan or ring mold, follow the same procedure, but unmold on a platter, slice in the kitchen, and serve on individual plates.

THE CURRIED TOAST: Assemble and prepare all ingredients.

1. Preheat the oven to 300 degrees.
2. Blend the softened butter thoroughly with the curry powder and spread generously on each slice of bread.
3. Cut each slice into 4 triangles. Place on a baking sheet on the middle rack of the oven. Bake for 25 to 30 minutes or until golden-brown and crisp. Can be served hot or cold.

TO SERVE: Cross 2 pimiento strips on top of each portion. Arrange 3 slices of curried toast around each plate. Tuck 1 or 2 sprigs of watercress or parsley around the toast. Pass a small bowl of India relish separately.

SUGGESTED MAIN COURSE:
Pompano en Papillote
OR *Baked Pork Chops*

Vegetables

ARTICHOKE BOTTOMS WITH SOUR CREAM AND RED CAVIAR

8 SERVINGS

You will need a 2-quart saucepan made of enameled ironware, stainless steel or earthenware: do not use aluminum—it will discolor the artichokes.

The artichoke bottoms may be prepared and cooked up to 4 days ahead and refrigerated.

Assemble just before serving.

Serve chilled.

Assemble and prepare all ingredients.

1. Place the water, oil, lemon juice, and salt in a saucepan of at least 2-quart capacity, and put the vinegar into a separate small bowl. Set both aside.

2. Prepare the artichokes one at a time, as follows: Trim off the stem of an artichoke even with the base.

3. Hold the artichoke in the palm of your left hand, base side toward you. Using a sharp paring knife, cut and snap off the leaves, rotating all around, as close as you can without taking too much of the "meat" from the bottom. Easiest done by inserting the knife between each leaf and the artichoke. Discard the leaves as you cut them away. The little edible portion left is not worth saving.

4. When you reach the pale yellow cone, turn the artichoke on its side and cut off the cone just above where it attaches to

The Artichoke Bottoms
COLD WATER *1½ quarts*
SALAD OR OLIVE OIL
  ¼ cup
FRESH LEMONS *Juice of 2*
SALT *1 tablespoon*
WHITE VINEGAR *About ⅓ cup*
FRESH ARTICHOKES *8*

The Filling
RED CAVIAR *1 jar (4-ounce size); reserve about 2 teaspoons for garnishing*
COMMERCIAL SOUR CREAM *¾ to 1 cup, depending on the size of the artichoke bottoms*

The Garnish
HARD-COOKED EGG YOLKS *3, pressed through a medium-mesh sieve*
RESERVED CAVIAR
PARSLEY SPRIGS

the hairy choke. Do not remove the choke. This will be done just before serving.

5. With a sharp knife, trim the ragged outside edges, removing all the green part, but retaining as much of the cream-colored surface underneath as possible. Dip frequently into the reserved vinegar as you work.

6. Drop each bottom into the reserved seasoned water as it is finished and repeat until all the bottoms are prepared.

7. Bring the artichokes and seasoned water to a boil and simmer, uncovered, for about 15 to 20 minutes, or until tender when pierced with the point of a sharp knife.

8. Cool in the liquid in which they cooked. They may be used at once, or refrigerated up to 4 days in their cooking liquid.

9. Remove the bottoms from the liquid. Using your fingers or a spoon (a grapefruit spoon is ideal), pull or scrape out the hairy choke a little at a time. Try and retain all the creamy bottom. Trim the top smoothly.

TO ASSEMBLE AND SERVE: 1. Reserve 2 teaspoons of the caviar and blend the balance with the sour cream.

2. Mound each artichoke bottom generously with part of the mixture.

3. Sprinkle some of the egg yolk in a circle around the filling and place 1 bottom on each small chilled plate. Put a dab of the reserved caviar in the center of each. Garnish with a few sprigs of parsley.

SUGGESTED MAIN COURSE:
Broiled Shrimp in Brochette
OR *Roast Duck*

COLD LEEKS WITH TAPENADE

8 SERVINGS

The Tapénade may be
made up to 4 days
ahead.

The leeks may be cooked
a day ahead.

Serve very cold.

———————

TAPENADE *½ of the
recipe, page 148*
TENDER LEEKS *8 medium*
CHICKEN BROTH *1½ cups*
SALT
BLACK PEPPER, GROUND
FRESH

The Garnish
RESERVED TAPENADE
MINCED PARSLEY
CANNED PIMIENTOS
*Cut to make 24 strips,
each about ⅛ inch wide
and 3 inches long*

*Leeks are often the forgotten vegetable,
yet they are delicious, especially with our
slightly tangy Tapénade.*

Assemble and prepare all ingredients.

1. Make the Tapénade and refrigerate
it until ready to serve.

2. Clean the root ends of the leeks but
do not cut them off. Then trim off all but
about 1 inch of the green tops. Remove
any withered leaves and a layer or two of
the white skins. The leeks should be about
5 inches long after trimming.

3. Starting at the leaf end, cut each in
half lengthwise being careful not to cut all
the way through the root end. You will do
this later.

4. Wash them thoroughly under cold
running water, spreading the leaves apart.
Leeks manage to trap a good deal of sand
between their leaves.

5. Place the leeks in a medium skillet,
making 2 or 3 layers. Heat the chicken
broth to boiling and pour it over them.
Season to taste with salt and pepper, and
simmer, covered, for about 15 minutes or
until the leeks are tender when pierced
with the tip of a small, pointed knife.

6. Remove from the heat, uncover, and
let them cool in the broth.

7. When cool enough to handle, drain them, reserving the broth. Transfer to a shallow dish or platter and pour a little of the reserved broth over them—just enough to moisten. Save the remaining broth to use as a soup base.

8. Cover tightly and refrigerate up to a day ahead.

TO SERVE: 1. Remove the leeks from the broth with a slotted spoon, and let them drain well. Arrange 1 whole leek in the center of each of 8 chilled serving plates. Trim off and discard the root end. Split any remaining end through and spread to form 2 halves; the cut side should be up.

2. Spread each half lengthwise with a wide ribbon of the tapénade, and sprinkle with a little minced parsley.

3. Drape 3 pimiento strips diagonally over each serving, covering both halves with each strip. Serve very cold.

SUGGESTED MAIN COURSE:
Crown Roast of Pork
OR *Chicken Paprika*

ZUCCHINI IN SALSA VERDE

6 SERVINGS

Make at least 4 hours or up to 2 days ahead.

Serve at room temperature or chilled.

The green sauce, with its anchovy flavor, adds zest to the normally bland zucchini.

Assemble and prepare all ingredients.

1. Heat about ½ inch of salad or olive oil in a medium skillet. Add the zucchini

SALAD OR OLIVE OIL FOR
  FRYING
ZUCCHINI 6 *medium: trim
  off the ends, but do not
  peel them; cut in strips
  about ⅜ by ⅜ inches
  wide and 1½ inches long*
FRESH PARSLEY *To make
  ¼ cup when minced*
GARLIC *1 clove, minced
  almost to a paste with a
  little salt*
FLAT ANCHOVY FILLETS
  IN OIL *1 can (2-ounce
  size): drain, reserve the
  oil, mash 6 to a paste
  and chop the rest for
  garnishing*
OLIVE OIL *¼ cup*
RESERVED ANCHOVY OIL
RED WINE VINEGAR
  2 tablespoons
BLACK PEPPER, GROUND
  FRESH

The Garnish
LETTUCE CUPS *6*
RESERVED CHOPPED
  ANCHOVIES
CANNED PIMIENTOS
  About 3, chopped coarse

strips, a handful at a time, and fry over medium-high heat until they just start to color. They should be slightly soft but still crisp.

2. Remove them with a slotted spoon and drain on paper towels, in a single layer. Repeat until all are fried. Cool.

3. In a small bowl, combine the parsley, garlic, 6 mashed anchovies, olive oil, reserved anchovy oil, vinegar, and black pepper to taste. Beat to blend with a fork or wire whisk.

4. In a medium bowl, pour the sauce over the zucchini and toss until they are well covered. Let the mixture marinate at room temperature for about 4 hours, turning occasionally. Then cover and refrigerate for up to 2 days or until ready to serve. Serve at room temperature or chilled.

TO SERVE: Put the lettuce cups on 6 chilled plates and divide the zucchini among them. Garnish with the chopped anchovies and a sprinkling of chopped pimientos.

SUGGESTED MAIN COURSE:
  Lasagne
  OR *Jambalaya, page 201*

ANTIPASTO MISTO

10 TO 12 SERVINGS

Best made a day ahead,
but it must marinate
for at least 4 hours.

Serve slightly chilled or
at room temperature.

———————

OLIVE OIL *1 cup*
CELERY STALKS *To make
1 cup when scraped of
strings and cut in 1-inch
slices: cut the large base-
end slices in half*
GREEN BELL PEPPER
*1 large, cut in half
lengthwise: discard core,
seeds, and heavy veins,
then cut lengthwise in
¼-inch strips*
GREEN BEANS *¼ pound:
remove the ends and
string if necessary, then
slice diagonally in very
thin ovals about 1 inch
long (cut with your
knife at about a 20-
degree angle to the
beans)*
CAULIFLOWER *To make
2 cups when broken into
flowerets*

*Don't let the formidable list of ingredients
throw you. When all the flavors blend, it
turns out to be something pretty wonderful and beautiful to behold.*

Assemble and prepare all ingredients.

It's very important to remember that
the vegetables should be cooked only until *al dente:* just tender, but still firm to the
bite.

1. Heat the oil in a 12-inch skillet or
heatproof casserole at least 10 inches in
diameter. When very hot and just starting
to smoke, add the celery, green pepper,
green beans, cauliflower, and onions. Reduce the heat to medium-high. Toss and
turn frequently and cook for about 4 minutes.

2. Add the zucchini, mushrooms, and
garlic. Cook for 4 minutes longer, turning
frequently.

3. Add the tomato purée, wine, and
vinegar-and-sugar mixture. When the liquid starts to simmer, add the shrimp,
scallops (if using cooked fish, add it at the
end of the cooking time), basil, oregano,
parsley, black and green olives, and the
pimiento. Sprinkle with the salt and 2 or 3
grinds of the pepper mill. Turn frequently
for 6 to 8 minutes more, or until the
vegetables are tender but still crisp, and
the shrimp are opaque but still firm. Do
not overcook.

ONIONS *To make 2 cups (about ½ pound) when sliced in rounds about ¼ inch thick: cut rounds into quarters*

ZUCCHINI 6 *small, unpeeled: trim off ends, cut in 1-inch-thick slices, then cut each slice in half crosswise*

FRESH BUTTON MUSHROOMS ½ *pound: first wipe with a damp paper towel if necessary, then cut off the stem end flush with the caps*

GARLIC 5 *cloves, peeled and minced with a little salt*

TOMATO PUREE ⅔ *cup*

DRY WHITE WINE ½ *cup*

WINE VINEGAR ½ *cup* MIXED WITH:

SUGAR 1 *tablespoon*

UNCOOKED SHRIMP 1½ *pounds medium, shelled: devein only if you prefer*

BAY SCALLOPS, OR LARGER ONES CUT IN 1-INCH PIECES *To make 2 cups when drained (about 1 pound)*

OR COOKED, LEFTOVER FISH FILLETS FROM ANY FIRM, WHITE

4. Put the mixture into a large bowl and add the potatoes, pushing them down into the sauce. Refrigerate for at least 4 hours; a day ahead is better. Serve slightly chilled or at room temperature.

TO SERVE: Present this dish with a bit of drama. Transfer the mixture to your prettiest large bowl. Place the necessary number of individual small plates and a small bowl of lettuce cups in front of the host. The host will present the bowl of Antipasto Misto to be viewed by each guest, then put a lettuce cup on each plate, and fill it with a portion of the Antipasto. Or, the bowl could be placed on a side table or buffet, with each plate holding a lettuce cup. Let the guests help themselves. Pass the bread sticks and butter.

SUGGESTED MAIN COURSE:
   Coq au Vin
   OR *Baked Pork Chops*

FISH *To make 2 cups when cut in 1-inch chunks: remove any small bones*

DRIED BASIL LEAVES
¼ teaspoon, crumbled

DRIED OREGANO LEAVES
¼ teaspoon, crumbled

PARSLEY *To make ¾ cup when chopped coarse*

PITTED BLACK OLIVES
12 jumbo

PIMIENTO-STUFFED GREEN OLIVES *12 large*

CANNED SLICED PIMIENTOS *⅓ cup when drained (about a 4-ounce jar or can)*

SALT *1½ teaspoons*

BLACK PEPPER, GROUND FRESH

CANNED WHOLE SMALL POTATOES *About 2 cups when drained (1 can, 16- or 17-ounce size)*

The Garnish
LETTUCE CUPS

The Accompaniment
BREAD STICKS IN TALL GLASSES

BUTTER

PIMIENTOS FILLED WITH MUSHROOMS

8 SERVINGS

The filling must be
prepared a day ahead.

May be assembled several
hours before serving.

Serve at room tempera-
ture.

_____

FRESH MUSHROOMS
*1½ pounds: first wipe
with a damp paper
towel, if necessary*
BUTTER (NOT
MARGARINE) *2 table-
spoons*
SALAD OR MILD OLIVE
OIL *2 tablespoons*
RED ONION *To make ¼
cup when peeled and
chopped very fine*
SESAME SEEDS *2 table-
spoons*
DRIED BASIL LEAVES
½ teaspoon, crumbled
DRIED TARRAGON *½ tea-
spoon, crumbled*
DRIED THYME LEAVES
½ teaspoon, crumbled

Assemble and prepare all ingredients.

1. Trim and discard the dry tip of the
mushroom stems, cut off the remaining
stems at the base of the cap, and reserve.

2. Heat the butter and oil in a large
skillet. When it is very hot, add the mushrooms and stems. Sauté rapidly over moderately high heat, tossing and turning constantly, until the mushrooms start to color
and there is some liquid in the pan, about
5 minutes. They should be slightly firm.
Remove from the heat, strain off the liquid, and reserve it.

3. Cool the mushrooms and stems and
chop them fine. Put them into a bowl with
the onion, sesame seeds, basil, tarragon,
thyme, oregano, and the reserved mushroom liquid. Mix thoroughly and add salt
and pepper to taste. Cover and refrigerate
for at least a day so that the flavors will
blend and develop. It is surprising how
mild this may taste when you first make it
—the next day, what a difference!

4. Mix the oil and vinegar for the topping and reserve at room temperature until ready to serve.

TO ASSEMBLE: Carefully pat the pimientos
dry—they tear easily—and fill each with
part of the mushroom mixture, pressing it
down lightly, so that the pimientos will,

DRIED OREGANO LEAVES
  ½ teaspoon, crumbled
RESERVED MUSHROOM
  LIQUID
SALT
BLACK PEPPER, GROUND
  FRESH
CANNED WHOLE
  PIMIENTOS 8 (*2 cans,
  7 ounces each*): *use any
  extras in the can as
  "spares," in case 1 or 2
  tear while filling*

The Topping
SALAD OR OLIVE OIL
  ¾ cup
WINE VINEGAR *3 table-
  spoons*

The Garnish
SHREDDED LETTUCE

The Accompaniment
ANCHOVY CRESCENTS,
  page 303
OR BUTTER CRACKERS

8 SERVINGS AS A FIRST
  COURSE OR THE RECIPE
  MAY BE HALVED AND
  SERVED AS PART OF AN
  HORS D'OEUVRE TRAY

hopefully, stand upright. (A trick for this later.) If assembled ahead, put them into a wide bowl, propping them against the sides and each other to hold them upright. Keep at room temperature, well covered, or refrigerate until an hour before serving.

TO SERVE: 1. Here is the trick. Holding the pimientos one at a time in the palm of one hand, use the index finger of your other hand to press the bottom of the pimiento into itself, about ¼ inch deep, to form a little "belly button." Arrange them on individual plates. They should stand upright. If they don't, never mind, turn them on their sides like a cornucopia—no one will know the difference!

2. Surround each with some of the shredded lettuce. Stir the oil-and-vinegar mixture again, dribble about 2 teaspoons of it over the top of each pimiento and a tablespoon or so over the lettuce. Serve at once.

SUGGESTED MAIN COURSE:
  Cold Swedish Salmon Mousse, page 26
  OR *"Bones," page 211*

ONIONS MONACO

A perfectly delicious dish. The onions are a bore to peel. Enlist the help of a friend or the children.

Can be made up to 2 days
  ahead and refrigerated.

Serve cold.

———————

**PEARL ONIONS (PICKLING
  ONIONS) OR SMALL
  WHITE ONIONS ABOUT
  1-INCH IN DIAMETER**
  *1 ¼ pounds (or two
  10-ounce baskets), of
  uniform size, if possible*
BOILING WATER
WHITE WINE *1 cup*
WATER *1 cup*
CIDER VINEGAR *⅔ cup*
SALAD OIL *2 tablespoons*
OLIVE OIL *2 tablespoons*
TOMATO PASTE *¼ cup*
BAY LEAVES *2 whole*
GROUND THYME *Rounded
  ¼ teaspoon*
DARK SEEDLESS RAISINS
  ⅔ cup
SUGAR *2 tablespoons*
FRESH PARSLEY *2 sprigs*
**BLACK PEPPER, GROUND
  FRESH**

The Garnish
SMALL LETTUCE CUPS

The Accompaniment
FINGERS OF BUTTERED

Assemble all ingredients.

1. To peel the onions, plunge them into rapidly boiling water for 1 minute. Drain them and shave off both ends. The dry outer layers of skin can then be removed quite easily.

2. With a small, sharp knife, cut a tiny cross, about ¹⁄₁₆ inch deep, in the root end of each onion to help retain their shape while cooking.

3. In a saucepan put the onions, wine, water, vinegar, salad oil, olive oil, tomato paste, bay leaves, thyme, raisins, sugar, parsley, and a twist or two of the pepper mill. Simmer, uncovered, for 30 to 45 minutes, or until the onions are tender but still firm, and the liquid is reduced to a thick syrup. If the onions start to stick, add a little more water during the cooking. Or if the liquid is too thin when the onions are done, remove them and boil the liquid down to a thick syrup.

4. Transfer to a bowl and chill before serving.

TO SERVE: Put a small lettuce cup on each small, chilled plate, and divide the onions evenly among them. Put a finger or two of black bread on the side, and a rolled-up slice of *prosciutto*. Or pass a bowl of Anchovy Crescents.

SUGGESTED MAIN COURSE:
  Pâté de Campagne, page 144
  OR *Coulibiac*

BLACK BREAD AND
SMALL THIN SLICES OF
PROSCIUTTO
OR ANCHOVY CRESCENTS,
page 303

THE PRIEST FAINTED
(Imam Bayildi)

8 SERVINGS

Prepare and bake at least
4 hours ahead, but this
is at its best when
made a day ahead and
refrigerated.

Bring to room tempera-
ture before serving.

———

EGGPLANT *4 small, about
½ pound each or about
4¼ inches long*

SALT

OLIVE OIL *¼ cup, plus
more if needed: for best
flavor, don't use a
substitute*

ONIONS *To make 2 cups
when chopped medium-
fine (about 2 medium)*

GREEN BELL PEPPER
*1 large: core, remove
seeds and veins, and
chop medium-fine*

Imam bayildi literally means "the priest fainted." There are many versions of the origin of this favorite Turkish dish. The one we like best tells the story of the Moslem priest who, upon returning to the home of his proud host from the Fast of Ramadan, partook of this dish. He smelled the heavenly aroma, and, in an ecstasy of delight, ate portion after portion. In fact, he ate so much that he fainted, passing out prone on the floor, right then and there.

Some followers arrived for council and when they saw the prostrate priest, they asked, "What happened to the *Imam?*"

"*Imam bayildi,*" answered his host. And so the dish was named.

Assemble and prepare all ingredients.

1. Bring a large pot of water to a rapid boil. Put in the whole, unpeeled eggplant and boil vigorously, uncovered, for 5 minutes. If your pot isn't large enough, boil 2 at a time. Turn them over occasionally, using 2 spoons so that you won't pierce the skin. Then immediately plunge them into cold water to stop the cooking.

GARLIC 3 *large cloves,*
 peeled and minced very
 fine with a little salt
PARSLEY *To make 2 table-*
 spoons when minced,
 plus a little extra for
 garnishing
DRIED OREGANO LEAVES
 ½ teaspoon, crumbled
CAYENNE PEPPER
 2 or 3 dashes
PINE NUTS *¼ cup*
TOMATOES *4 medium,*
 peeled and cored: cut
 into halves, scrape out
 the seeds and juice, cut
 into small chunks, then
 put on several thicknesses
 of paper towels to drain
 thoroughly
SUGAR *⅛ teaspoon*
OLIVE OIL *3 tablespoons*
FRESH LEMON JUICE
 2 tablespoons
BLACK PEPPER, GROUND
 FRESH
SALT

The Garnish
RESERVED MINCED
 PARSLEY
PITTED SLICED BLACK
 OLIVES

2. Cut off the stems and cut each eggplant in half lengthwise. Scoop out and discard most of the center seed section, retaining as much of the pulp as possible. Using a small, sharp knife, cut around the inside of each half, about ¼ inch from the edge. Hold the knife at a slight inward angle as you cut, so that you won't pierce the skin. Gradually working downward (a grapefruit knife or spoon is very helpful), scoop out the remaining pulp in as large pieces as possible. Don't cut too deep, as you want about ¼ inch of pulp left on the bottom of the shell. Smooth off any thick places. If you pierce the skin in a spot or two, mend it by placing a small piece of eggplant over it.

3. Cut the pulp into medium-fine dice. Sprinkle very lightly with salt. Put into a colander to drain for at least 30 minutes. Drain the eggplant shells skin side up on paper towels. Reserve.

4. When ready, spread the diced eggplant in a single layer between several thicknesses of paper towels and pat dry.

5. Heat the ¼ cup of olive oil in a large skillet. When very hot add half the diced eggplant. Toss and turn until golden; do not let brown. Using a large slotted spoon, remove to a side dish. Repeat with the other half of the eggplant. Reserve.

6. If necessary, add more oil to the same skillet and when it is very hot, add the onions and green pepper. Sauté together for a few minutes, then add the minced garlic and continue to sauté, stir-

The Accompaniment
COMMERCIAL SOUR
   CREAM
COARSE DARK BREAD,
   BUTTERED

ring frequently, until the mixture is just beginning to soften.

7. Add the 2 tablespoons of minced parsley, the oregano, cayenne pepper, pine nuts, and the reserved eggplant. Cook together for a few minutes more. The mixture should be moist but with no visible liquid on the bottom of the pan.

8. Remove from the heat, stir in the well-drained pieces of tomato and the sugar.

9. Mix together 1 tablespoon of the remaining olive oil and the lemon juice. Pour it over the eggplant mixture and sprinkle with a few grinds of the pepper mill. Toss and taste; add salt if necessary.

WHEN READY TO BAKE: 1. Preheat the oven to 350 degrees.

2. Spread the remaining 2 tablespoons of oil in a shallow baking pan. Using a paper towel, pat the inside of the eggplant shells dry. Spoon the mixture into the shells and arrange them, filled side up, in the baking pan. Cover with foil, place on the middle rack of the preheated oven, and bake for 25 minutes.

3. Remove the foil and cool the eggplant in the pan. Then either cover and let them remain at room temperature for 4 hours before serving or refrigerate overnight and remove 2 to 3 hours before serving so that they will return to room temperature.

TO SERVE: Put the filled shells on individual plates. Sprinkle each serving with minced parsley, then place a few sliced olives on top. Pass the sour cream and the buttered bread separately.

SUGGESTED MAIN COURSE:
Crabmeat Mornay, page 98
OR *Beef à la Mode*

MARINATED CARROTS

The lowly carrot takes on fancy dress and more taste appeal in this dish.

Assemble and prepare all ingredients.

1. In a 1½-quart saucepan, combine the vinegar, wine, water, oil, sugar, salt, garlic, bay leaf, thyme, dill, parsley, and cayenne pepper.

2. Bring the marinade to a boil and add the carrots. When the water returns to a simmer, cook, uncovered, for about 15 to 20 minutes, or until the carrots are tender but still firm to the bite. They should bend only slightly.

3. Drain the carrots, set them aside, and reserve the marinade.

4. Put the mustard into a small bowl and add a little of the marinade to it. Stir well to make a thin paste. Add to the balance of the marinade, mixing well. Pour the marinade over the carrots, cover and refrigerate for at least 6 hours or up to 2 days.

SERVE: Either as part of an hors d'oeuvre tray or as a first course on a bed of lettuce.

2 CUPS

Make 6 hours ahead; 1 or 2 days is better

Serve cold.

_____

WHITE WINE VINEGAR
   ½ cup
DRY WHITE WINE *½ cup*
WATER *½ cup*
OLIVE OIL *½ cup*
SUGAR *1 teaspoon*
SALT *1 teaspoon*
GARLIC *2 cloves, peeled and minced almost to a paste with a little salt*
BAY LEAF *1, crumbled*
DRIED THYME LEAVES
   ½ teaspoon, crumbled
DILL *To make 1 tablespoon when chopped fine, if fresh or if dried, 1 teaspoon*
PARSLEY, PREFERABLY
   FLAT-LEAF *4 sprigs, minced*

CAYENNE PEPPER *Pinch*

FRESH CARROTS *1 pound,
peeled and cut in strips
about 3/8 inch thick and
2 inches long: baby
carrots are delicious left
whole, of course, but
allow a longer cooking
time*

DIJON MUSTARD *1 table-
spoon*

6 SERVINGS

Must be made a day
ahead, but may be
prepared up to 4 days
in advance and re-
frigerated.

You will need dampened
newspaper, a small,
sharp knife, and up to
4 kitchen forks or long
skewers.

Serve at room tempera-
ture.

GREEN OR RED BELL
PEPPERS OR A COM-
BINATION OF THE
TWO *4 large: choose*

SUGGESTED MAIN COURSE:
   Teriyaki Steak
   OR *Chicken Tetrazzini*

MARINATED GREEN PEPPERS AND BLACK OLIVES

*The peppers for this dish are peeled. We
warn you, you'll never be happy eating
the tough outer skin again!*

Assemble and prepare all ingredients.

1. Remove the skins from the peppers.
If you have a gas stove: spear the stem end
of a pepper with a kitchen fork or a long
skewer. Put the pepper directly on the
grate over a high flame. Leave until the
side touching the flame is blistered and
blackened. Turn and continue until the
skin is blistered and blackened all over,
and then turn to blacken on each end.
Watch carefully to prevent the flesh from
burning. Repeat with each pepper, or if
you are using separate burners, you can do
4 at one time.

If you have an electric broiler: put the
peppers directly under the heating unit, as
close as possible and almost touching the

*the fullest with the least
depressions for easier
peeling*

OLIVE OIL *⅓ cup*

RED WINE VINEGAR
1½ tablespoons

GARLIC *1 large clove
minced almost to a paste
with a little salt*

PITTED BLACK OLIVES
*To make ½ cup when
drained and sliced in
half*

SALT

BLACK PEPPER, GROUND
FRESH

ONIONS *3 thick slices:
these will be discarded
later*

The Garnish

WATERCRESS SPRIGS

MUENSTER OR MONTEREY
JACK CHEESE *Cut in
small cubes (about
⅓ pound)*

element. When the top side is blistered and blackened, turn and continue turning until the skin is blistered and blackened all over. Watch carefully to prevent the flesh from burning.

2. As each pepper is blackened, remove from the heat and immediately wrap them individually in wet newspaper. Let them remain for about 5 minutes. The steam will loosen the skin.

3. Unwrap the peppers 1 at a time. (Do not unwrap the second until you have peeled the first one, and so on.) Cut in half lengthwise. Remove and discard the stem, core, seeds, and heavy veins.

4. Lay the halves on a flat surface and, with a small, sharp knife, carefully scrape off all of the black. Then scrape under running cold water to remove any remaining specks. If there is any blistered green skin left, remove it by putting the tip of the knife just under the skin and carefully pulling it away. Rinse again under cold running water and dry on paper towels.

5. Repeat with the remaining peppers.

TO FINISH THE DISH: 1. Cut the peppers lengthwise into ⅜-inch strips and put them into a bowl.

2. In another bowl mix together the olive oil, vinegar, garlic, and olives. Add salt and pepper to taste and pour over the peppers, turning until they are well coated.

3. Lift the peppers and tuck the onion slices under them in several places.

4. Cover and refrigerate overnight or for up to 4 days. Turn occasionally.

5. About an hour before serving, remove from the refrigerator, discard the onion slices, and let the peppers come to room temperature.

TO SERVE: Drain and divide equally among 6 small plates. Surround each serving with 3 or 4 sprigs of watercress and top with several cubes of cheese.

SUGGESTED MAIN COURSE:
> *Chupe—a Seafood Casserole, page 203*
> OR *Cold Poached Fish with Aïoli Sauce, page 12*

CAPONATA WITH MARINATED ARTICHOKE HEARTS

6 TO 8 SERVINGS

The artichokes must marinate 6 hours, or for up to 2 days.

The Caponata is at its best when made 1 or 2 days in advance, but it will keep for up to 1 week, refrigerated.

Can be assembled about ½ hour before serving.

Serve at room temperature or chilled.

Caponata *is an Italian peasant dish. Try serving it sometime without the artichokes as part of an* antipasto *plate, or in larger portions as a main course garnished with hard-cooked eggs, shrimp or tuna fish, and accompanied with toasted garlic bread or Herb Bread, page 316.*

THE ARTICHOKE: Assemble and prepare all ingredients.

Put the prepared artichoke hearts into a small, deep bowl. Mix the ¾ cup of olive oil with the garlic and pour it over them. Toss and turn gently until all the artichokes are well coated. Cover and marinate for at least 6 hours at room tem-

The Artichokes

FROZEN ARTICHOKE
HEARTS 2 *packages*
(*9-ounces each*): *cooked*
according to package
directions, then drained
and turned, cut side
down, on paper toweling
to cool

MILD OLIVE OIL ¾ *cup*

GARLIC 2 *cloves, peeled*
and minced to a paste
with a little salt

The Caponata

EGGPLANT *To make 4 cups*
when peeled and cut in
¼-inch dice (about
¾ pounds)

SALT

MILD OLIVE OIL ⅓ *cup,*
or more if necessary

CELERY *To make 1 cup*
when chopped very fine:
use the tender inside
stalks only

ONIONS *To make ⅓ cup*
when chopped very fine

FRESH TOMATOES *To make*
1½ cups when chopped
fine (2 or 3 medium):
first peel and cut in half
crosswise, then gently
squeeze and shake to

perature. If made 2 days in advance, refrigerate the first day and let stand at room
temperature the second day. Stir occasionally.

THE CAPONATA: Assemble and prepare all
ingredients.

1. Sprinkle the eggplant lightly with
salt. Spread a double thickness of paper
towels on a flat surface. Place the eggplant
cubes on it in a single layer. Cover with
more paper towels and press together.
Place either a breadboard, plates, or pots
on top. The idea is to weight the eggplant
slightly so that some of the bitter juice will
be pressed out. Let drain for 30 minutes.

2. In the meantime, in a large skillet,
heat about 2 tablespoons of the ⅓ cup of
olive oil. Add the celery and sauté over
medium-low heat for about 8 minutes, or
until slightly soft but not brown. Stir frequently. Add the onions and sauté, turning
frequently, for another 5 to 8 minutes, or
until the onions are soft and just starting
to color. Transfer to a small bowl and reserve.

3. Wipe the skillet with a piece of paper toweling. Put half the remaining oil
into it and heat until a haze starts to form.
Add half the drained eggplant cubes and
sauté over high heat, tossing and turning
constantly until most of them are golden-
brown on all sides. Remove with a slotted
spoon and transfer to the bowl containing
the celery and onions. Add the remaining
oil to the skillet and the remaining egg-

*remove the seeds and
juice*
PIMIENTO-STUFFED
 GREEN OLIVES *½ cup
 when chopped fine*
CAPERS *To make 1 table-
 spoon when drained
 and chopped*
CANNED FLAT ANCHOVY
 FILLETS IN OIL *About
 4, mashed to a paste*
DRY RED WINE *½ cup,
 or more if necessary*
RED WINE VINEGAR
 3 tablespoons
MIXED WITH:
SUGAR *2 teaspoons*
PINE NUTS (OPTIONAL)
 1½ tablespoons
SALT
BLACK PEPPER, GROUND
 FRESH

The Garnish
CANNED PIMIENTOS,
 CHOPPED
LEMON OR LIME WEDGES

plant and cook the same way. If the egg-plant starts to stick, add a little more oil, but as little as possible, because the Caponata should not be oily.

4. Turn the heat to low and return the reserved eggplant cubes, celery, and onions to the skillet. Add the tomatoes, olives, capers, anchovies, the ½ cup of wine, and vinegar-sugar mixture. Blend thoroughly so that the anchovies will be well distributed.

5. Bring the mixture to a gentle simmer and cook, uncovered, for 15 minutes or more, stirring frequently, until the Caponata is thick and condensed and there is no visible liquid on the bottom of the pan. If the mixture gets dry before the Caponata is thick, add a little more red wine.

6. Stir in the pine nuts, if desired, salt, and a few grinds of the pepper mill. Cool, and taste for seasoning. The Caponata should have a sweet-sour taste. Add more pepper if you like, but be cautious before adding more salt. Refrigerate in a covered bowl for 1 or 2 days.

TO ASSEMBLE AND SERVE: Drain the artichoke hearts. Place 4 half sections, cut side up, on a small plate. Space evenly in a circular pattern, like the spokes of a wheel, putting the base ends inward and the pointed ends outward. Space the base ends about 1 or 2 inches from the center of the plate. Mound about ⅓ cup of Caponata over the base ends, partially covering them. Top with a dab of chopped pimiento. Place 2 or 3 lemon or lime wedges on the side of the plate. Repeat for each serving.

SUGGESTED MAIN COURSE:
Ham Loaf
OR *Goulash*

AILEEN'S AVOCADOS AND HOT SAUCE

8 SERVINGS

The sauce may be made 1 or 2 days in advance and reheated just before serving.

Serve in small, shallow cereal bowls, or in saucers placed on a serving plate.

The sauce is served very hot and the avocados well chilled.

———————

CHILI SAUCE *½ cup*
WORCESTERSHIRE SAUCE
    6 tablespoons
FRESH LIME JUICE
    6 tablespoons
BUTTER *½ cup*
SUGAR *6 tablespoons or a little more, to taste*

This is quick and easy. The bland and the biting, the hot and the cold, make a taste-provoking combination.

Assemble and prepare all ingredients except the avocados.

1. Put the chili sauce, Worcestershire sauce, lime juice, butter, and sugar in the top section of a double boiler.

2. Heat over simmering water until the sauce is very hot. Stir occasionally to dissolve the sugar and distribute the butter.

3. Taste for seasoning and add more sugar to your liking, if necessary. The sauce should have a sweet-sour taste and be very piquant. It will mellow when eaten with a spoonful of avocado.

4. Keep hot until ready to serve, or refrigerate and reheat in a double boiler.

JUST BEFORE SERVING: 1. Reheat the sauce, if necessary.

2. Line 8 small, shallow cereal bowls or saucers with lettuce leaves and put them on service plates.

AVOCADOS 4 *medium, well chilled*

The Garnish
LETTUCE LEAVES
CORN OR TORTILLA CHIPS

3. Cut the chilled avocados in half lengthwise. Remove and discard the seed and cut a sliver off the bottom of each so that they will stand upright. Place in the bowls, and when the sauce is very hot, stir it well and put a tablespoon or so into the center cavity of each avocado half. Put the extra sauce into a small, warm pitcher. Serve at once.

4. Pass the corn or tortilla chips, and the extra sauce separately.

SUGGESTED MAIN COURSE:
Cold Poached Salmon
OR *Couscous*

TOMATO ICE ELEGANTE IN TOMATO SHELLS

8 SERVINGS

A blender is a must.

May be made ahead and frozen.

Defrost to a mush before serving.

It must be made at least 10 hours ahead.

The tomato shells may be prepared in the morning.

Assemble and prepare all ingredients.

1. Put 1 cup of the tomato juice, the Worcestershire sauce, Tabasco sauce, lemon juice, sugar, onion, Roquefort, and cream cheese into a blender and whirl together until smooth. Remove to a medium bowl.

2. Add the balance of the tomato juice, salt and pepper to taste, and a dash or two more Tabasco sauce or Worcestershire sauce, if necessary. Stir thoroughly. The mixture should be rather highly seasoned as it will lose a little flavor as it freezes.

3. Transfer the mixture to a flat-bottomed pan. A bread pan about 5 by 9 by 3 inches is ideal. Put in the freezer and chill

TOMATO JUICE *2 cups*

WORCESTERSHIRE SAUCE
*1 teaspoon, or a little
more*

TABASCO SAUCE *3 or 4
dashes, or more*

LEMON JUICE *2 table-
spoons*

SUGAR *¼ teaspoon*

ONION *To make ½ tea-
spoon when grated*

ROQUEFORT OR BLUE
CHEESE *3 tablespoons*

CREAM CHEESE *1 package
(3-ounce size), cut in
chunks*

SALT

WHITE PEPPER, GROUND
FRESH

EGG WHITES *2, at room
temperature*

FIRM TOMATOES *8, about
2½ inches in diameter:
they should be of a size
to fit into a stemmed
sherbet or martini glass*

The Accompaniment

BENNE SEED WAFERS,
page 313

OR MARINATED SODA
CRACKERS, *page 311*

OR ANY COMMERCIALLY
PREPARED THIN, NON-
SWEET WAFER (NOT
CHEESE FLAVOR)

until all but the center portion is frozen, or at least 4 hours.

4. Beat the egg whites until they form soft peaks when the beater is lifted.

5. Remove the partially frozen tomato mixture from the refrigerator and transfer it to a bowl. Break it up with a fork and then beat it until smooth, using a rotary or electric mixer. Stir in a third of the beaten egg whites. Then quickly fold in the remaining egg whites.

6. Put the mixture back into the freezing pan, cover tightly, and return to the freezer. Freeze until about ¾ of an hour before serving. Then let it defrost to a mush—about the consistency of an ice or sherbet. (If it is to be used within 2 or 3 hours of the second freezing, freeze only until it reaches the mushy stage.)

7. In the meantime cut off and discard about ½ inch of the top of each tomato. Do not peel them.

8. Using a spoon and a small, sharp knife, scoop out the liquid, seeds, and meaty pulp to form a shell, leaving only the firm outer walls. Save the tops, liquid, and pulp for another use. Drain the tomatoes, cut side down, on a rack or paper-lined plate until ready to serve.

TO SERVE: Put a tomato shell into each of 8 stemmed sherbet or martini glasses. Spoon a generous portion of the tomato ice into each, mounding it a little. Serve on individual plates accompanied, if you wish, with Benne Seed Wafers, Marinated

Soda Crackers, or any other nonsweet, non-cheese crackers of your choice.

SUGGESTED MAIN COURSE:
A Greek Salad, page 156
OR *Standing Rib Roast*

Salads

MARINATED HEARTS OF PALM WITH ANCHOVY TOAST

8 SERVINGS

You will need a blender.

The hearts of palm may
 be marinated for up to
 2 days, but they must
 be marinated at least
 for 6 hours in advance
 of serving.

May be assembled in the
 morning and chilled
 on individual plates
 until ready to serve.

The anchovy toast may
 be prepared in the
 morning and put in the
 oven 20 to 25 minutes
 before serving.

Serve the hearts of palm

Assemble and prepare all ingredients for
the hearts of palm.

1. Put the oil, vinegar, onion, garlic,
and mustard into a blender, adding salt
and pepper to taste. Blend at high speed
for 3 or 4 minutes, or until the mixture is
creamy and smooth.

2. Split the 8 drained hearts of palm in
half lengthwise. Place them, split side
down, in a stainless-steel, glass, or ceramic
flat-bottomed pan, preferably just large
enough to hold them in a single layer.
Handle them gently so that they don't
come apart.

3. Pour the seasoned oil over them and
cover with plastic wrap. Marinate for at
least 6 hours, or up to 2 days. Occasionally
spoon a little of the marinade over the top.
Serve chilled.

THE ANCHOVY TOAST: Assemble all ingredients.

very cold and the toast warm.

SALAD OIL *1 cup*
WHITE WINE OR
   TARRAGON VINEGAR
   2 tablespoons
ONION *½ medium, peeled
   and cut in small chunks*
GARLIC *2 cloves, peeled
   and cut in small pieces*
DIJON MUSTARD
   ½ teaspoon
SALT
WHITE PEPPER, GROUND
   FRESH
HEARTS OF PALM (THE
   BEST QUALITY AVAIL-
   ABLE SO THAT THEY
   WILL BE EVENLY
   SIZED) *8, well drained
   (2 cans, 14-ounces, each)*

The Anchovy Toast
SOFTENED SWEET BUTTER
   ¼ cup
ANCHOVY PASTE *1½ tea-
   spoons*
LEMON JUICE *A few drops*
FIRM SLICED WHITE
   BREAD *4 slices, crusts
   removed*

The Garnish
LETTUCE LEAVES

1. Preheat the oven to 300 degrees.

2. Thoroughly mix the softened butter, anchovy paste, and lemon juice. Cover each slice of bread generously with the seasoned butter, spreading it to the edges. It will seem like a lot of butter, but it will melt down into the bread as it bakes.

3. Cut each slice of bread into 4 triangles. Bake on a foil-lined baking sheet on the middle rack of the oven for 20 to 25 minutes or until golden-brown and crisp. Serve warm.

TO SERVE: Place flattened lettuce leaves on individual salad plates. Using a slotted spoon, carefully lift a split palm heart and put 2 halves on each plate. Sprinkle with the remaining marinade. Cross 2 strips of pimiento on each serving and garnish with 3 black olives and 2 anchovy toast triangles.

SUGGESTED MAIN COURSE:
   Shrimp Crêpes
   OR *Chicken Curry*

**CANNED PIMIENTO
STRIPS** *16, cut about ⅛
inch wide and about 2½
inches long*
PITTED BLACK OLIVES 24

TABBOULEH
(Lebanese Salad)

8 SERVINGS

Must be made at least 6
hours ahead, but it is
better marinated over-
night.

At its best served
thoroughly chilled.

———————

**BULGHUR, FINE OR
MEDIUM-FINE** *1 cup*
BOILING WATER *2 cups*
**FRESH PARSLEY, PREFER-
ABLY FLAT-LEAF**
*To make 1 cup when
chopped fine*
SCALLIONS *To make 1 cup
when chopped fine: in-
clude about 3 inches of
the green stems*
MINT, PREFERABLY FRESH
*To make ½ cup when
chopped fine, or, if
dried, 4 tablespoons,
soaked in water for ½
hour, then well drained*

*Bulghur is the unforgettable ingredient in
this salad. It's a free-wheeling, beautifully
seasoned dish. The versions and proportions of the "makings" vary with the cook.
Bulghur may be purchased in most health-
food stores or in shops carrying Middle
Eastern food products.*

Assemble and prepare all ingredients.

1. Put the bulghur into a large 2- or 3-
quart bowl and pour the boiling water
over it. Let it soak for 1½ to 2 hours, until most of the water is absorbed. All of the
water will be absorbed eventually, but you
do not have to wait before completing the
salad.

2. Add the parsley, scallions, mint,
tomatoes, olive oil, and lemon juice to the
bulghur and mix gently but thoroughly.
Add salt and pepper to taste and mix
again.

3. Cover tightly and allow to marinate
in the refrigerator for at least 6 hours or
overnight.

TO SERVE: Put 3 small or 1 large leaf of
romaine lettuce on each of 8 chilled plates

FIRM RIPE TOMATOES
  3 large, chopped coarse:
  first peel and cut them
  in half crosswise, then
  squeeze gently and shake
  to extract the juice and
  seeds
OLIVE OIL *½ cup*
FRESH LEMON JUICE
  ⅓ cup
SALT
BLACK PEPPER, GROUND
  FRESH

The Garnish
CENTER LEAVES OF
  ROMAINE LETTUCE
  About 24 small (3 per
  person), or 8 large (1
  per person)

The Accompaniment
BREAD STICKS AND
  BUTTER

and divide the salad among them. Pass the
bread sticks and butter.

SUGGESTED MAIN COURSE:
  Pitta Bread with Meat Filling, page
  166
  OR *Barbecued Spareribs*

LENTIL SALAD

12 SERVINGS

May be made up to a
  week ahead and re-
  frigerated, but must
  marinate several hours
  before serving.

Serve cold.

This is from Caroline Tupper, who serves
it with cocktails or whenever anyone is
slightly hungry. The first time we had it,
it was the first course of a "drinking din-
ner," eaten with cocktails, and followed
by raw vegetables with a sour-cream dip.
Then her "All-Day Soup," and finally fruit
and cheese for dessert, both with a good

DRY LENTILS 2 *cups*
WATER 5 *cups*
SALT 2 *teaspoons*
FRESH PARSLEY *To make
½ to ¾ cup when
minced (about 1 to 1½
cups of parsley sprigs)*
SCALLIONS 4 *or* 5, *chopped
fine, include a little of
the pale green stems*
SAFFLOWER OR OTHER
LIGHT SALAD OIL
¼ *cup*
LEMON JUICE 3 *table-
spoons*
CURRY POWDER (THE
BEST QUALITY AVAIL-
ABLE) 3 *teaspoons*
DIJON MUSTARD 2 *to* 3
teaspoons
GARLIC 1 *clove, peeled and
minced almost to a paste
with a little salt*
SALT

The Garnish
LETTUCE LEAF CUPS
RADISH ROSES (*page 320*)
24
OR CELERY STUFFED WITH
SOFTENED ROQUEFORT
CHEESE 24 *pieces, each
about 3 inches long*

*hearty red wine. We ate and drank for 3
hours and the conversation was brilliant.
The Lentil Salad started it all!*

Assemble and prepare all ingredients.

1. Wash the lentils and put them into
a large pot with the water. Cover and
bring to a simmer. Add the salt after about
20 minutes. Continue cooking for 20 minutes more, until the lentils are tender but
still crunchy. If necessary, add more water
to keep the beans covered. Don't let them
get too soft. The pleasure of this dish is in
the texture as well as the flavor.

2. Drain the lentils thoroughly and
chill.

3. Add the parsley and the scallions
and fold together. Put aside while you
make the dressing.

4. Mix the oil, lemon juice, curry powder, mustard, and garlic until well blended.
Add salt to taste. Pour over the lentils and
mix gently but thoroughly.

5. Marinate for several hours in the refrigerator before serving. Toward the end
of the marinating time, taste again and
add more salt if necessary. Beans seem to
absorb a lot of salt.

TO SERVE: Put a lettuce leaf cup on each
of 12 small, chilled plates. Spoon a portion
of the salad on each and garnish with 2
radish roses or 2 sticks of stuffed celery.

SUGGESTED MAIN COURSE:
Osso Buco
OR *Brunswick Stew*

SPICED RED ONION RINGS

SERVES AT LEAST 10 TO
12 (MAKES 5 CUPS)

Must be made the day
before serving.

Halve the recipe if serving
as part of a tray of hors
d'oeuvre.

Serve cold.

_____

BROWN SUGAR *1¼ cups*
CIDER VINEGAR *2 cups*
RED ONIONS *2½ pounds,*
peeled and sliced thin
crosswise into rounds,
about ⅛ inch thick, then
separated into rings,
cutting any large rings
in half: for easier slicing,
cut a sliver from the side
of each onion and put
cut side down on a
chopping board; they
won't roll as easily while
you slice
WHOLE CLOVES *¼ cup*
MUSTARD SEED *2 table-*
spoons

The Garnish
LETTUCE LEAVES

*A Hawaiian Islands favorite that has be-
come very popular with us. Also makes a
dandy sandwich.*

Assemble and prepare all ingredients.

1. Combine the sugar and vinegar in a
large bowl and stir until the sugar is dissolved.

2. Add the onions, cloves, and mustard
seed. Mix well. Cover and marinate overnight in the refrigerator. Stir occasionally.

TO SERVE: Place a lettuce leaf on each
small, chilled plate. Using a slotted spoon,
put a portion of the onions on top. Pass
the mayonnaise-spread French bread separately.

SUGGESTED MAIN COURSE:
    Swedish Meat Balls
    OR *English Mixed Grill*

The Accompaniment
FRENCH BREAD, SLICED
   THIN, SPREAD WITH
   MAYONNAISE AND
   DUSTED WITH MINCED
   PARSLEY

8 SERVINGS

The radishes and the
   marinade may be pre-
   pared several hours
   ahead and refrigerated
   separately.

Serve chilled.

_____

SMALL RED RADISHES
   50 to 60, to make about
   2 cups when smashed
CIDER VINEGAR *½ cup*
DRY MUSTARD *1 teaspoon*
SUGAR *3 tablespoons, plus*
   a little more, to taste
MONOSODIUM GLUTA-
   MATE *1 teaspoon*
IMPORTED LIGHT SOY
   SAUCE* (U.S.A. MANU-
   FACTURED "REGULAR"
   SOY SAUCE MAY BE
   SUBSTITUTED, BUT THE

AVOCADO WITH SMASHED RADISHES

Never smashed a radish? Do it and you'll be a confirmed radish-smasher and consumer.

Assemble and prepare all ingredients except the avocados.

1. Wash and dry the radishes, remove any blemishes, and cut off the root and stem ends. Save a few of the smallest tender inside leaves, if your radishes have them, and set aside.

2. Cut each radish in half lengthwise, and lay it on a board *cut side down* (or they'll fly all over the kitchen when you clobber them). Give each 1 or 2 hard blows with the side of a mallet. When all are smashed, gather them in a mound and cut across them 2 or 3 times so that they are in ½-to-¾-inch chunks.

3. Chop the reserved small radish leaves fine, if you have them, and add them to the radishes. Put into a small bowl, cover, and refrigerate.

4. In a separate small bowl, mix a little

COLOR WON'T BE
QUITE AS ATTRACTIVE)
6 *tablespoons*
PEANUT OIL *3 tablespoons*
AVOCADOS *4 medium*

The Garnish
SNIPPED CHIVES

* Available in Oriental food shops.

of the vinegar and all of the mustard to a paste. Add the remaining vinegar, 3 tablespoons of the sugar, the monosodium glutamate and the soy sauce. Mix well to dissolve the sugar. Taste and add a little more sugar if you like. The sauce should not be too sweet and should have a little "bite." Cover with plastic wrap and refrigerate.

TO ASSEMBLE AND SERVE: 1. Fifteen minutes before serving time, pour the marinade over the radishes. Add the oil and toss until all the radishes are well coated. Refrigerate again until serving time. They should be served very cold.

2. Halve the avocados lengthwise and remove and discard the seeds. Cut a sliver from the bottom of each half so that they won't tip, being careful not to cut through the "meat."

3. Using a slotted spoon, divide the marinated radishes among the avocado halves. Put each half on an individual plate. Spoon a little of the remaining marinade over each serving and sprinkle with a bit of snipped chives. Serve at once.

SUGGESTED MAIN COURSE:
Jambalaya, page 201
OR *Roast Chicken*

GREEN BEANS WITH SHALLOT DRESSING

6 SERVINGS

Fresh shallots are necessary (usually available in large supermarkets or specialty food shops).

The dressing, except for the vinegar, may be made up to 1 day ahead.

The beans should be marinated at room temperature for 30 minutes to 1 hour before serving.

Serve cold.

FRESH SHALLOTS *To make ¼ cup when peeled and sliced very thin*
LIGHT OLIVE OR SALAD OIL *¼ cup*
DIJON MUSTARD *2 teaspoons*
SALT *⅛ teaspoon*
BLACK PEPPER, GROUND FRESH *⅛ teaspoon*

Assemble and prepare the dressing.

Place the shallots, oil, mustard, salt, and pepper in a small bowl or screw-top jar. Stir well or shake to mix. *Do not add the vinegar.* Cover and refrigerate for up to 1 day. Let stand at room temperature for at least 1 hour.

30 MINUTES TO 1 HOUR BEFORE SERVING: 1. Add the vinegar to the salad dressing. Stir or shake again to mix.

2. Pour the dressing over the cooked green beans. Toss and turn to combine. Let marinate at room temperature.

TO SERVE: Put a lettuce leaf on each of 6 chilled plates. Mound part of the salad on each. Put a few crackers on the side of each plate.

SUGGESTED MAIN COURSE:
    Crabmeat Gumbo
    OR *Grilled Lamb Chops*

NOTE: The Shallot Dressing is equally good with raw zucchini, mushrooms, or tomato slices, and with cooked carrots or beets.

WHITE WINE VINEGAR
   2 tablespoons
GREEN BEANS *½ pound,*
   cut in 1-inch pieces,
   cooked until tender, then
   rinsed in cold water and
   drained

The Garnish
LETTUCE LEAVES

The Accompaniment
COMMERCIAL CHEESE
   CRACKERS
OR BENNE SEED WAFERS,
   page 313
OR POPPY SEED CRACKETS,
   page 315

8 SERVINGS

Can be made several days
   ahead and refrigerated,
   but must marinate for
   at least 6 hours before
   serving.

Serve well chilled.

Basic Sauce à la Grecque
OLIVE OIL *⅓ cup*
LEMON *Juice of 1*
DRY WHITE WINE *⅓ cup*

VEGETABLES A LA GRECQUE

While any one of the vegetables makes an excellent first course, they are especially good on a tray of hors d'oeuvre and as garnishes for other dishes. We're not sure of the maximum time they can be kept, but we've kept some for 10 days with no deterioration.

THE BASIC SAUCE A LA GRECQUE: Assemsemble and prepare all the ingredients and combine them in a bowl.

THE VEGETABLES: 1. Put the prepared vegetable of your choice into a saucepan.

GARLIC *1 large clove,*
peeled and minced
almost to a paste with a
little salt
PARSLEY SPRIGS *2*
GROUND THYME *½ tea-*
spoon
WHOLE CORIANDER SEEDS
½ teaspoon
DRIED TARRAGON LEAVES
¼ teaspoon, crumbled
SALT *½ teaspoon*
BLACK PEPPERCORNS
12 whole

The Vegetables: Choose One

CELERY HEARTS *8, each*
about 4 inches long,
halved: do not cut off
the bulb at the bottom;
it will be removed just
before serving
OR LEEKS *8, trimmed of*
the green stems and
halved: wash very
thoroughly to remove
all grit, but do not cut
off the root end; it will
be removed just before
serving
OR FRESH ASPARAGUS
2 pounds, cut in 4-inch
lengths, measuring from
the tip (discard the
lower part): use a swivel-

Pour enough boiling water over it to al-most cover.

2. Add the sauce à la Grecque and sim-mer for the time suggested below.

3. Transfer the vegetable and its cook-ing liquid to a bowl. Cool, and refrigerate for from 6 hours to several days.

COOKING TIME FOR THE VEGETABLES:

Celery hearts: 20 minutes
Leeks: 15 minutes
Asparagus: 15 minutes
Mushrooms: 10 minutes

TO SERVE: If using the celery hearts or the leeks, trim off the root ends. Put a lettuce leaf on each of 8 chilled plates and divide the vegetable among them. Spoon a little of the sauce over each and garnish with watercress or parsley sprigs and 2 radishes.

SUGGESTED MAIN COURSE:
Baked Whole Fish
OR *Grilled Veal Chops*

NOTE: If you wish to serve as a part of a tray of hors d'oeuvre, cook 3 or 4 of the above or the following vegetables. Cook each vegetable separately and make 1 recipe of the sauce for each of the veg-etables. Cool and refrigerate separately.

Artichokes: 12 tiny: cut off about ½ inch of the tops, all of the stem and the tough outside leaves; sim-mer 25 minutes.

bladed peeler to trim off
the tough outer fibers
OR FRESH MUSHROOMS
*1 pound: first wipe with
a damp paper towel if
necessary, and trim off
the tough end of the
stem*
BOILING WATER

The Garnish
LETTUCE LEAVES *8 large*
**WATERCRESS OR PARSLEY
SPRIGS**
RED RADISHES *16, washed,
trimmed, and crisped*

Small white onions: 20, about 1 inch
in diameter: peel and simmer 15
minutes

Carrots: 5 medium, peeled and cut in
⅓-inch rounds: simmer 15 minutes

Scallions: About 20: remove the
tough outer skins and the upper
part, leaving about 2 inches of the
pale-green stem; simmer 15 minutes

Cauliflower flowerets: 15: simmer 15
minutes

FRUITS

CURRIED MELON

10 TO 12 SERVINGS
(ABOUT ½ CUP EACH)

The sauce may be made a
day ahead.

Combine with the fruit
and refrigerate several
hours before serving.

Serve well chilled.

_____

The Sauce

BUTTER *1 tablespoon*

SALAD OIL (NOT OLIVE
OIL) *1 tablespoon*

ONION *To make ½ cup
when chopped very fine:
the finer they are
chopped now, the easier
it will be to push them
through a sieve later*

CURRY POWDER (THE
BEST BRAND AVAIL-

Assemble and prepare all ingredients.

1. Heat the butter and oil in a small
skillet and add the onions. Sauté over low
heat until the onions are very soft and a
very light gold, but not brown.

2. Add the curry powder and continue
to cook, stirring constantly, for 2 minutes
more.

3. Remove from the heat and, when
cold enough to handle, press through a
medium-mesh sieve into a small bowl, using either the back of a spoon or a pestle.
(We use our fingers!) Do not use a blender.
Keep pressing until all is through, except
a very small amount of pulp. Scrape the
bottom of the sieve with a knife to gather
all the mashed onion.

4. Add the mayonnaise and mix well.
Then gradually add the cream. The amount
to use depends upon whether you have
used homemade or commercial mayonnaise. The homemade will be stiffer and
require a larger amount of cream. The re-

ABLE) *1 tablespoon,
more or less, to taste: see
note at end of recipe*
MAYONNAISE, PREFER-
ABLY HOMEMADE
(*page 296*) *½ cup*
LIGHT CREAM *2 table-
spoons, or more*

The Fruit
RIPE CANTALOUPE OR
HONEYDEW MELON
*To make 3 cups when
cut in ½-inch dice (1
large cantaloupe or 1
medium honeydew
melon): first remove
seeds, filament, rind, and
any unripe flesh*
MIXED WITH:
WATERMELON *To make 3
cups when cut in ½-inch
dice (1 small or ½
medium): first remove
seeds and rind*

The Garnish
FRESH MINT SPRIGS

The Accompaniment
ROQUEFORT SHORTBREAD,
page 310

sultant blend should be quite thick. When
it is marinated with the fruit, it will thin
out to the consistency of light cream.

5. Put the combined cantaloupe or
honeydew and watermelon into a large
bowl, pour the sauce over it, and fold together. Cover tightly and refrigerate for
several hours.

TO SERVE: Put about ½ cup of the melon
mixture into each of 10 or 12 stemmed
cocktail glasses or small bowls. Garnish
with a sprig of mint and pass the shortbread separately.

NOTE: If after testing the sauce with the
amount of curry suggested in the recipe,
you decide to add more, sauté the additional curry powder for a few minutes in a
little butter before adding.

SUGGESTED MAIN COURSE:
Deviled Crab
OR *Stuffed Baked Fish*

GUADALAJARA FRUIT CUP

8 TO 10 SERVINGS

The dressing and all the ingredients, except the avocados, may be prepared a day ahead and refrigerated separately.

Prepare the avocados, blend all, and let marinate 1 hour before serving.

Serve chilled.

———————

CUCUMBERS *To make 1⅔ cups when peeled, seeds and pulp removed and discarded, and cut in ½-inch dice (about two 6-to-7-inch cucumbers)*

PAPAYA *To make 1⅔ cups when peeled, cut in half, seeds removed and discarded, and cut in ½-inch dice (about ¾ pound)*

FIRM, RIPE AVOCADOS *To make 1⅔ cups when peeled, seed removed, and cut in ½-inch dice (about 3 medium, each about 4 inches long)*:

We were served this, on a large plate, with cocktails late one afternoon at the Guadalajara Marriott Hotel. Toothpicks were handy for spearing. We think it makes a simple and lovely first course, even without the toothpicks.

Assemble and prepare all the ingredients except the avocados.

1. Mix together the prepared cucumbers and papaya and refrigerate.

2. Combine the pineapple juice, chili sauce, salad oil, and lime juice and refrigerate.

3. Cut the bacon for the garnish into 3- or 4-inch lengths, and fry slowly until crisp. Drain and crumble it. Keep at room temperature until ready to use, or refrigerate. (Allow to come back to room temperature for 1 hour before serving.)

1½ HOURS BEFORE SERVING: 1. Prepare the avocados and put them in a large bowl along with the chilled cucumbers and papayas. (If the cucumbers and papayas were prepared ahead, pour off any juice that has accumulated.)

2. Stir the dressing and pour it over all. Toss and turn to coat well. Refrigerate for 1 hour or a little more.

TO SERVE: Using a slotted spoon, divide

*do not prepare until 1
hour before serving*

Dressing
UNSWEETENED PINE-
APPLE JUICE *1 cup*
CHILI SAUCE OR TOMATO
CATSUP *¼ cup*
SALAD OIL *¼ cup*
LIME JUICE *¼cup*

The Garnish
BACON *6 slices*
HOT RED PEPPER FLAKES

the mixture evenly into chilled sherbet or martini glasses. Add a little extra dressing to each serving. (Save any leftover dressing for a fruit salad.) Sprinkle with some of the crumbled bacon, and then with a few red pepper flakes.

SUGGESTED MAIN COURSE:
  Sole Meunière
  OR *Shrimp Creole*

Before Dinner: First Courses

HOT

Soups

TOMATO BURGUNDY SOUP

This is an unusual, aromatic soup. It is served in the Garden Café of the Honolulu Academy of Arts. A talented, enthusiastic group of ladies prepare and serve a gourmet luncheon of soup, salad, sandwiches, and an irresistible dessert every Tuesday for the benefit of the Academy. Patsy Gibson, chairman, very generously gave us the recipe—to serve 80! We have adapted it here.

6 SERVINGS (1 CUP EACH)

You will need a piece of cheese cloth to tie the spices and seasonings.

The soup may be prepared a day ahead, but do not add the Burgundy until just before reheating.

TOMATO JUICE 3½ *cups*
ONION *1 medium, peeled and chopped coarse*
CELERY 2 *stalks with leaves, chopped coarse*
WHOLE CLOVES ¼ *teaspoon*
BAY LEAF ½, *crushed*
FULL-FLAVORED BEEF BROTH, *page 291,* OR CANNED BEEF BROTH,

Assemble and prepare all ingredients.

1. Put the tomato juice into a pot that will hold at least 2 quarts. Tie the onion, celery, cloves, and bay leaf in a piece of cheesecloth and add it to the tomato juice. Cover and simmer for 30 minutes.

2. Remove from the heat and, when cool enough to handle, remove the cheesecloth bag and squeeze the juices back into the tomato juice. Discard the bag.

3. Add the broth and bring it to a boil. At this point the soup may be cooled, cov-

UNDILUTED *1¾ cups*
BURGUNDY *1 cup*
BLACK PEPPER, GROUND
    FRESH
SALT

The Accompaniment
SEASONED CRACKERS
OR MARINATED SODA
    CRACKERS, *page 311*
OR TINY CHEESE PUFFS,
    page 305

ered, and refrigerated for up to 24 hours.

4. Just before serving add the Burgundy and 5 or 6 grinds of the pepper mill. Reheat but *do not boil* the soup. Add salt to taste or more pepper, if desired.

TO SERVE: We serve this from a pitcher, into small mugs or cups, to guests standing or sitting in the living room, patio, or garden, before going in to a sit-down dinner; informal and very convenient. Everyone will want more—resist their requests. One cup is enough as a first course. Serve with the accompaniment of your choice. The Marinated Soda Crackers are especially good, as they are highly spiced.

SUGGESTED MAIN COURSE:
    Brazilian Sardine Pudding, page 139
    OR *Shish Kabobs*

BISQUE OF HEARTS OF PALM

6 SERVINGS

A blender is a must.

May be prepared up to
    8 hours ahead, but no
    longer.

Cover, refrigerate, and
    heat just before serving.

May also be served cold.

We first tasted this bisque at a late lunch in the newest resort hotel in Lake Chapala, Mexico. The chef could not be disturbed at siesta, so we bravely and accurately duplicated the subtle flavor at home. It is so simple—try it!

Assemble and prepare all ingredients.

1. Put the chicken broth and chopped hearts of palm into a blender and blend at high speed for about 20 seconds or until the mixture is very smooth and creamy. Blend in 2 batches if necessary.

CANNED CHICKEN BROTH,
  DILUTED ACCORDING
  TO THE MANUFAC-
  TURER'S DIRECTIONS
  2 cups
CANNED HEARTS OF PALM
  To make 3 cups when
  drained and measured
  after chopping into
  coarse pieces (1-pound
  14-ounce can): reserve
  2 or 3 of the smaller
  stalks for garnishing
MILK *1 cup*
HEAVY CREAM *1 cup*
WORCESTERSHIRE SAUCE
  ⅛ teaspoon
SALT
WHITE PEPPER, GROUND
  FRESH

The Garnish
THE RESERVED HEARTS OF
  PALM *Cut in rounds*
  about ¼ inch thick and
  then cut each round in
  quarters or halves de-
  pending upon the size
SNIPPED CHIVES

The Accompaniment
ANCHOVY CRESCENTS,
  page 303
OR ROQUEFORT SHORT-
  BREAD, *page 310*
OR BUTTER CRACKERS

2. Pour the purée into a 2-quart bowl. Add the milk, cream, and Worcestershire sauce. Stir well to combine. Add salt and pepper to taste. Add a little more milk or chicken broth if you desire, but the soup should be fairly thick and very creamy. If preparing in advance refrigerate for up to 8 hours.

3. *If you are serving it hot:* heat in the upper section of a double boiler over simmering water. Stir frequently, and do not let the bisque boil. *If you are serving it cold:* refrigerate, covered, for at least 4 hours or until serving time.

TO SERVE: Divide the wedge-shaped pieces of hearts of palm among 6 soup cups or small bowls. Pour a little less than a cup of the bisque into each. Sprinkle with a bit of snipped chives and serve. Pass the accompaniment of your choice separately.

SUGGESTED MAIN COURSE:
  London Broil
  OR *Roast Cornish Game Hens*

JANE'S CREAM OF CHICKEN SOUP

6 TO 8 SERVINGS

Full-flavored chicken
  broth is a must—the
  goodness of the soup
  depends upon it: use
  your own recipe, or
  ours on page 293

The soup may be partially
  cooked up to 24 hours
  in advance and finished
  about ½ hour before
  serving.

—————

BUTTER ¼ *cup*
CELERY *To make ¼ cup*
  when chopped very fine:
  use only the tender in-
  side stalks
ONION *To make ¼ cup*
  when peeled and chopped
  fine
ALL-PURPOSE FLOUR
  ¼ *cup*
FULL-FLAVORED CHICKEN
  BROTH (*page 293*) 4
  cups
LIGHT CREAM 2 *cups*
COOKED CHICKEN
  To make 1 cup when cut
  in small chunks

This recipe has traveled widely, but we traced it to its source—a friend in Guadalajara. The olives add a unique flavor to a good thick soup.

Assemble and prepare all ingredients.

  1. Put the butter into a 1½- or 2-quart saucepan. When it is very hot, add the celery and, stirring frequently, sauté over moderate heat until the celery just begins to soften but is still firm to the bite.

  2. Continuing to stir, add the onions and sauté until they are slightly soft. Do not let the mixture brown.

  3. Sprinkle with the flour and stir well. Turn the heat to low and cook for 3 minutes, stirring constantly.

  4. Remove the pan from the heat and slowly add the chicken broth, stirring until smooth. At this point the soup may be refrigerated for up to 24 hours.

½ HOUR BEFORE SERVING TIME: 1. Warm the broth in a saucepan. Add the cream and mix well. Bring the broth to *just under a simmer.* Keeping the heat very low, cook slowly, partially covered, for 15 minutes. Do not let it boil or the texture will become unpleasant. Stir frequently.

  2. Remove from the heat and add the chicken, rice, and olives. Add salt and pep-

COOKED RICE *½ cup*

PIMIENTO-STUFFED
   GREEN OLIVES *To make*
   ½ cup when sliced

PITTED RIPE OLIVES
   *To make ½ cup when
   sliced*

SALT

WHITE PEPPER, GROUND
   FRESH

per to taste. The olives are salty, so be careful. Let stand 10 minutes to blend the flavors. Reheat to just warm, stirring often.

TO SERVE: Ladle into warm cups and top each serving with a sprinkling of parsley.

SUGGESTED MAIN COURSE:
   Broiled Fish
   OR *Pork Loin with Orange Sauce*

The Garnish
MINCED PARSLEY

Seafoods

STEAMED SHRIMP ROLLS

You will need a flat-bottomed skillet or *crêpe* pan, measuring 6 inches at the bottom.

You will also need a steamer: to improvise one, see note at end of recipe.

May be prepared a day ahead (but no more), refrigerated, and steamed just before serving.

Or may be made ahead, frozen uncooked, and thawed to room temperature before steaming.

The tender egg wrappers are what make these unique and especially good—a welcome change from the usual flour paste.

Assemble and prepare all ingredients.

THE FILLING: Mix together the shrimp, pork, water chestnuts, scallion, and monosodium glutamate. Stir the cornstarch-and-sherry mixture and add. Add salt and pepper to taste, combine thoroughly, and set aside.

THE WRAPPERS: 1. Place a 6-inch skillet on medium-low heat and brush with a film of oil.

2. Measure 2 tablespoons of the beaten egg-and-water mixture. (Either measure 2 tablespoons into a small cup, or use a ⅛-cup measure.) Lift the pan off the heat and pour the egg into the center. Quickly rotate the pan so that the egg covers the bottom as evenly as possible.

May also be served cold, but at its best when warm.

The Filling

UNCOOKED SHRIMP

To make ¾ cup when shelled and chopped fine (about ½ pound): it's not necessary to remove the veins unless you prefer

COOKED PORK *To make ½ cup when minced*

CANNED WATER

CHESTNUTS *14, drained and minced*

SCALLION *1, minced: use some of the light-green upper part*

MONOSODIUM GLUTA-

MATE *1 teaspoon*

CORNSTARCH *1 tablespoon*

MIXED WITH:

DRY SHERRY *1 tablespoon*

SALT

BLACK PEPPER, GROUND

FRESH

The Wrappers

OIL *For brushing skillet and steamer*

EGGS *5 large, lightly beaten: beat only until most of the stringiness has disappeared and there is a*

3. Return the pan to the heat and cook slowly until the bottom of the wrapper is light gold and the top is still shiny. Do not turn or overcook or the wrapper will be tough.

4. Transfer to a flat surface or a large pastry board.

5. Brush the skillet again with oil, and repeat until you have 8 wrappers. Do not stack one on the other.

TO ASSEMBLE: 1. Divide the reserved shrimp-and-pork mixture into 8 parts. Spread each wrapper with one part, leaving a border of about 1 inch around the edge (figure A).

2. Fold about 1 inch of the right, left, and bottom edges toward the center (figure B).

3. Roll up from the bottom to within 1 inch of the top. Spread the flap with beaten egg white and press down to seal (figure C). Place on a flat surface, seam side down. Refrigerate, well covered, for up to 24 hours, freeze, or steam at once.

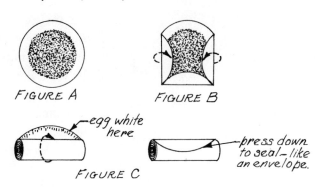

FIGURE A   FIGURE B

egg white here

FIGURE C

press down to seal – like an envelope.

minimum of froth
WATER *1 tablespoon*
EGG WHITE *1, lightly
beaten, for sealing the
rolls*

The Garnish
FRESH CORIANDER
   (CHINESE PARSLEY
   OPTIONAL) MUSTARD
MAYONNAISE, *page 140*

TO STEAM: Put water into the lower section of a steamer and bring to a boil Brush the inside bottom of the upper section with oil and place 3 or 4 shrimp rolls on it, seam side down. They should be separated by at least ½ inch so that the steam will penetrate evenly and they will have room to swell. Cover and steam over high heat for 15 to 20 minutes. Remove to a plate and keep warm. Repeat until all are steamed. They may be kept warm up to 30 minutes if covered with foil.

TO SERVE: Take 8 small plates and put 1 roll on each. Garnish with a sprig or two of fresh coriander. Pass a small bowl of the Mustard Mayonnaise separately. Serve warm or cold. *For an alternate serving:* cut each roll in ½-inch slices and divide evenly on the plates, putting a cut side down.

NOTE: If you don't have a steamer, you can improvise one. Place a tall, empty tin can, with top and bottom removed, in the bottom of a large pot. Add water, being sure the water does not come more than a third of the way up the height of the can. The water must not come in contact with the food. Put a large plate or close-meshed rack on top of the can. Oil lightly, place 3 or 4 shrimp rolls on it, cover and cook as directed. If using a plate, the cooking time will be a little longer.

SUGGESTED MAIN COURSE:
   Chicken and Long Rice, page 214
   OR *Kedgeree, page 202*

SHRIMP ONO ONO

6 TO 8 SERVINGS

You will need a blender.

The shrimp-cream mixture and the sauce may be prepared a day ahead and refrigerated separately.

Serve in small bowls, not more than 4 inches in diameter at the top, in scallop shells, or stemmed martini glasses.

Serve the shrimp warm and the sauce cold.

BUTTER 2 *tablespoons, or more if necessary*
SALAD OIL 2 *tablespoons, or more if necessary*
UNCOOKED SHRIMP
1½ pounds, shelled: devein only if you wish; dry well on paper toweling
MONOSODIUM GLUTA-
MATE *½ teaspoon*
HEAVY CREAM *¾ cup*
LARGE LIME *Juice of ½*

Ono ono means "delicious" in Hawaiian, and that's just what this is; elegant and easy, a subtle blend of Hawaiian and European cooking with a sauce that makes the dish. Our version of a first course served in a well-known New York restaurant.

Assemble and prepare all ingredients.

THE SHRIMP: 1. In a large skillet, heat the butter and the 2 tablespoons of oil. When very hot add approximately half of the shrimp and sauté for about 6 minutes or until they are tender but still firm to the bite. If you are preparing them ahead to serve later, undercook them a little, so that they will not be overcooked when reheated. Turn and toss frequently so that they will color evenly. Sprinkle with ¼ teaspoon of the monosodium glutamate as they sauté.

2. Remove from the pan with a slotted spoon and set aside.

3. Sauté the remaining shrimp in the same manner, using the remaining ¼ teaspoon of monosodium glutamate. Add a little more butter or oil if necessary. Remove them with a slotted spoon and add to the first half.

4. Discard all but about 1 teaspoon of the oil remaining in the skillet, but leave any brown bits that cling to the bottom of the pan.

SALT

WHITE PEPPER, GROUND
    FRESH

The Sauce

SOY SAUCE *½ cup*

CIDER VINEGAR *¼ cup*

ONION *To make ½ cup
    when peeled and
    chopped coarse*

GINGER *To make 1 tea-
    spoon when minced, if
    fresh, or, if powdered,
    ¼ teaspoon*

SUPERFINE SUGAR
    1 teaspoon

The Garnish

MINCED PARSLEY OR
    FRESH CORIANDER
    (SOMETIMES CALLED
    CHINESE PARSLEY)

12 SERVINGS (2 SHRIMP
    EACH)

You will need toothpicks.

5. Cut the shrimp into bite-sized pieces, about 1 inch, and put them back into the skillet. Add the cream and lime juice. Mix well, scraping the bottom to incorporate all the nice brown bits. Cook until hot but not boiling. Salt lightly (the sauce will be quite salty) and add pepper to taste. Refrigerate if not to be used at once. Before serving reheat in the upper section of a double boiler over warm but not boiling water.

THE SAUCE: Put all the sauce ingredients into a blender. Whirl for a minute, or until all is liquid. Refrigerate until serving time.

TO SERVE: Divide the warm shrimp mixture among 6 or 8 small bowls, scallop shells, or stemmed martini glasses. Be sure to divide the cream also. (It's the combination of the cream and the sauce that gives this dish its goodness.) Spoon about 1 tablespoon of the cold sauce over each serving and sprinkle with a little minced parsley or coriander. Pass the remaining sauce separately.

SUGGESTED MAIN COURSE:
    Teriyaki Chicken
    OR *Curried Lamb*

STUFFED SHRIMP

Jumbo shrimp, the larger the better, are a must. Don't attempt this recipe with anything smaller. We stole the idea from

May be assembled ready
for broiling several
hours in advance.

Broil just before serving.

_____

UNCOOKED JUMBO
SHRIMP 24, *remove
shells by splitting with
scissors, but leave the
shrimp intact*
SWISS CHEESE 24 *pieces
when cut in chunks
¾ by 1½ by ¼ inch
thick*
BACON 12 *thin slices: each
cut in half crosswise*

The Garnish
PARSLEY OR WATERCRESS
SPRIGS

Carlos Anderson's chain of restaurants in Mexico.

Assemble and prepare all ingredients.

1. Prepare the shrimp. Using a small, sharp knife, split each shrimp lengthwise along the inner curve, *about three-quarters of the way through,* no more.

2. Put a piece of waxed paper on a counter or cutting board and sprinkle it with a little water. Lay the peeled shrimp split side down in a single layer, and flatten each with the heel of your hand. Turn split side up.

3. Taking 1 shrimp at a time, lay it on a board with the long side toward you. Place a piece of the cheese on one side and fold the other side over it.

4. Wrap each shrimp spirally in a half slice of the bacon, enclosing the cheese completely. Fasten with a toothpick on each end to secure it. Place the stuffed shrimp on a broiling rack in 1 layer, not touching. At this point they may be refrigerated until shortly before serving.

JUST BEFORE SERVING: Broil about 2 inches from the heat for 5 minutes on each side. Serve at once.

TO SERVE: Put 2 shrimp on each individual warm serving plate and garnish with a sprig or two of parsley or watercress.

SUGGESTED MAIN COURSE:
Chicken Paprika
OR *Herbed Meat Loaf*

SCANDINAVIAN FISH PUDDING WITH SHRIMP SAUCE

Light in texture, delicate in flavor, this pudding is beautiful when done in a ring mold as the center of attraction for a luncheon or dinner. Fresh buttered peas would be good to fill the center.

12 SERVINGS

You will need 12 molds of ½-cup capacity and a food grinder or food mill.

The pudding may be prepared a day ahead, refrigerated, and baked 45 minutes before serving, or it may be frozen uncooked, and thawed before baking.

The sauce may be prepared several hours in advance and kept at room temperature, then reheated before serving, or it may be frozen, separate from the pudding, and thawed before reheating.

___

The Fish Pudding
BUTTER FOR MOLDS
FINE DRY BREAD CRUMBS
  3 tablespoons or more
FRESH FILLETS OF
  HADDOCK, CODFISH,
  SEA BASS, OR ANY
  OTHER LEAN, FIRMLY

Assemble and prepare all ingredients.

THE FISH PUDDING: 1. Using a piece of waxed paper, thoroughly butter the inside of the molds. Put about 2 tablespoons of the bread crumbs in a mold, and rotate it until the inside is evenly coated. Pour any remaining crumbs into the next mold, and repeat, adding another tablespoon or more of bread crumbs as necessary, until all the molds are coated. Set aside.

2. Put the fish through the coarse blade of a food grinder or food mill. Then put it through the grinder again, using the finest blade.

3. Using an electric mixer, gradually add the flour, salt, and pepper to the fish. Add the combined creams little by little and continue to beat at medium speed until the mixture is very light and fluffy.

4. Spoon into the prepared molds, banging each one on the counter to settle it and eliminate any air pockets. Smooth the top of each and cover tightly with foil. At this point either refrigerate them until ready to bake, or freeze. If frozen, thaw in the refrigerator overnight before baking.

TEXTURED FISH WITH
A SLIGHTLY GELATIN-
OUS QUALITY 2 *pounds,*
cut into small pieces
FLOUR 3 *tablespoons*
SALT 1½ *teaspoons*
WHITE PEPPER, GROUND
FRESH *About* ¼ *tea-*
spoon
LIGHT CREAM 1 *cup*
MIXED WITH:
HEAVY CREAM 1 *cup*
HOT WATER

The Shrimp Sauce
BUTTER ¼ *cup*
ONION 1 *medium, peeled*
and chopped fine
UNCOOKED SHRIMP
1 *pound, medium,*
shelled: devein only if
you prefer
ALL-PURPOSE FLOUR
¼ *cup*
FISH STOCK OR CHICKEN
BROTH 1 *cup*
HEAVY CREAM 1 *cup*
DILL 4 *teaspoons if dried,*
or, if fresh, to make
2½ *tablespoons when*
chopped fine
SALT

TO BAKE: Preheat the oven to 350 degrees. Put the foil-covered molds into a baking pan and place on the middle rack of the oven. Add enough hot water to the baking pan to come two-thirds of the way up the sides of the molds. Bake about 45 minutes, or until the tops of the puddings are firm to the touch and a toothpick or skewer inserted in the center of one comes out clean. Remove the molds from the water and let stand at room temperature for a few minutes before removing the puddings from the molds.

TO UNMOLD: Remove the foil and pour off any liquid from the molds. Using the tip of a small sharp knife, loosen the edge of each pudding. Don't go down more than a quarter of an inch. Center a small, warm serving plate upside down over each. Invert plate and mold, holding them firmly together and giving a sharp downward shake. Repeat for each mold. If necessary, blot up any damp spots with the torn edge of paper toweling.

THE SHRIMP SAUCE: Prepare while the pudding is baking.

1. Melt the butter in a 1½-quart saucepan. Add the onion and shrimp and sauté, stirring constantly, for 3 minutes. Remove from the heat, sprinkle with the flour and blend well. Return to heat for a minute or two, stirring constantly.

2. Remove from the heat, mix the fish stock or chicken broth with the cream, and add to the shrimp-and-flour mixture, stirring constantly. Add the dill and cook un-

til thick. Then simmer slowly for 3 or 4 minutes longer. Remove from heat and add salt to taste. At this point the sauce may be put into a container and frozen. Before serving, thaw and reheat in the top section of a double boiler over simmering water.

3. If made several hours in advance, fold a piece of plastic wrap to fit the top of the saucepan and press it against the top of the sauce to keep a skin from forming. Set aside at room temperature. When ready to serve, reheat in the top section of a double boiler, over simmering water.

TO SERVE: Pour a portion of the shrimp sauce over each pudding, making sure to put 1 or 2 of the shrimp on the top for garnishing.

SUGGESTED MAIN COURSE:
Roast Turkey
OR *Roast Beef*

CRABMEAT MORNAY

6 SERVINGS

You will need a heatproof 1½-quart casserole pretty enough to come to the table, or 6 individual ramekins.

May be prepared in the morning, refrigerated,

When Dungeness crab was in season and fresh in the San Francisco area, this was by far our favorite way of preparing it. Uncommonly smooth and delicious, it can be served frequently without palling.

Assemble and prepare all ingredients.
1. Butter or oil the casserole or ramekins.

and broiled about 20 minutes before serving.

BUTTER OR OIL FOR
  BAKING DISH
FRESH CRABMEAT (MOST
  PREFERABLE), CANNED
  LUMP CRABMEAT, OR
  FROZEN CRABMEAT,
  THAWED 1 *pound,*
  thoroughly drained: pick
  out and discard any
  cartilage or shell
FRESH MUSHROOMS
  ½ pound, sliced thin:
  wipe clean with a damp
  paper towel if necessary,
  then slice vertically, in-
  cluding the stems

The Mornay Sauce
BUTTER 4 *tablespoons*
ALL-PURPOSE FLOUR
  4 *tablespoons*
MILK 1 *cup*
HALF-AND-HALF OR
  LIGHT CREAM 1 *cup*
MONOSODIUM GLUTA-
  MATE ½ *teaspoon*
SHERRY ⅓ *cup*
SWISS CHEESE *To make*
  ¾ cup when grated fresh
  (about ¼ pound)
SALT
WHITE PEPPER, GROUND
  FRESH

2. Fill with the crabmeat and arrange the mushrooms on top. Set aside.

THE MORNAY SAUCE: 1. Melt the butter in a heavy 1-quart saucean. Add the flour and cook, stirring, for several minutes over low heat. Do not let it brown.

2. Remove from the heat and add the milk and cream while stirring vigorously with a wire whisk. Return to the heat and bring to a simmer, stirring constantly, and scraping the bottom and edges of the pan so that there are no lumps, for about 3 to 5 minutes or until thick.

3. Add the monosodium glutamate and sherry and fold in the grated cheese. Simmer until the cheese is melted and the sauce is smooth and velvety. Add salt and pepper to taste.

4. Pour the sauce over the crabmeat and mushrooms. The dish may now be refrigerated, well covered, or broiled at once for 5 to 10 minutes.

ABOUT 15 MINUTES BEFORE SERVING TIME: 1. Preheat the broiler.

2. Place the casserole or ramekins on a baking sheet and set under the broiler, about 3 inches from the source of heat, until slightly browned and bubbly. If prepared earlier and refrigerated, this will take about 20 minutes.

SUGGESTED MAIN COURSE:
  Broiled Lamb Chops
  OR *Broiled Steak*

ANN'S CURRIED CRABMEAT

6 SERVINGS

You will need 6 ramekins
of ½-cup capacity.

May be made up to a day
ahead, tightly covered,
refrigerated, and baked
before serving.

Serve either warm or hot.

———————

CRABMEAT (FRESH,
CANNED, OR FROZEN
AND DEFROSTED)
*1½ pounds, thoroughly
drained by pressing it
lightly against a sieve:
shred medium-fine and
discard any bits of
cartilage or shell*

CANNED PIMIENTOS
*To make ⅓ cup when
chopped fine*

GREEN BELL PEPPERS
*To make ⅓ cup when
chopped fine: first re-
move the seeds and pith*

SCALLIONS *To make ¼
cup when minced*

SALT

BLACK PEPPER, GROUND
FRESH

MAYONNAISE, PREFER-

*A subtly flavored dish that Ann Golden-
berg serves as a buffet casserole, tripling
the quantities we have given.*

Assemble and prepare all ingredients.

1. Mix together the crabmeat, pimientos, green peppers, scallions, and salt and
pepper to taste.

2. Into a separate small bowl, put the
¾ cup of mayonnaise, the mustard, curry
powder, and egg yolk. Beat well.

3. Pour the mixture over the crabmeat
and mix thoroughly. Taste for curry flavor;
add a little more if necessary—you should
know the flavor is there, but it should not
be too prominent. The mixture should also
be very well moistened but not "soupy." If
necessary, add a little more mayonnaise.

4. At this point you may refrigerate it,
tightly covered, for up to 24 hours.

ABOUT 45 MINUTES BEFORE SERVING: 1.
Preheat the oven to 350 degrees, and heat
some water.

2. Butter the 6 ramekins generously
and divide the crabmeat mixture among
them, smoothing the tops.

3. Taking a well-rounded tablespoonful from the ¾ cup of mayonnaise, spread
the top of each ramekin with it, as if you
were frosting a cake. Wipe the edges if
they have smeared.

4. Sprinkle the top of each generously
with paprika.

ABLY HOMEMADE
(*page 296*) *¾ cup, plus
a little more if necessary*
DRY MUSTARD *1 teaspoon*
CURRY POWDER *1 teaspoon*
LARGE EGG YOLK *1*
HOT WATER
BUTTER FOR RAMEKINS

The Topping
MAYONNAISE, PREFER-
ABLY HOMEMADE
¾ cup or a little more
PAPRIKA

5. In a baking pan large enough to hold the 6 ramekins, put enough boiling water to reach halfway up the sides of the ramekins. Place the ramekins in it and put it on the bottom third of the preheated oven. Bake for 25 to 40 minutes, or until the tops are slightly puffed and starting to turn a very light gold.

TO SERVE: Place a ramekin on each of 6 small, warm plates. Serve warm or hot.

SUGGESTED MAIN COURSE:
Beef Wellington
OR *Veal Birds*

ROULADE OF SOLE

8 SERVINGS

May be prepared and assembled in the morning and refrigerated, tightly covered.

Bake just before serving.

———————

BUTTER OR OIL *For pan*
FILLETS OF SOLE *8, about
7 inches long and 2½
inches wide*
FRESH LEMON *Juice of ½*
BUTTER *4 tablespoons*
ALL-PURPOSE FLOUR
4 tablespoons
MILK *2 cups*

A classic, not served often enough. Easy, pretty, delicious—it should become one of your favorites.

Assemble and prepare all ingredients.

1. Generously butter or oil a 7-by-11-inch baking pan and set aside.

2. Sprinkle the fillets with the lemon juice and let them stand while you prepare the sauce.

3. Melt the butter in a 1-quart saucepan. Add the flour and cook over medium heat, stirring constantly, for 2 or 3 minutes. Do not let it brown.

4. Remove from the heat, add the milk all at once, and stir vigorously with a wire whisk until all the lumps are dissolved. Return to the heat and cook for about 3

SWISS CHEESE *To make
½ cup when grated*
CAYENNE PEPPER *Several
shakes*
SALT
WHITE PEPPER, GROUND
FRESH
COOKED BAY SHRIMP OR
SMALL SHRIMP, PEELED
1 cup
THOMPSON SEEDLESS
GRAPES (IF OUT OF
SEASON, SUBSTITUTE
SLICED FRESH MUSH-
ROOMS, STEMS RE-
MOVED) *1 cup*
PARMESAN CHEESE,
GRATED FRESH *¼ cup*

The Garnish
SMALL PARSLEY SPRIGS

minutes, stirring, until the sauce is very thick. It will thin out during the baking.

5. Add the grated Swiss cheese and the cayenne pepper and cook until the cheese has melted. Add salt and pepper to taste, stir well, remove from the heat, and set aside.

6. Lay the fillets out flat and, using about a rounded tablespoon for each, spread the shrimp over them, leaving a ½-inch border on 3 sides and a 2-inch border on the narrowest end. Drizzle about 2 teaspoons of the sauce over each.

7. Roll the fillet from the widest end. Don't worry if some of the shrimp and sauce escape; save it and add it to the sauce that remains.

8. Place the rolls, seam side down, in a single layer in the prepared baking dish.

9. Sprinkle the grapes (or mushrooms) over the rolled fillets. Cover with the remaining sauce and sprinkle with the grated Parmesan cheese. Refrigerate, tightly covered, or bake at once.

WHEN READY TO BAKE: 1. Preheat the oven to 350 degrees.

2. Put the sole on the middle rack of the oven and bake for 40 minutes (a little longer if chilled), or until lightly brown on top. If it does not brown within this time, put the dish under the broiler for 1 or 2 minutes.

TO SERVE: Put a rolled fillet and some of the sauce on each heated serving plate. Garnish with sprigs of parsley.

NOTE: This is also delicious using crab-meat instead of shrimp, in the same quantity.

SUGGESTED MAIN COURSE:
Broiled Filet Mignon
OR *Roast Veal*

ANN'S OYSTERS AND ARTICHOKES

6 TO 8 SERVINGS

May be prepared a day ahead and refrigerated, or may be frozen.

Bake just before serving in ½-cup ramekins or 5-inch scallop shells.

WATER *About 4 quarts*
LARGE ARTICHOKES *3*
LEMON *Juice of ½*
BUTTER *3 tablespoons*
MUSHROOMS *To make ¾ cup when sliced vertically (2 or 3 ounces): wipe clean with a damp paper towel if necessary, and remove the stems even with the base of the cap (save the stems for another use)*
SCALLIONS *To make ¼*

This is an unusually compatible "marriage."

Assemble and prepare all ingredients.

1. In an enamel or stainless-steel saucepan (do not use aluminum), bring the water to a rapid boil. Remove the stems of the artichokes even with the base and snap off and discard any small bottom leaves. Put the artichokes in the boiling water along with the lemon juice. Push them down so that they fill with water. If they fit tightly, they will remain under water and be less apt to darken. However, this is not essential. Boil rapidly for 30 to 45 minutes, or until the bases are very tender when pierced with a small, sharp knife or fork.

2. Immediately remove them with a slotted spoon and turn them upside down in a colander to drain.

3. When the artichokes are cool enough to handle, begin at the outside of each one and remove the leaves one by one. Re-

cup when minced

PARSLEY *To make ¼ cup when minced*

GARLIC *3 cloves, peeled and minced with a little salt*

ALL-PURPOSE FLOUR *1½ tablespoons*

HEAVY CREAM *¾ cup*

RESERVED OYSTER LIQUOR *¼ cup, plus a little more if necessary*

DRIED OREGANO LEAVES *¼ teaspoon, crumbled*

TABASCO SAUCE *¼ teaspoon*

WORCESTERSHIRE SAUCE *1 teaspoon*

SHUCKED OYSTERS *To make 2 cups when well drained: reserve the liquor and if the oysters are large, cut in half or thirds*

SALT

WHITE PEPPER, GROUND FRESH

BUTTER *For baking dishes and dotting top*

FINE DRY BREAD CRUMBS *2 to 3 tablespoons*

The Garnish

PAPRIKA

RESERVED ARTICHOKE LEAVES

serve 18 to 24 of the largest and sturdiest leaves for garnishing.

4. Using the edge of a spoon, scrape off the inside, lower tender part of the balance of the leaves, discarding the tough outer skin. Reserve the scrapings.

5. When you get to the feathery "choke," remove it with a sharp-edged spoon or knife and discard it. Reserve the bottoms.

6. Chop the scrapings and the bottoms into medium-fine chunks and reserve.

7. Put the 3 tablespoons of butter into a large skillet and, when it is hot, add the mushrooms and sauté for a minute or so. Then add the scallions, parsley, and garlic. Lower the heat, and continue sautéeing, stirring frequently, until the onions are limp. Do not let them brown.

8. Add the reserved chopped artichokes and mix well.

9. Sprinkle the mixture with the flour and turn for a minute or two. Then add the cream, the ¼ cup of reserved oyster liquor, oregano, Tabasco sauce, and Worcestershire sauce.

10. Cook together, stirring until the mixture is quite thick. Remove from the heat and reserve.

11. Put the oysters and their remaining liquor into a saucepan. Add a little water, if necessary, to cover them. Bring to a simmer and cook only until the edges of the oysters start to curl. Drain them and save the liquor for another use, if you wish.

12. Add the drained oysters to the

creamed artichoke mixture and blend well. Add salt and pepper to taste. The mixture should be very moist. Add a little more oyster liquor if necessary. The dish may now be refrigerated, covered, for up to 24 hours, or frozen. If frozen, defrost before baking.

WHEN READY TO BAKE: 1. Preheat the oven to 400 degrees.

2. Butter 6 to 8 five-inch scallop shells or ramekins of ½-cup capacity. Divide the mixture among them. Sprinkle the top of each with about 1 teaspoon of the dry bread crumbs and dot with butter. Place on a baking sheet and bake for about 10 minutes, or until heated through.

TO SERVE: Put the ramekins on individual serving plates. Sprinkle with a dash or two of paprika. Surround with 3 of the reserved artichoke leaves to use as a scoop. But better have a fork handy, too!

SUGGESTED MAIN COURSE:
Chicken Breasts Supreme
OR *Ham Steak*

SCALLOPS FLORENTINE

8 SERVINGS

You will need 8 large scallop shells or rame-kins of ½-cup capacity.

May be prepared and

The spinach makes the colorful difference in our rendition of scallops in shells.

Assemble and prepare all ingredients.
1. Butter the scallop shells and set aside.
2. In a saucepan combine the wine,

assembled a day ahead and refrigerated tightly covered.

Broil just before serving.

BUTTER FOR SCALLOP SHELLS

DRY WHITE WINE *1½ cups, plus a little more if necessary*

WATER *½ cup*

CARROT *1 small, peeled and sliced*

ONION *About 5 slices, peeled*

BAY LEAF *1 whole*

BAY SCALLOPS (SEA SCALLOPS MAY BE SUBSTITUTED) *1½ pounds, drained: if using sea scallops, cut into bite-sized pieces*

The Sauce

RESERVED AND REDUCED POACHING LIQUID *1 cup*

LIGHT CREAM *1 cup, plus a little more if necessary*

BUTTER *2 tablespoons*

FLOUR *3 tablespoons*

FROZEN CHOPPED UN-COOKED SPINACH *To make 1½ tablespoons when thawed and well*

water, carrots, onion, and bay leaf. Cover and simmer slowly for 5 minutes. Add the scallops, cover, and simmer for 3 minutes more. The scallops should be just covered with the liquid. If not, add a little more wine.

3. Remove the scallops with a slotted spoon and set aside. Strain the cooking liquid and reserve it. Discard the vegetables and bay leaf.

THE SAUCE: 1. Put the reserved cooking liquid into a saucepan and boil it rapidly, uncovered, until reduced to 1 cup. Cool, and then add the light cream. Set aside.

2. In another saucepan melt the butter, add the flour, stirring vigorously, and let them sizzle together very slowly for 2 minutes. Stir constantly and do not let the flour color.

3. Take the butter-and-flour mixture off the heat and add the wine-and-cream mixture all at once. Stirring vigorously with a wire whisk, return it to the heat. Continue stirring and scraping the bottom of the pan for about 2 or 3 minutes, or until the sauce is quite thick.

4. Remove from the heat and add the spinach, chives, parsley, tarragon, and a few drops of lemon juice. Add salt and pepper to taste and mix well. Set aside until cold.

5. Combine the scallops with the cooled sauce. The mixture should be thickly coated and moist; if not, add a little more cream.

6. Spoon into the prepared scallop shells, dividing the mixture equally among

drained: *as you need such a small amount, just break off a piece of the frozen block*

CHIVES *To make 1½ tablespoons when snipped*

PARSLEY *To make 1½ tablespoons when minced*

TARRAGON *Generous ¼ teaspoon, crumbled, if dried, or, if fresh, to make 1½ teaspoons when minced*

LEMON JUICE *A few drops*

SALT

WHITE PEPPER, GROUND FRESH

Topping

PARMESAN CHEESE *To make ½ cup when grated fresh*

BUTTER *About 2 tablespoons, cut in 8 pieces, for dotting*

The Garnish

LEMON OR LIME WEDGES *8*

them. Sprinkle each with some of the grated cheese and dot with a bit of butter. At this point they may be refrigerated, well covered, for up to 24 hours.

ABOUT 20 MINUTES BEFORE SERVING:
1. Preheat the broiler.

2. Place the scallop shells under it, about 2 or 3 inches from the source of heat. Broil for about 10 to 15 minutes, or until they are heated through and the cheese is lightly browned. Serve at once.

TO SERVE: Arrange on small plates and garnish each with a lemon wedge.

SUGGESTED MAIN COURSE:
Ham Loaf
OR *Herb Baked Chicken*

Meat and Poultry

CHICKEN LIVERS ON CROUTES

8 SERVINGS

The sauce may be made
up to a day ahead, re-
frigerated, and reheated
in a double boiler just
before serving.

Cut the *croûtes* a few
hours in advance and
let them dry a little
at room temperature
before frying.

Prepare the apples for
the garnish, cook the
livers, fry the *croûtes,*
and assemble just be-
fore serving; this will
only take about 15
minutes.

*The sauce for this dish is adapted from
one created by the famous Colony Restaurant in New York. It is also delicious
on any grilled meat or chicken.*

Assemble and prepare all ingredients.

THE SAUCE: 1. Off the heat, put the mustard in the upper section of a double
boiler. Add the cream, a little at a time,
stirring well after each addition. When all
is well blended, add the bottled sauce and
the lime juice and stir well.

2. Put just enough water in the lower
section of the double boiler to barely touch
the bottom of the upper section. Bring the
water to a slow simmer, put the upper part
of the boiler over it, and cook the sauce
for 15 minutes, stirring frequently and
scraping down the sides of the pan. Remove from the heat.

3. Put the beaten egg yolk into a small
mixing bowl. Taking the mustard-cream

The Sauce
DIJON MUSTARD
  1½ tablespoons
HEAVY CREAM *¾ cup*
ESCOFFIER SAUCE DIABLE,
  SAUCE ROBERT, OR ANY
  OTHER GOOD BOTTLED
  MEAT SAUCE *1 table-
  spoon*
LIME *Juice of ½*
EGG YOLK *1, slightly
  beaten*
SALT
BLACK PEPPER, GROUND
  FRESH
CREAM OR MILK FOR
  THINNING *If necessary*

The Chicken Livers
BUTTER *1½ tablespoons*
SALAD OIL *1½ tablespoons*
ONION *To make ¼ cup
  when chopped fine*
CHICKEN LIVERS *12 whole
  livers (about 1¼
  pounds): separate each
  half and remove any
  greenish spots or con-
  nective tissue, rinse under
  cold water, drain well,
  and pat dry between
  paper towels*
DRY SHERRY *¼ cup*
PAPRIKA *1 teaspoon*

The Croutes
SALAD OIL

mixture, about 1 teaspoon at a time, beat about ¼ cup of it into the egg yolk. Then beat in the balance of the mixture in a very thin stream.

4. Pour back into the upper section of the double boiler. Keep the water in the lower section warm but not simmering, and cook, stirring and scraping the bottom and sides of the pan constantly, until the sauce is thick enough to coat a spoon, or about the consistency of hollandaise sauce.

5. Add salt and pepper to taste. If the sauce is too thick, mix in a little cream or milk.

NOTE: *If the sauce is to be used within 1 or 2 hours:* cover and put near, but not on, the heat of a gas pilot, or over a pan of lukewarm water. Just before serving reheat it in a double boiler over slowly simmering water. If necessary, thin with a little milk or cream to the proper consistency.

If the sauce is to be used the next day: put into a small bowl. Cool in the refrigerator, then put a piece of plastic wrap, folded to fit, directly on top of the sauce to keep a film from forming. Cover the bowl and return it to the refrigerator. About 10 minutes before serving, reheat it in a double boiler over slowly simmering water. If necessary, add a little cream or milk to make the sauce the proper consistency.

THE CHICKEN LIVERS: 1. Heat the butter and oil in a large skillet. When very hot

DAY-OLD WHITE BREAD
*8 slices, cut ½ to ¾
inch thick: a few hours
ahead, cut each slice into
3-inch rounds and allow
them to dry slightly at
room temperature*

The Garnish

**RED- OR GREEN-SKINNED
APPLE** *1 medium, cored
and cut vertically in 24
wedges about ¼ inch
thick: do not peel*
PAPRIKA
**WATERCRESS OR PARSLEY
SPRIGS**

add the chopped onions and sauté over medium heat until they are just starting to turn golden. Turn frequently and do not let them burn.

2. Turn the heat to high. Add the chicken livers. Turning and tossing continually, sauté for 2 to 3 minutes until the centers are pink or well done, as you wish. Add the sherry and paprika and cook, stirring, for a minute more. Keep warm.

THE CROÛTES: Put enough oil in the bottom of another skillet to cover it generously. Place over high heat. When the oil is very hot and a haze forms over it, add 3 or 4 bread rounds. Quickly fry to a golden-brown on one side. Turn and brown the other side. Watch carefully, this only takes a second or two. Immediately remove from the skillet with a slotted spoon and drain on paper toweling. Repeat, adding more oil if necessary, until all the rounds are browned.

TO ASSEMBLE AND SERVE: Cut and slice the apples. Place a crisp *croûte* on each of 8 small plates. Top the *croûtes* with the hot chicken livers, dividing them equally. Mound with a spoon or two of sauce and sprinkle with paprika. Garnish with a sprig of watercress or parsley and 3 apple slices. Repeat for each plate. Serve at once.

SUGGESTED MAIN COURSE:
Braised Lamb Shanks
OR *London Broil*

VEGETAbLES

CURRIED MUSHROOMS

8 SERVINGS

The mushrooms may be cooked up to 8 hours ahead and reheated just before serving.

Fry the bread rounds just before serving.

Mushrooms are a popular first course. These are easy, subtly flavored, and especially tasty.

Assemble and prepare all ingredients.

The Mushrooms

BUTTER *3 tablespoons, plus a little more for reheating*

SALAD OIL *1 tablespoon*

CURRY POWDER (THE BEST QUALITY AVAILABLE) *1 teaspoon or more*

FRESH MUSHROOMS *1 pound, cut vertically into ⅛-inch slices: wipe clean with a damp paper*

THE MUSHROOMS: 1. Put the 3 tablespoons of butter and the oil in a large skillet over medium-high heat. When hot add 1 teaspoon of curry powder and stir constantly for about 1 minute.

2. Add the sliced mushrooms. Stirring and turning constantly, sauté for about 5 minutes or until golden.

3. Add the lemon juice, cayenne, and salt and pepper to taste. Mix and sauté a minute more. Taste again and add more curry, if desired. The taste of curry should be faint but not predominant. Use immediately or refrigerate until just before serving.

THE BREAD ROUNDS: 1. A few minutes

towel and remove and
discard the stems (or
save for another use)
LEMON JUICE 1 table-
spoon
CAYENNE PEPPER 2 dashes
SALT
BLACK PEPPER, GROUND
FRESH

The Bread Rounds
SALAD OIL
DAY-OLD WHITE BREAD
8 slices, ½ to ¾ inch
thick, cut in 3-inch
rounds: let stand at room
temperature a few hours
before frying to dry out

The Garnish
HARD-COOKED EGG YOLKS
2, pressed through a
medium-mesh sieve

before serving, heat enough salad oil in a heavy skillet to cover the bottom ⅛ inch deep. When it is very hot and a haze is just visible, put in the bread rounds, 3 or 4 at a time, and fry quickly on both sides until a light golden-brown. It will take less than a minute. Be careful not to burn them. Add more oil if necessary.

2. Drain on paper towels until all are fried. Keep warm in a very low oven or on an electric plate.

TO ASSEMBLE AND SERVE: 1. To reheat the mushrooms, put a little butter in a large skillet. When it has melted, add the cooked mushrooms. Stir over low heat until hot, adding a little more butter if necessary. They should not be dry.

2. Put a fried bread round on each of 8 small individual plates and divide the mushrooms equally among them. Top each serving with a sprinkling of the sieved egg yolks. Serve immediately.

SUGGESTED MAIN COURSE:
*Crêpes with Crabmeat and Avocado,
page 119*
OR *Veal Scaloppine*

FRESH ASPARAGUS

SERVE 6 TO 8 SPEARS
PER PERSON

The asparagus may be
cleaned ahead, but

There is almost no better first course than steaming spears of properly prepared and cooked fresh asparagus with a simple, good dressing. Just in case you haven't run into

should be cooked just before serving.

The sauces may be prepared up to 24 hours ahead.

FRESH ASPARAGUS *6 to 8 per person*
BOILING WATER
SALT *½ teaspoon*
MELTED BUTTER *3 table-spoons per person*
FRESH LEMON JUICE *1 tablespoon per person*

it, here is a perfect method to serve asparagus at its delicious best and with almost no waste at all.

Assemble and prepare all ingredients.

1. Cut off any white or dry stalk from the bottom of each spear of asparagus. With a vegetable peeler or a small, sharp knife, peel each spear. At the blossom end of the spear you may remove only the skin, but at the bottom half, you will need to remove several layers to get down to the tender part. The object is to be able to eat all of the spear when cooked.

2. Put the peeled spears into a large skillet. Cover with boiling water and add the salt. Bring to a boil and cook, uncovered, until the asparagus is barely tender, about 10 to 15 minutes. Do not overcook.

3. Lift out each spear and drain on a paper towel.

4. Combine the melted butter with the lemon juice.

TO SERVE: Put 6 to 8 spears on a hot plate for each person. Pass the lemon-butter sauce in a small pitcher or bowl.

AN ALTERNATE SAUCE: Creamy Dill Dressing, page 297.

SUGGESTED MAIN COURSE:
Herbed Lamb Chops
OR *Cold Poached Salmon*

CHEESE

SPINACH CHEESE PUFFS
(Spanakopetes)

A Greek treat, and not as difficult as it sounds.

Before starting this recipe, read the directions for handling *phyllo* pastry on page 319.

Assemble and prepare all ingredients except the *phyllo* pastry sheets.

1. Melt the 2 tablespoons of butter in a medium skillet. Add the grated onion and sauté until soft but not colored.

2. Add the drained spinach and sauté for several minutes more, or until all the liquid has evaporated. Remove from the heat.

3. Put the crumbled feta cheese into a large mixing bowl and add the eggs, spinach, nutmeg, and bread crumbs. Add salt to taste. Mix well and set aside while you prepare the *phyllo* sheets.

4. Unfold the *phyllo* sheets and place

10 SERVINGS
(3 PUFFS EACH)

You will need a pastry brush (a 2-inch paintbrush will do nicely), 2 damp kitchen towels, and waxed paper.

May be prepared several hours ahead, tightly covered with plastic wrap, refrigerated, and baked just before serving.

May also be frozen before baking and baked unthawed.

Serve warm.

BUTTER *2 tablespoons*

ONION *1 small, grated*

FROZEN CHOPPED
　SPINACH *2 packages*
　(*10 ounces each*),
　thawed and well drained

FETA CHEESE *½ pound,*
　crumbled fine

EGGS *4 whole, plus 2 yolks,*
　beaten

NUTMEG, GRATED FRESH
　¼ teaspoon

FINE DRY BREAD CRUMBS
　⅓ cup

SALT

PHYLLO PASTRY SHEETS
　½ pound (12 sheets
　about 12 by 18 inches)

BUTTER FOR BRUSHING
　PASTRY *½ pound,*
　melted

The Garnish

BLACK OR GREEK OLIVES

vertically on a working surface. Using a straight-edge guide and the tip of a very sharp, small knife, cut a 3-inch strip vertically through all the sheets (about 12 layers). Cover the remainder of the sheets with waxed paper and a damp kitchen towel.

5. Take one 3-inch strip to work with and cover the rest with waxed paper and a damp kitchen towel. Place it vertically on a pastry board. Using a pastry brush and the melted butter, butter the entire length thoroughly.

6. Put a heaping tablespoon of the spinach mixture about 1 ½ inches from the top edge and slightly to the left (figure 1).

FIGURE 1

7. Fold the top right corner over the filling to form a triangle. Don't worry if a little of the filling oozes out. It will be completely enclosed when you finish the pastry (figure 2).

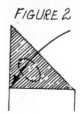

FIGURE 2

8. Continue to fold the triangle: down, then to the right, down, then to the left,

etc., making sure that with each fold, the top or bottom edge makes a right angle with the side. If you practice with a long, narrow strip of paper, the folding will be quite clear (figure 3).

FIGURE 3

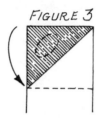

9. Continue to turn the triangle until you reach the end of the strip. Lightly butter the finished triangle and place it, open edge down, on a baking sheet. Repeat the filling and folding process until the first stack of strips is used.

10. Cut more strips and repeat, using the remainder of the filling or the *phyllo* sheets. Don't worry if a sheet tears. The tear will probably be covered by the next fold. If 2 or 3 sheets come off the stack together, just make 2 triangles from 1 strip by cutting the strip in half, horizontally across the middle, and putting a little extra butter on it. It won't be quite as flaky, but it will turn out fine. The triangles may now be refrigerated for several hours, or frozen in a single layer.

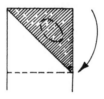

WHEN READY TO BAKE: 1. Preheat the oven to 375 degrees.

2. Place the puffs on the center rack of the preheated oven. If they were refrigerated, bake for 25 to 30 minutes until golden and crisp. If they were frozen and

are to bake unthawed, allow about 40 minutes.

TO SERVE: Serve 3 per person on a small plate, or pass to guests in the living room before the main course is served.

SUGGESTED MAIN COURSE:
Stuffed Baked Fish
OR *Lake Chapala Fish Market Pâté,*
page 137

CHEESE PIE WITH PHYLLO PASTRY
(Tiropete)

12 SERVINGS

You will need waxed paper, a damp kitchen towel, and a pastry brush (a 2-inch paintbrush works nicely).

May be prepared up to 4 hours ahead, covered with plastic wrap, refrigerated, and baked about 30 minutes before serving time.

Serve warm.

FETA CHEESE *½ pound, crumbled*

RICOTTA CHEESE, POT CHEESE, OR DRY COTTAGE CHEESE (SEE

After your first experience wtih phyllo *pastry, you'll keep coming back for more. Another recipe that can be an impressive entrée for a luncheon or buffet supper, also.*

Before starting the recipe, read the directions for handling *phyllo* pastry on page 319.

Assemble and prepare all ingredients except *phyllo* pastry sheets.

1. Mix the feta cheese with the ricotta, pot, or dry cottage cheese and the ⅓ cup of melted butter.

2. Gradually add the beaten eggs and stir well, then stir in the parsley.

3. Taking 1 sheet at a time, line a 10-by-8-by-2-inch pan with about 10 *phyllo* pastry sheets, buttering each sheet generously before putting the next one on top. Keep the unbuttered sheets covered with

NOTE BELOW) ½
pound
BUTTER *⅓ cup, melted and*
cooled
EGGS 6, *beaten until thick*
FRESH PARSLEY *To make*
¼ cup when minced
PHYLLO PASTRY SHEETS
18 (about ½ pound)
BUTTER FOR BRUSHING
PASTRY *About ½ cup,*
melted

waxed paper and a damp kitchen towel. Fold the excess *phyllo* into the pan, covering only the bottom.

4. Fill with the cheese mixture.

5. Taking 1 sheet at a time, place about 8 *phyllo* pastry sheets on top of the filling, again buttering each sheet generously.

6. Trim the top layers of the *phyllo* to about 1 inch larger than the pan and tuck the excess into the sides. Butter the top generously, cover tightly with plastic wrap, and refrigerate for up to 4 hours, or bake at once.

WHEN READY TO BAKE: 1. Preheat the oven to 350 degrees.

2. Put the pie on the middle rack and bake for about 30 minutes or until crisp and golden. Let stand 5 minutes and serve warm.

TO SERVE: Using the tip of a small, sharp knife, cut in 4 parts parallel to the long side, and in 3 parts the other way, to make 12 rectangles. Each rectangle may be speared with a toothpick to keep the pastry and filling together.

SUGGESTED MAIN COURSE:
Moussaka
OR *Vitello Tonnato*

NOTE: If ricotta or pot cheese isn't available, put *large curd* cottage cheese in a strainer and rinse under cold running water to remove the cream. Drain well. Buy a little extra, as you will lose some of the weight.

Crêpes and Pasta

CREPES WITH CRABMEAT AND AVOCADO

16 TO 20 CREPES
(ENOUGH FOR 8 FIRST
COURSE SERVINGS OR
6 AS AN EVENING
SNACK)

The *crêpes* may be made ahead, and kept at room temperature, refrigerated, or frozen; bring to room temperature before filling and rolling.

The filling and topping may be made up to a day ahead and refrigerated separately.

The *crêpes* may be prepared and assembled, ready for the oven, in the morning.

We use crabmeat with a cheese sauce in many ways because it is simply delicious. The addition here of the avocado and the crêpes *just enhances the pleasure.*

THE CREPES: Prepare and cook, then let them stand at room temperature, refrigerate or freeze.

THE FILLING AND SAUCE: Assemble and prepare all ingredients except the avocados.

1. Melt the butter in a medium skillet and when it is quite hot, add the celery and sauté until it is just beginning to soften but is still crisp. Stir frequently.

2. Add the shallots or scallions and continue to sauté, stirring, for 1 or 2 minutes more, or until the shallots just start to soften. Do not let the vegetables overcook; you want them to add crispness to the filling.

Add the topping and
bake just before serving.

---

*The Crepes 1 full
recipe, page 306*

The Filling and Sauce

BUTTER (NOT
  MARGARINE) *⅓ cup*

CELERY *To make 1½ cups
when cut in very small
dice (⅛ by ⅛ inch)*

SHALLOTS OR SCALLIONS
  *To make 3 tablespoons
when minced*

RESERVED BUTTER (FROM
  COOKING THE CELERY
  AND SHALLOTS) PLUS
  ENOUGH EXTRA TO
  MAKE *¼ cup*

FLOUR *¼ cup*

LIGHT CREAM *2 cups*

SWISS CHEESE *To make ⅓
cup when grated*

MONOSODIUM GLUTA-
  MATE *½ teaspoon*

FRESH LEMON *A good
squeeze of juice*

SALT

WHITE PEPPER, GROUND
  FRESH

CRABMEAT *¾ pounds,
shredded coarse, if fresh,
or, if canned, 2 cans (6
ounces each), shredded
coarse: remove all
cartilage and bits of shell*

3. Remove from the heat and drain.
Reserve the butter in which the vegetables
were cooked. Put the celery and shallots
into a medium bowl and set aside.

4. Add enough additional butter to the
reserved butter from the sautéeing to
make ¼ cup. Put it into a heavy-bottomed
saucepan and place over low heat. Sprinkle
with the flour, blend, and cook slowly, stirring, for 1 or 2 minutes. Do not let the
mixture color.

5. Remove from the heat and add the
cream. Immediately beat vigorously with
a wire whisk to blend, being sure to
gather in all the flour from the inside
edges and bottom of the pan.

6. Place the saucepan over moderate
heat and continue stirring with the whisk
until the sauce thickens to about the consistency of a very heavy syrup and coats the
whisk well.

7. Remove from the heat and add the
grated cheese, monosodium glutamate,
and a good squeeze of lemon. Stir until the
cheese melts. Add salt and pepper to taste
and set aside.

8. Combine the crabmeat with the reserved celery and shallots. Then add and
mix in just enough of the sauce to bind the
solids, about 1 cup. Reserve the remainder
of the sauce for the topping. The mixture
should be moist, soft, and sticky. Set aside.
You will add the avocado slices and the
additional lemon juice when you fill the
crêpes.

THE TOPPING: Assemble and prepare all
ingredients.

and drain thoroughly
AVOCADOS 2 *small or 1
large, prepared just be-
fore filling and rolling
the* crêpes: *peel, seed,
and cut lengthwise in
slices about ¼ by ¼ by
4 inches long; you will
need 16 to 20 slices (the
short ends may be used
to make equivalent-size
slices)*
LEMON *Juice of 1*

The Topping
BUTTER 2 *tablespoons*
OIL 1 *tablespoon*
FRESH MUSHROOMS
*½ pound, to make 2
cups when sliced thin
vertically: wipe them
clean with a damp paper
towel, then remove the
stems even with the base
of the cap (save the
stems for another use)*
RESERVED CHEESE SAUCE
BUTTER FOR BAKING PAN
MILK IF NECESSARY

1. In a medium skillet, melt the 2 table-spoons of butter and the oil. When it is quite hot, add the mushrooms and sauté, turning frequently, until they are soft, a light gold, and most of the liquid has evaporated.

2. Add the mushrooms and any remaining liquid to the reserved cheese sauce and mix well.

3. At this point you may cover and refrigerate the crabmeat filling and the topping, separately, until ready to fill and roll the *crêpes*. Press a piece of plastic wrap directly on the topping so that a film will not form. Or, if you wish, you may continue with the recipe, filling and rolling the *crêpes* several hours in advance. Do not cover with the topping until just before baking.

TO FILL AND ROLL THE CREPES: 1. Bring the *crêpes* to room temperature.

2. Butter a 9-by-14-inch baking dish or 2 pie pans and set aside.

3. Prepare the avocado slices and sprinkle them with lemon juice.

4. Line up 8 or 10 *crêpes* on a flat surface, *spotty side up.* Using half of the crabmeat mixture, put about a heaping tablespoon on each, placing it on the lower third of the *crêpe* and spreading it to about ½ inch of the outside edges.

5. Lay a strip of avocado on top of the

crabmeat and start rolling from the lower third. When each is rolled, place them close together, seam side down, on the prepared baking dish.

6. Repeat with the remaining *crêpes* and the other half of the filling. You may now refrigerate them, covered, until ready to bake.

TO BAKE THE CREPES: 1. About 40 minutes before serving, preheat the oven to 375 degrees.

2. Put the topping in the upper section of a double boiler, over simmering water. It will have thickened while in the refrigerator. Heat, stirring frequently. If it seems too thick after heating, blend in a little milk to bring it back to the original consistency.

3. Spoon the sauce over the *crêpes* and place on the middle rack of the preheated oven for 15 to 20 minutes, or until heated through and bubbly.

TO SERVE: As a first course, put 2 *crêpes* on each warm individual plate. As an evening snack, serve 3 to each guest.

SUGGESTED MAIN COURSE:
   Baked Ham
   OR *Veal and Kidney Chops*

SWEDISH PANCAKES
WITH A CHOICE OF FILLINGS

10 SERVINGS
(ABOUT 40 TO 45
PANCAKES, 4
PANCAKES A
SERVING)

You should have a
Swedish pancake pan:
they are widely
available in housewares
and imported-
kitchenware stores.

Make the batter for the
pancakes at least an
hour before cooking.

The pancakes and filling
may be made up to 2
days ahead and
refrigerated separately.

May be assembled early on
serving day, covered,
and refrigerated: bake
just before serving.

Or they may be made,
filled, and frozen, then
thawed and baked just
before serving.

*Don't let us intimidate you. If you don't
have a Swedish pancake pan, try these any-
way—just make tiny pancakes on a griddle or in a skillet. They're such tasty little
morsels that they'll be a hit however ir-
regular in size.*

THE PANCAKES: Assemble and prepare all
ingredients.

1. Beat the eggs slightly, add the milk,
and combine. Add the sugar and the salt
to the flour and sift the mixture into the
eggs and milk, beating with a wire whisk
or hand mixer until well blended and
free from lumps. The mixture should be
smooth as velvet and the consistency of
light cream. Cover and let stand at room
temperature for at least 1 hour, preferably
2.

2. When ready to cook the pancakes,
put the pan over medium-low heat and
brush each indentation lightly with oil.
Continue heating until it is hot enough to
make a drop of cold water jump and evaporate.

3. Stir the batter. Using a measuring
tablespoon, scoop up a very scant measure
(about 2 teaspoons) of the batter and,
lifting the pan off the heat quickly, pour
it into 1 indentation. Immediately tip and
tilt the pan to distribute the batter evenly.

The Pancakes

EGGS *2*

MILK *1 cup*

SUGAR *½ teaspoon*

SALT *¼ teaspoon*

ALL-PURPOSE FLOUR
   ¾ cup, unsifted

VEGETABLE OIL

The Spinach and Mushroom Filling

BUTTER *1 tablespoon*

SHALLOTS OR SCALLIONS
   To make 1 tablespoon when chopped fine

FRESH MUSHROOMS
   ¼ pound, chopped very fine: first wipe with damp paper towel, if necessary

FROZEN CHOPPED
SPINACH *To make 1 cup, cooked (2 packages, 10 ounces each): after cooking, drain well and chop again*

IMPORTED GRUYERE
CHEESE *To make ¼ cup when grated fine*

HEAVY CREAM *2 tablespoons*

NUTMEG, GRATED FRESH
   1 generous pinch

SALT

BLACK PEPPER, GROUND
   FRESH

The pancakes must be very thin. Repeat with the other indentations.

4. As soon as the pancakes set, which will be almost at once, little holes will appear on top and they will start to color very lightly underneath. Turn them with a spatula and cook the other side until very lightly colored. This side will be more or less spotty.

5. Stack the pancakes on a towel as they are removed from the pan, placing the side that was baked first down. This is the prettier side, and the side that you will want outside when you roll it. Cover with the towel as you cook each batch to keep them soft and pliable.

6. If necessary, brush each indentation again with oil as you bake the subsequent batches. One oiling will probably be sufficient for 3 or 4 batches. Stir the batter occasionally.

7. When all are cooked, put them aside until you are ready to fill them. If they are to be kept an hour or less, cover and let stand at room temperature so that they will not dry out. If they are to be kept longer, cover and refrigerate for up to 2 days.

THE FILLING: Choose whichever filling you desire. Each recipe is enough to fill 40 pancakes. Or if you are really ambitious, halve the recipes and make some of each!

THE SPINACH AND MUSHROOM FILLING: Assemble and prepare all ingredients:

1. Heat the butter in a medium-sized

BUTTER FOR BAKING
   SHEET

The Topping
MELTED BUTTER *¼ cup*
GRUYERE OR PARMESAN
   CHEESE, GRATED FRESH
   ¼ cup

The Shrimp and
Bacon Filling
BUTTER *3 tablespoons*
FLOUR *3 tablespoons*
HEAVY CREAM *½ cup*
   MIXED WITH:
MILK *1 cup*
MADEIRA *2 tablespoons*
MONOSODIUM GLUTA-
   MATE *¼ teaspoon*
SALT
WHITE PEPPER, GROUND
   FRESH
COOKED SHRIMP *Enough*
   to make 1½ cups when
   shelled and minced in
   ⅛-inch chunks (about
   1 pound uncooked)
BACON *8 slices, fried crisp*
   and crumbled
BUTTER FOR BAKING
   SHEET

The Topping
RESERVED SAUCE *¾ cup*

saucepan. When it starts to foam, add the shallots or scallions and sauté until they are limp and just starting to color.

2. Add the mushrooms and sauté, stirring constantly for about 3 or 4 minutes more, or until all the moisture has evaporated.

3. Remove from the heat, add the spinach, Gruyère, cream, and nutmeg. Stir vigorously to blend. Add salt and pepper to taste. Reserve, covered, until ready to fill the pancakes. If the filling is to be kept more than 2 or 3 hours, cover and refrigerate for up to 2 days.

THE SHRIMP AND BACON FILLING: Assemble and prepare all ingredients.

1. Melt the butter in a 1-quart saucepan. Add the flour and cook slowly, stirring constantly, for about 2 minutes. Do not let the mixture color.

2. Remove from the heat and add the cream-and-milk mixture all at once. Beat vigorously with a whisk until smooth, then return the pan to medium heat. Beating constantly, simmer until the sauce is medium thick. It should be thick enough to coat a spoon heavily, or about the consistency of hollandaise sauce. Remove from heat.

3. Add the Madeira, monosodium glutamate, and salt and pepper to taste. Mix well.

4. Measure ¾ cup of the sauce and put it in a small bowl. Place a piece of plastic wrap directly on top to keep a skin from

forming. Reserve to spoon on top of the pancakes.

5. To the remaining sauce, add the cooked shrimp and bacon. Check for seasoning, adding salt and pepper to taste. Reserve, covered, until ready to fill the pancakes, or, if it is to be kept more than 2 or 3 hours, cover and refrigerate for up to 2 days.

TO FILL THE PANCAKES: 1. Taking 20 pancakes, line them up on a counter or pastry board. Divide the filling in half (about ¾ cup). Spread about 1 heaping teaspoon of the filling on the half of each pancake that is nearest you. Roll into a cylinder and place on a buttered baking sheet, seam side down, in a single layer. If some of them won't stay rolled, insert a toothpick vertically through the center. Remove the toothpicks before serving. Repeat until all are filled and rolled.

TO FREEZE: Place them in a single layer, seam side down, on a flat surface, not buttered, and freeze for 2 hours. Remove them and pack in a container with freezer paper, foil, or plastic wrap between the layers. Return them to the freezer. If you are freezing the shrimp-and-bacon pancakes, put the reserved sauce in a separate container and freeze separately. On serving day thaw and bake as directed.

TO BAKE: 1. Preheat the oven to 350 degrees.

2. For the spinach-and-mushroom pan-

cakes, drizzle a little of the ¼ cup of melted butter over each roll. Then sprinkle them evenly with the grated Parmesan cheese.

3. For the shrimp-and-bacon pancakes, spoon a wide strip of the reserved ¾ cup of sauce down the center of the pancakes.

4. Bake uncovered for about 15 minutes or until heated through. (Bake a little longer if they have been refrigerated.)

TO SERVE: Put 4 pancakes on each warm individual plate and serve at once.

SUGGESTED MAIN COURSE:
> Cold Swedish Salmon Mousse, page 26
> OR Scandinavian Fish Pudding with Shrimp Sauce, page 96

STUFFED PASTA SHELLS

12 SERVINGS
  (3 SHELLS PER
  PERSON)
You will need a pot large enough to hold about 7 quarts, and 1 large or 2 smaller shallow baking dishes.

May be prepared up to a day ahead: bake just before serving.

THE PASTA SHELLS: Assemble all ingredients.

1. Bring the water to a boil in a large pot. Add the olive oil, salt, and pasta shells. Keep the water at a rapid boil and stir from time to time with a wooden fork.

2. When the shells are just *al dente* (tender but still firm to the bite), remove them with a slotted spoon, drain, and cool.

THE SAUCE: Assemble and prepare all ingredients.

1. In a heavy-bottomed saucepan, melt the butter over low heat. Add the chopped

The Pasta Shells

WATER 7 *quarts*
OLIVE OIL *1 tablespoon*
SALT 2 *tablespoons*
"JUMBO" PASTA SHELLS
 (ABOUT 2 INCHES IN
 LENGTH) 40 (*this will
 allow a few extra for
 tearing*)

The Sauce

BUTTER 6 *tablespoons*
GARLIC 6 *cloves, peeled
 and chopped very fine
 with a little salt*
FLOUR 6 *tablespoons*
MILK *3 cups*
 MIXED WITH:
HEAVY CREAM *1 cup*
PARSLEY *To make ½ cup
 when minced*
FLAT ANCHOVY FILLETS
 IN OIL *To make 3 table-
 spoons when minced*
SALT
WHITE PEPPER, GROUND
 FRESH

The Stuffing

RICOTTA CHEESE 2 *cups*
 (*about 1 pound*)
SMALL CURD COTTAGE
 CHEESE *1 cup*
PARMESAN CHEESE,
 GRATED FRESH *¼ cup*
PARSLEY *To make 3 table-
 spoons*
BASIL *To make 3 table-*

garlic and sauté until it just starts to turn golden. Stir frequently and do not let the garlic brown.

2. Remove from the heat and, when the butter has stopped bubbling, add the flour. Return to the heat and cook, stirring constantly, for about 2 minutes. Do not let the flour color.

3. Remove from the heat again and add the milk-and-cream mixture all at once. Immediately beat vigorously with a wire whip until smooth.

4. Replace the pan over moderate heat and add the parsley and anchovies. Cook, stirring constantly, until the sauce is the consistency of heavy cream.

5. Remove from the heat. Salt lightly (remember the anchovies are salty) and add pepper to taste. Reserve uncovered.

THE STUFFING: 1. Put about 2 cups of the sauce in the bottom of a baking dish (1 cup in each if using smaller pans). Set aside.

2. In a large bowl, combine the ricotta cheese, cottage cheese, Parmesan, parsley, basil, *prosciutto,* and egg yolks. Add salt and pepper to taste and mix well.

3. Stuff each shell with some of the cheese mixture, pressing it down lightly to fill out the shape.

4. Using your fingers press the top of the 2 long sides slightly together so that the shape of the shell is as it was before boiling. Wipe off any excess filling that may be squeezed out.

5. Place the stuffed shells in a single

*spoons when minced, if
fresh, or, if dried,*
1 *tablespoon, crumbled*
PROSCIUTTO 6 *very thin
slices, cut in ⅛-by-⅛-
inch squares*
EGG YOLKS 2, *beaten*
SALT
WHITE PEPPER, GROUND
    FRESH

layer in the prepared baking dish. Pour the remaining sauce over them.

6. Cover with foil or plastic wrap and refrigerate until about 25 minutes before you are ready to serve. If made a day ahead, press a piece of plastic wrap directly on top of the sauce so that a film will not form.

TO BAKE: Preheat the oven to 375 degrees. Bake for 15 minutes or until the sauce bubbles.

TO SERVE: Put 3 shells with some sauce on each plate and serve at once.

SUGGESTED MAIN COURSE:
    Steak Diane
    OR *Osso Buco*

FETTUCCINE CON PESTO

6 SERVINGS

You will need a blender
    and a deep pot large
    enough to hold 7 quarts.

The *pesto* may be made
    up to a week in advance
    and refrigerated, or
    frozen for up to 6
    months, but the *fet-
    tuccine* must be cooked
    just before serving.

Most attractive when

Pesto *is a fragrant Italian sauce of basil, cheese, and oil, delicious on pasta, but with many other uses. Try some of those suggested at the end of the recipe.*

THE PESTO: Assemble and prepare all ingredients.

1. Put the olive oil, basil, garlic, and walnuts into the jar of a blender.

2. Turning the motor on and off, blend on low speed and then on high speed until smooth. Stop the blender every few seconds and push the ingredients down with a rubber spatula. The sauce should be quite

served in individual ramekins or small bowls.

The Pesto (1⅔ cups)

OLIVE OIL (NO SUBSTITUTE) *1 cup, plus up to ½ cup more if necessary*

FRESH BASIL LEAVES *2 cups, tightly packed: remove the stems and chop coarse*

GARLIC *8 cloves, peeled and chopped coarse*

WALNUTS *To make ½ cup when chopped coarse*

IMPORTED PARMESAN, SARDO, OR ROMANO CHEESE *To make 1 cup when fresh and grated fine, plus about ½ cup more for topping (about 8 ounces): do not use the packaged, grated Parmesan—it will make the texture too rough*

SALT

BLACK PEPPER, GROUND FRESH

The Fettuccine

WATER *6 to 7 quarts*

SALT *2 tablespoons*

OLIVE OIL *1 tablespoon*

IMPORTED FETTUCCINE

thick and drop sluggishly off the spoon. If it is too thick, add up to ½ cup more olive oil.

3. Spoon into a bowl and mix in 1 cup of the cheese. Add salt and pepper to taste. If not used within several hours, this will keep, refrigerated, up to a week with about ¼ inch of oil poured over it; or it may be frozen, also covered with oil. The color will darken slightly, but it will taste just as good. Bring to room temperature before serving.

THE FETTUCCINE: *Just before serving,* assemble all ingredients.

1. Put the ramekins, small bowls, or plates, along with a large bowl, in the oven to warm.

2. Put the water into a large pot and bring it to a rapid boil. Add the salt, olive oil, and the *fettuccine,* gently pushing it down until all is submerged. Keep the water at a rapid boil and stir from time to time with a wooden fork.

3. After about 3 minutes of cooking, fork out a strand and bite it. Cook only until *al dente* (slightly firm to the bite). As a guide, it will probably take 5 or 6 minutes to cook, but test by biting a strand frequently.

4. Quickly drain the *fettuccine* into a colander or sieve, shaking it as it drains. Lift the strands with 2 forks to make sure that no water remains.

5. Immediately put into the large warmed bowl and pour ½ cup of the warmed cream over it. Gently and quickly

(1-INCH-WIDE EGG
NOODLES MAY BE
SUBSTITUTED) *1 pound*
HEAVY CREAM *½ cup,
warmed, plus a little
more if necessary*
SALT
BLACK PEPPER, GROUND
FRESH

The Topping
RESERVED PESTO SAUCE
*About ¾ cup; the re-
maining sauce to be
passed at the table*
RESERVED GRATED CHEESE

toss until each strand glistens. Add a little more cream if necessary. Each strand should be well coated, but there should be no moisture at the bottom of the bowl. Add salt and pepper to taste—it should be very well seasoned.

TO SERVE: Immediately divide the *fettuc-cine* among the 8 warm ramekins or bowls. Put a generous tablespoon of the *pesto* on top of each serving. The sauce is mixed with the pasta, individually, at the table. Put the extra ½ cup of grated cheese, and the balance of the Pesto, in separate bowls and pass for those who wish them. Serve at once.

SUGGESTED MAIN COURSE:
Cold Poached Salmon
OR *Sole Meunière*

NOTE: *Pesto* has many uses. Try putting a tablespoon on each serving of vegetables, or about 2 tablespoons in an oil-and-vine-gar salad dressing, or 2 tablespoons mixed with ½ cup of mayonnaise, or a table-spoon into a serving of any hot soup.

6 SERVINGS OF 4
GNOCCHI EACH

The *gnocchi* may be
prepared up to 8 hours

GNOCCHI PARISIENNE

Still another tasty way to use pâte à choux. *This version of* gnocchi *is strictly French. In Italy they are made with cheese or po-tatoes. Try the alternative serving sugges-*

in advance and refrigerated, lightly covered.

Add the melted butter and Parmesan cheese and heat just before serving.

BUTTER FOR BAKING PAN
WARM PATE A CHOUX
    ½ recipe, page 304
SWISS OR PARMESAN
    CHEESE *To make ½
    cup when fresh grated*
WATER *8 cups*
MELTED BUTTER *¼ cup*
PARMESAN CHEESE,
    GRATED FRESH *½ cup*

tions at the end: they are velvety rich and memorable.

Assemble and prepare all ingredients.

1. Butter a shallow baking pan about 8 inches square or 9 inches in diameter and set aside.

2. Add the ½ cup Swiss or Parmesan cheese to the *pâte à choux* and mix well.

3. Bring the water to a simmer in a large skillet. With a teaspoon and a small spatula, slip spoonfuls of the paste into the simmering water. Do not let the water boil. Cook the *gnocchi* about 15 minutes, testing one to see if it is done—it should be light and fluffy and cooked through. Remove with a slotted spoon and drain on paper towels.

4. Arrange the *gnocchi* in the buttered baking pan in one layer. At this point they may be refrigerated, covered, for up to 8 hours.

JUST BEFORE SERVING: 1. Preheat the broiler.

2. Pour the melted butter over all and sprinkle with the Parmesan cheese.

3. Broil about 2 inches below the source of heat until brown, about 15 minutes.

TO SERVE: Divide among 6 warmed plates. No accompaniment is needed.

SUGGESTED MAIN COURSE:
    Baked Whole Fish
    OR *Ham Steaks*

TWO ENHANCED VERSIONS:

GNOCCHI MORNAY: Arrange the cooked *gnocchi* in a shallow, buttered pan and cover with hot Mornay Sauce, page 98. Sprinkle with a little grated Parmesan cheese and heat under the broiler until brown and bubbly.

GNOCCHI PIE: Prepare as for *Gnocchi* Mornay above, but put the *gnocchi* and sauce into a baked 9-inch pie shell, page 299. Broil as above. One pie will make 6 servings.

After Dinner: Evening Snacks

Cold

Seafood

LAKE CHAPALA FISH MARKET PATE

ABOUT 20 WEDGES

You will need a 2-quart casserole, pretty enough to come to the table (we like a round one).

Must be made at least a day ahead, but may be made up to 2 days before serving.

Does not freeze well.

Serve cold.

BUTTER *For casserole*
FRESH SKINLESS AND
    BONELESS FISH
    FILLETS—NOT FROZEN
    (USE HALIBUT, SEA
BASS, FLOUNDER, COD,

Pierre is the unusual French-Mexican chef of an exclusive club on Lake Chapala, Mexico, and the co-owner of our local fish market. An unusual feature of the tiny fish market is the occasional specialty that Pierre whips up and serves at the one small table. One morning we tried his fish pâté. It intrigued us, so we asked for the ingredients, bought the seafood, went home, and immediately concocted our own version. We've never seen or tasted one quite like it. It is fairly well seasoned, yet delicate to the taste, with a medium-coarse texture that is solid and pleasing.

Assemble and prepare all ingredients.

1. Preheat the oven to 375 degrees. Lightly butter a 2-quart casserole and set aside.

2. In a large bowl, combine the ground fish, scallions, shrimp, parsley, garlic, dill, thyme, bay leaves, and salt and pepper to taste. Set aside.

OR ANY OTHER FIRM,
SLIGHTLY GELATINOUS
WHITE FISH)
*2¼ pounds, well dried
and ground through the
finest disk of a meat
grinder (about 4 cups,
packed, after grinding)*
SCALLIONS *To make ½
cup when sliced very
thin: include a little of
the green stems*
COOKED AND PEELED
SMALL OR TINY
SHRIMP (CANNED,
DRAINED SHRIMP MAY
BE USED) *1 cup (about
¾ pound uncooked) or
2 cans (4½ ounces
each)*
PARSLEY *To make ¼ cup
when minced*
GARLIC *3 cloves, peeled
and minced almost to a
paste with a little salt*
DRIED DILL WEED *½ tea-
spoon*
DRIED THYME LEAVES
⅛ teaspoon, crumbled
BAY LEAVES *2 small or
1 large, whirled in a
blender until very fine
or crushed with a mortar
and pestle*
SALT
BLACK PEPPER, GROUND
FRESH *We like 10 grinds*

3. In a small saucepan, sprinkle the gelatin over the wine and let stand 5 minutes to soften. Put the pan over low heat and stir the gelatin until it is completely dissolved.

4. Add the melted gelatin, eggs, and cream to the fish mixture and blend very thoroughly by hand. Do not use an electric mixer.

5. Spoon the mixture into the prepared casserole, packing it down lightly so that there are no air bubbles, and distributing the shrimp as evenly as possible. Cover tightly with foil.

6. Put the foil-covered casserole into a baking pan large enough to hold it and almost as deep as the casserole, and set on the middle rack of the oven. Add enough hot water to the lower pan to come about two-thirds up the sides of the casserole.

7. Bake 50 to 60 minutes, or until a knife inserted near the center comes out clean.

8. Take the casserole from the oven and remove the foil. The top of the *pâté* will look very moist. This is as it should be. The liquid will gel as it cools. Refrigerate for at least a day.

TO SERVE: Run a small, sharp knife around the edge of the *pâté* to loosen it. Decorate the top with lemon and onion slices. Bring the casserole to the table. Cut in wedges or slices and put on individual chilled plates. Pass the accompaniment of your choice separately, along with a glass of chilled dry white wine or beer.

UNFLAVORED GELATIN
   1 *tablespoon* (1 *enve-*
   lope)
DRY WHITE WINE 1/4 *cup*
EGGS 2 *whole, slightly*
   beaten
LIGHT CREAM 2/3 *cup*
HOT WATER

The Garnish
LEMON CIRCLES, CUT
   THIN
THIN ONION RINGS, CUT
   FROM A SMALL ONION

The Accompaniment
CRUSTY FRENCH OR
   ITALIAN BREAD
OR BENNE SEED WAFERS,
   page 313

BRAZILIAN SARDINE PUDDING

10 TO 12 SERVINGS

You will need a large
   rectangular baking pan
   and a large mixing
   bowl or pot that will
   hold at least 2½ quarts.

The pudding should be
   made early in the day
   and refrigerated, but
   do not put the topping
   or garnish on more than
   1 hour before serving.

Sardines are one of life's better sources of high flavor and nourishment. We feature them here in our version of a Brazilian dish.

Assemble and prepare all ingredients.

1. Preheat the oven to 400 degrees.
2. Butter a 9-by-13-by-2-inch baking pan well and coat it with bread crumbs, revolving it so that the bottom and sides are well covered. Give it a sharp shake, upside down, to remove the excess crumbs.
3. Heat the oil in a large skillet. Add

Serve cold.

The Pudding

BUTTER FOR BAKING PAN

FINE DRY BREAD CRUMBS
For coating pan

SALAD OIL *1 cup*

ONIONS *To make 1⅓ cups when chopped fine (about 2 medium)*

PARSLEY *To make 2 tablespoons when minced*

INSTANT MASHED POTATOES *To make 6 cups, when prepared according to package directions and cooled*

SKINLESS AND BONELESS SARDINES IN OIL *4 cans (3¾ ounces each), mashed with their canning oil—but not to a paste: you want some texture*

MILK *If necessary*

EGGS *6, beaten until fluffy*

SALT

WHITE PEPPER, GROUND FRESH

The Topping

MAYONNAISE, PREFERABLY HOMEMADE *(page 296) 1¼ cups* **MIXED WITH:**

DIJON MUSTARD *1 table-*

the onions and sauté for 2 or 3 minutes over medium heat. Add the parsley and continue sautéeing until the onions are soft but not colored.

4. Put the cooled potatoes into a large mixing bowl. Add the onion-parsley mixture along with all of the cooking oil and mix thoroughly. This will take a little time. Add the mashed sardines. Combine, folding and stirring, until all is well mixed. If the mixture seems dry, add a little milk. It should be moist and sticky but not wet.

5. Add the beaten eggs and fold together, until all is evenly distributed. Add salt and pepper to taste.

6. Spoon into the prepared baking dish and put on the middle rack of the preheated oven. Bake 30 to 40 minutes, or until the top is golden-brown, the edges are sizzling, and a knife inserted in the center has just a trace of potato on it.

7. Remove from the oven and put on a rack. Run a small, sharp knife around the edges, but do not remove the pudding from the pan. It will flatten a little as it cools. When cool, refrigerate in the pan until an hour or less before serving.

TO ASSEMBLE AND GARNISH (NO MORE THAN 1 HOUR AHEAD): 1. Again, run a knife around the edges. Center a large platter over the top of the pudding, and, holding the platter and baking pan firmly together, invert, giving a sharp downward shake. If the pudding sticks, poke it underneath with a spatula and invert again,

spoon, plus 2 teaspoons

The Garnish

SHREDDED LETTUCE
  To make about 3 cups,
  well dried and crisped

UNCOOKED CARROTS
  About 3 medium, cut
  lengthwise into match-
  size strips

UNCOOKED FROZEN PEAS
  1 cup, thawed

RED RADISHES 10 to 14,
  washed and root end re-
  moved: leave on a few
  of the smallest green
  leaves and crisp

**PARSLEY OR WATERCRESS
  SPRIGS**

PAPRIKA

or if it breaks in a place or two, just patch it together and don't worry. All will be covered with the mustard mayonnaise.

2. Spread the mustard mayonnaise over the top and sides, like frosting on a cake. Surround the base with the shredded lettuce. Place the julienne carrots on the lettuce, and spoon the peas in little mounds here and there. Spot the radishes, equally spaced, between the other vegetables. Arrange the parsley or watercress sprigs on the *top* of the pudding, in a single row, around the outside edge to form a wreath. Sprinkle the top with paprika, shaking it on or sifting it between your fingers to make 5 or 6 diagonal stripes. Return to the refrigerator until serving time. Serve cold.

TO SERVE: Bring to the buffet or coffee table, along with a knife, chilled plates, and a serving spoon and fork. Cut lengthwise in half and crosswise in 5 or 6 parts. Each guest will help himself to a piece of the pudding and some of the garnishes. If the night is warm, why not accompany it with a glass of iced coffee, and a decanter of rum or brandy to be added according to taste?

MEAT AND POULTRY

COLD MEAT WITH ANCHOVY SAUCE

1 ½ CUPS OF SAUCE
(ENOUGH TO COAT
MEAT FOR 6 TO 8
SERVINGS)

You will need a blender.

Homemade mayonnaise is
a must.

Make the sauce several
hours or up to a day
ahead.

Assemble and garnish just
before serving.

Serve cold.

_____

The Sauce
**FLAT ANCHOVY FILLETS
IN OIL** *1 can* (*2 ounces*)
COOKED SPINACH *To make*

A tangy sauce to serve with the brisket left over after you have made our rich, good beef broth, page 291; a delicious late-evening snack. Other cold meats are suggested in the recipe. The amount of sauce given will cover a 2- or 3-pound brisket nicely. Double the sauce recipe if you have more meat. Any leftover sauce can be used for an unusual dip for raw vegetables.

THE SAUCE: Assemble and prepare all ingredients.

1. Put the anchovies, their canning oil, spinach, capers, and onion into a blender. Whirl until you have a smooth paste and transfer to a bowl.

2. Add the mayonnaise and cream to the paste, with a few grinds of the peppermill. Mix well and refrigerate several hours to blend the flavors.

THE MEAT: 1. Slice the meat thin and ar-

2 tablespoons when
chopped and very
thoroughly drained by
pressing against a sieve:
since you need such a
small amount, it's best to
break off a piece from a
package of frozen
spinach
CAPERS 2 teaspoons,
drained
ONION To make 2 table-
spoons when chopped
fine
HOMEMADE MAYON-
NAISE, page 296 (NOT
COMMERCIAL) ¾ cup
HEAVY CREAM ¾ cup
WHITE PEPPER, GROUND
FRESH

The Meat
COLD COOKED MEAT
Brisket, lamb, pork, veal,
or any combination

The Garnish
CANNED PIMIENTOS
1 or 2 whole, drained,
dried, and cut lengthwise
in strips about ⅜ inch
wide

The Accompaniment
HERB BREAD, page 316

range the slices, overlapping, on a large
platter. Refrigerate tightly covered.

JUST BEFORE SERVING: 1. Spread the
sauce evenly and thickly on the meat, covering the top and sides like the frosting on
a cake. Ideally it should cover all with no
bits of meat showing.

2. Arrange the pimiento strips radiating from the center, like the spokes on a
wheel, or in horizontal and vertical lines
forming squares or diamonds. Serve cold.

TO SERVE: Serve at the table accompanied
by warm Herb Bread.

PATE DE CAMPAGNE

SERVES 10 TO 12

You will need a 2-quart loaf pan, about 10 by 5 by 3 inches, and a larger and deeper pan to put it in.

Bake and chill at least 3 hours before serving.

At its best after 2 days of refrigeration, but will keep well up to 5 days.

Does not freeze well.

Serve chilled.

BACON *About ½ pound to line the baking pan, plus 2 slices, diced*

CHICKEN BREASTS *3 halves, boned*

COGNAC *3 tablespoons*

ONION *1 large, peeled and chopped fine*

GARLIC *3 cloves, peeled and minced with a little salt*

UNCOOKED GROUND TURKEY (CHICKEN MAY BE SUBSTITUTED)

There are many combinations of ingredients for pâtés, almost all of them good. We have worked out this one—highly seasoned, very pretty when sliced and served, and delicious.

Assemble and prepare all ingredients.

1. Preheat the oven to 350 degrees.
2. Line the loaf pan with overlapping slices of bacon. Let the bacon hang over the sides of the pan. Set aside.
3. Put the boned chicken breasts into a shallow dish and sprinkle them with the Cognac. Allow them to marinate while the rest of the filling is being cooked and combined.
4. In a small skillet, fry the diced bacon over moderate heat until it is crisp. Remove and drain on paper towels. Retain the drippings.
5. In the same skillet, heat the drippings, add the onions and garlic, and sauté over moderate heat until they are soft but not brown. Stir frequently.
6. In a large bowl, combine the reserved bacon bits, sautéed onions and garlic, ground turkey, ground pork, nutmeg, ginger, salt, pepper, eggs, and cream. Mix well and set aside.
7. Slice the marinated chicken in strips about 1 inch wide. Set aside.
8. Blend the excess marinade with the meat mixture, and divide into 5 parts.

1 pound

GROUND PORK *1 pound*

GROUND NUTMEG *½ teaspoon*

GROUND GINGER *½ teaspoon*

SALT *2 teaspoons*

BLACK PEPPER, GROUND FRESH *½ teaspoon*

EGGS *2, beaten*

HEAVY CREAM *½ cup*

HAM *¼ pound, cut in strips ½ inch wide by ½ inch thick*

BAY LEAVES *3 medium*

HOT WATER

HEAVY FILLED CANS OF FRUIT OR VEGETABLES *2 or 3 for weighting the* pâté

The Accompaniment

FRESH, CRISP FRENCH BREAD

BUTTER PATS OR CURLS

9. Layer the ingredients in the prepared loaf pan as follows:

a. Spread one-fifth of the meat mixture as evenly as possible on the bottom.

b. Arrange half of the ham slices, lengthwise, in a single layer over it.

c. Spread with another fifth of the meat mixture, disturbing the ham as little as possible.

d. Arrange half of the chicken strips lengthwise over it.

e. Spread with another fifth of the meat mixture without disturbing the chicken.

f. Arrange the remaining half of the ham, lengthwise, in a single layer on top.

g. Spread with another fifth of the meat mixture.

h. Arrange the remaining half of the chicken, lengthwise, in a single layer over it.

i. Finish with the remaining fifth of the meat mixture, and space the 3 bay leaves at equal intervals on top.

10. Fold over the flaps of bacon so that the Pâté is covered. If there is not sufficient excess to cover the top, cut additional slices of bacon and fit them in.

11. Cover the pan tightly with aluminum foil. Place the filled pan in a larger, deep pan and put on the middle rack of the preheated oven. Fill the bottom pan with about 2 inches of hot water.

12. Bake for 2 hours. Remove the Pâté pan from the water, take off the foil, and put the pan on a rack to cool.

13. When cool, pour off some of the fat

and juices and replace the foil. Put 2 or 3 heavy cans of fruit or vegetables on top to weight it. Chill in the refrigerator at least 3 hours or for up to 5 days.

TO SERVE: Cut the Pâté in the pan in slices about ½ inch thick. Put 1 or 2 slices on individual chilled plates and accompany with crisp French bread—warmed or not, as you wish—butter pats, and a glass of rich red wine, such as a Burgundy. If you don't care for the bacon on the outside, remove it before serving.

CHICKEN-CURRY DEEM SUM

This is a sample of Chinese deem sum, snacks, which are either baked or steamed pastries with a wide variety of fillings. Try your own filling, substituting shrimp or leftover pork or beef for the chicken. The curry-flavored pastry is unique and appealing.

18 PASTRIES

May be made several days ahead and refrigerated.

May be frozen: thaw before serving or warming.

Serve either cold or warm.

Assemble and prepare all ingredients.

The Pastry

MARIE'S MAGIC BASIC PASTRY MIX (*page 299*) *3 cups; stir well before measuring*
CURRY POWDER *1 teaspoon*
ICE WATER *3 tablespoons, or a little more*

THE PASTRY: 1. Put the pastry mix into a chilled bowl, add the curry powder, and combine thoroughly with a pastry blender or fork.

2. Sprinkle the 3 tablespoons of ice water over the mix and combine. Do this quickly, adding a little more water if necessary to form the pastry into a ball with your hands. Cover and refrigerate while you prepare the filling.

The Filling

COOKED CHICKEN
To make 1½ cups when minced
WATER CHESTNUTS
8, chopped fine
BACON 3 *slices, fried crisp and crumbled*
SOY SAUCE 3 *tablespoons*
CORNSTARCH *1 tablespoon*
MONOSODIUM GLUTA-MATE ¼ *teaspoon*

FLOUR FOR ROLLING
OIL FOR BAKING SHEET
EGG *1, well beaten, for glaze*

THE FILLING: Put all the ingredients into a bowl and mix well.

TO MAKE THE PASTRIES: 1. Preheat oven to 375 degrees.

2. Divide the pastry dough in half and refrigerate one half while using the other.

3. On a lightly floured board, roll out the pastry to about ⅛ inch thick. If it starts to stick, sprinkle it with a little more flour.

4. Cut rounds 4½ inches in diameter. You may need to make a paper pattern for this. Press the trimmings together, roll out, and cut as many more rounds as you can.

5. Put a pastry round into the palm of your left hand, and in the center place a generous tablespoon of the filling. Bring the pastry edges to the center to form a ball. Squeeze it if necessary, to seal the edges. Put it on an oiled baking sheet folded side down.

6. Repeat with the rest of the rounds and the other half of the pastry. Brush each ball well with the beaten egg.

7. Bake for about 30 minutes or until nicely browned. Serve with hot tea.

HARD-COOKED EGGS IN TAPENADE

6 SERVINGS

You will need a blender.

You may hard-cook the eggs up to a day ahead and refrigerate.

The sauce may be made up to 4 days ahead, refrigerated, and brought to room temperature before serving.

Assemble just before serving.

Serve cold.

The Tapenade
FLAT ANCHOVY FILLETS
IN OIL *1 can (2-ounce*

A tapénade is a highly flavored and versatile sauce. This version makes a tasty light snack. The sauce may be used also over cooked vegetables, cold or hot, and as a dip with raw vegetables.

THE TAPENADE: Assemble and prepare all ingredients.

1. Put all the ingredients for the Tapénade except the olive oil and black pepper into a blender.

2. Turn the blender on for a few seconds, then off, repeating until the mixture is fairly smooth.

3. With blender on, add the olive oil gradually to form a thick purée. Scrape down with a rubber spatula, if necessary, until the mixture moves freely.

4. Transfer to a small bowl and season to taste with a few grinds of the pepper mill. Cover tightly and refrigerate for up to 4 days. Bring to room temperature before serving. Makes 1 full cup.

size), *plus the oil from the can*

LEMON JUICE *2 teaspoons*

BRANDY *1 tablespoon*

DIJON MUSTARD *2 teaspoons*

CHOPPED RIPE OLIVES *1 can (4½-ounce size): reserve 3 tablespoons for the garnish*

CHUNK OR GRATED CANNED TUNA *½ cup (about half of a 6¼-ounce can)*

CAPERS *2 tablespoons, drained*

OLIVE OIL *¼ cup*

BLACK PEPPER, GROUND FRESH

The Eggs

HARD-COOKED EGGS *12, do not shell them until just before serving*

The Garnish

RESERVED CHOPPED OLIVES

MINCED PARSLEY

The Accompaniment

BREAD STICKS

SWEET BUTTER CURLS OR PATS

TO ASSEMBLE AND SERVE: 1. Shell the eggs and cut each in half lengthwise.

2. Spread a little of the Tapénade over the bottom of each small, chilled, individual serving plate. Place 4 hard-cooked egg halves on each plate, yolk side down. Spread a generous ribbon of the sauce lengthwise on top of each egg. Garnish each with a sprinkle of the reserved olives, and a little minced parsley.

3. Tie 3 or 4 bread sticks in 6 brightly colored napkins and put them at each place. Pass the butter separately. Accompany with a cold beer or a glass of dry red wine.

ONION PIE
(*Zwiebelkuchen*)

SERVES 8 AT LEAST;
  MORE IF APPETITES
  ARE SMALL

The pastry may be made
  ahead and either
  refrigerated for a day or
  two or frozen for about
  a month.

The onions and bacon for
  the filling may be
  cooked ahead and kept
  at room temperature
  for several hours, or
  refrigerated up to a day
  and brought back to
  room temperature just
  before completing the
  pie.

You may even prepare and
  bake the whole thing,
  cool it, and then
  refrigerate several
  hours ahead.

Serve slightly warm or at
  room temperature, not
  cold.

———————

*This onion pie is German and is always
served in the spring with May wine, which
is sweet, new, and unfermented. We be-
came addicted to this combination in Ger-
many, and spent many happy hours with it
on the terrace of a medieval castle and
restaurant overlooking the Neckar River.
You don't need a castle, and you can make
a version of May wine too. See recipe below. Woodruff may be purchased in many
gourmet food shops.*

THE PASTRY (easy because you don't have
to roll it out—just press it into the pan):
Assemble and prepare all ingredients.

  1. Sift the 2 cups of flour, baking powder, and salt together into a medium bowl.

  2. Add the chilled butter. Using the
tips of your fingers, a large fork, or 2
knives, scissors-fashion, work the butter
into the flour until the mixture resembles
coarse crumbs.

  3. Add the beaten egg, and, using a
fork, stir and scrape the flour into it. If the
mixture seems dry, gradually add up to 1
tablespoon of cream, but just enough to
make a dough that leaves the sides of the
bowl and forms a ball. It should be moist
and pliable but not wet.

  4. Lightly press and pat the dough as
evenly as possible into the bottom and
sides of a 9-inch layer-cake pan.

The Pastry

ALL-PURPOSE FLOUR
  2 cups
BAKING POWDER *1 tea-
  spoon*
SALT *½ teaspoon*
BUTTER *¾ cup, chilled and
  cut in small cubes*
EGG *1 whole, beaten*
CREAM *1 tablespoon, if
  necessary*
EGG WHITE *1, lightly
  beaten for sealing the
  pastry*

The Filling

BUTTER *2 tablespoons*
BACON *3 slices, diced*
ONIONS (PREFERABLY
  YELLOW-SKINNED)
  *To make 4 to 4½ cups
  when chopped fine
  (about 6 large)*
FLOUR *1 tablespoon*
SUGAR *2 teaspoons*
SALT *½ teaspoon*
CARAWAY SEEDS *1 teaspoon*
EGGS *3, well beaten*
HEAVY CREAM *¾ cup*

5. Using a pastry brush, brush the egg white over the bottom and sides. Refrigerate, covered, until ready to fill or freeze.

THE FILLING AND BAKING: Assemble and prepare all ingredients.

1. Preheat the oven to 375 degrees.

2. Place a heavy skillet over medium heat, and, when it is hot, add the butter. When the butter starts to sizzle, add the diced bacon and fry it, stirring frequently, for about 3 minutes.

3. Add the onions, mix well, and sauté until the onions are golden and translucent but not brown. Stir frequently.

4. Sprinkle the 1 tablespoon of flour, the sugar, and salt over the onions. Stir, and cook a minute more. Add the caraway seeds and combine. Remove from the heat and allow to cool, uncovered.

5. Put the beaten eggs into a large bowl. Mix in the cream. Add the cooled onion mixture and stir well.

6. Pour the mixture into the chilled pastry shell. (If the pastry has been frozen, it may be filled and baked without thawing.)

7. Bake on the middle rack of the preheated oven until the shell is a light tan, the filling is firm and golden, and a knife or skewer inserted in the center comes out clean, about 45 minutes.

8. Remove from the oven and allow to cool on a rack. Serve slightly warm or at room temperature.

TO SERVE: Cut into wedges and serve to

8 or 10 eager people, accompanied by a glass of new wine, May wine, or a semi-sweet white wine. The pie is also good the next day if there should happen to be any left over.

TO MAKE YOUR OWN MAY WINE: You will need dried woodruff, sugar, and dry white wine in the following proportions: 1 bottle white wine, 3 tablespoons sugar, 3 tablespoons dried woodruff. Put the woodruff into a quart bowl, sprinkle with the sugar, and add 1 cup of the wine. Let it marinate at room temperature for 2 hours. Add the remaining wine, and refrigerate until you are ready to serve it. One bottle of wine will usually serve 4.

Salads

SALADE RUSSE

A handy recipe for making leftover meats and vegetables festive. We use our scraps of meat from making beef broth, but almost anything goes. It is "Russe" if it has meat, potatoes, and vegetables.

THE SALAD: Assemble and prepare all ingredients.

1. In a large bowl, at least 3-quart size, put the meat, green beans, carrots, pickles, scallions, olives, and, last, the potatoes.

2. In a separate small bowl, combine the mayonnaise, yogurt, and dill. Pour the dressing over the salad and toss lightly but thoroughly. Add salt and pepper to taste.

3. Now, cautiously add about half of the vinegar and lemon juice. Toss again and taste. It should be tart but not too sharp. If necessary, add more vinegar and lemon juice (we use the full amount), but a lot depends upon how tart the pickles and yogurt are. Just keep gently tossing and tasting until it's just right for you.

6 TO 8 SERVINGS

Prepare and refrigerate at least 2 hours or up to 6 hours ahead.

The garnish may be prepared ahead, but arrange it just before serving.

Serve slightly chilled.

The Salad
LEAN, COOKED COLD
   MEAT *To make about 2
   cups when cut in ½-inch
   pieces: use leftover beef,
   pork, lamb, veal, sausage,
   ham, or any combination*
COLD, BARELY COOKED
   GREEN BEANS
   (SHELLED GREEN PEAS

MAY BE SUBSTITUTED)
*To make 1 cup when cut
in 1/3-inch dice*

COLD, BARELY COOKED
CARROTS *To make 1 cup
when cut in 1/3-inch
dice (about 2 medium)*

CRISP DILL PICKLES
(JEWISH-STYLE PRE-
FERRED) *To make 1 1/2
cups when drained and
cut in 1/3-inch dice
(about 3 large)*

SCALLIONS *To make 3/4
cup when sliced into
thin rounds: discard the
coarse outer leaves, but
use a little of the pale-
green stems (8 to 10)*

PITTED GREEN OLIVES
10, *sliced lengthwise,
then each slice cut in
half*

COLD, COOKED BOILED
POTATOES *To make 2
cups when peeled and
cut in 1/2-inch dice
(about 2 medium): do
not peel before cooking,
and cook only until
barely tender or they will
fall apart*

MAYONNAISE, PREFER-
ABLY HOMEMADE
(*page 296*) *1/2 cup*

UNFLAVORED YOGURT
1/2 cup

4. Refrigerate, tightly covered, for from 2 to 6 hours.

THE GARNISH: Assemble and prepare all ingredients.

1. Put the anchovies, eggs, and olives into small separate bowls. Wash the lettuce, roll in a towel, and refrigerate to dry and crisp.

2. Put the beets into a slightly larger bowl. Mix the oil and vinegar. Add salt and pepper to taste and beat with a fork. Pour over the beets and toss so that all are coated.

3. Cover all tightly and refrigerate.

ABOUT 1/2 HOUR BEFORE SERVING: 1. Mound the salad on a large platter or round plate.

2. Place 8 of the anchovy slices, evenly spaced, radiating lengthwise down from the top, like spokes of a wheel. Add the remaining anchovy slices to them, ends touching, to make long strips.

3. Place the egg slices casually between the strips, about 2 to each section. Press lightly on the salad so that they will adhere.

4. Arrange the sliced olives prettily over all. Press lightly on the salad to make them adhere.

5. Surround the base of the salad with the lettuce cups, and put about 1/4 cup of the beets into each.

TO SERVE: Bring to the table or sideboard along with chilled plates and a large glass

DILL WEED *To make ½*
tablespoon when minced,
if fresh, or, if dried,
½ teaspoon

SALT

BLACK PEPPER, GROUND
FRESH

RED WINE VINEGAR
1 tablespoon or less

LEMON JUICE *1 teaspoon*
or less

The Garnish

FLAT ANCHOVY FILLETS
IN OIL 8, *drained and*
cut in half lengthwise,
to make 16 slices

HARD-COOKED EGGS
2, peeled and sliced thin,
with an egg slicer if
possible

PITTED BLACK OLIVES
8 to 12, sliced crosswise,
³⁄₁₆ inch thick

LETTUCE CUPS 8

COLD, COOKED DICED
BEETS (CANNED OR
COOKED FRESH)
To make 2 cups when
drained and cut in ¼-
inch dice (1-pound can
or, if fresh, about 4
medium beets)

OIL ¼ *cup*

WINE VINEGAR *1 table-*
spoon

or tall narrow bowl filled with bread
sticks. Serve approximately 1 section of
salad to each guest, being sure that each
gets some of the anchovies. Let your guests
help themselves to bread sticks. Vodka,
hot black tea, or beef bouillon served with
it tastes just right.

SALT

BLACK PEPPER, GROUND
  FRESH

The Accompaniment
BREAD STICKS

8 TO 10 SERVINGS

You will need a large plate
  or platter, preferably
  round, 14 to 16 inches
  in diameter.

The potato salad and the
  other garnishes—
  except the avocados—
  may be prepared a day
  ahead: all should be
  thoroughly chilled.

The salad may be
  assembled and
  refrigerated up to 4
  hours before serving.

Serve cold.

————————

The Potato Salad
POTATOES *To make about
  7 cups, when cooked and
  sliced (about 3 pounds):
  see text for cooking
  instructions*

A GREEK SALAD

*Here is your chance to be an artist. Your
canvas is a base of potato salad and your
palette a whole range of colorful vegetables and seafood. We adapted this from
one served at Pappa's in Tampa and sent
us by artist friends there.*

THE POTATO SALAD: Assemble and prepare all ingredients.

1. Boil the whole, unpeeled potatoes in
enough water to cover until barely tender;
don't overcook or they will fall apart when
sliced—about 20 to 30 minutes, depending on their size.

2. When the potatoes are cooked, drain
them, and while they are still hot, peel and
cut them into quarters, then slices, and put
into a large bowl. Over the still-warm potatoes, pour first the ¼ cup of vinegar and
then the ½ cup of oil.

3. When cool, add the scallions, parsley, and mayonnaise. Add salt and pepper
to taste. Toss gently but thoroughly. Refrigerate, covered, up to a day ahead.

THE GARNISHES: Assemble and prepare
all the garnishes except the avocados. Put

WHITE WINE VINEGAR
¼ cup
SALAD OR OLIVE OIL, OR
A MIXTURE OF BOTH
½ cup
SCALLIONS *To make a full
½ cup when peeled and
sliced into thin rounds,
include about 2 inches
of the pale-green stems
(10 to 12)*
PARSLEY *To make ½ cup
when minced*
MAYONNAISE, PREFER-
ABLY HOMEMADE
(page 296) 1 cup
SALT
BLACK PEPPER, GROUND
FRESH

The Garnishes

LETTUCE *1 small head, to
line the plate: washed,
dried, and rolled in a
towel to crisp*
SHREDDED LETTUCE
*To make 3 cups, about 1
small head*
WATERCRESS *20 sprigs*
FIRM, FRESH TOMATOES
*4 medium, each cut in
6 wedges*
CUCUMBERS *2, each about
5 inches long, peeled and
cut lengthwise into 8
fingers each: scrape off
the seeds but leave the*

in small, separate, covered bowls, or wrap separately and refrigerate up to a day ahead.

TO ASSEMBLE: 1. Prepare the avocados and set aside.

2. Line the rim of a large plate or platter with lettuce leaves.

3. Place the potato salad in a mound in the center of the plate.

4. Cover the potato salad with the shredded lettuce and dot with the watercress sprigs.

5. Now for the fun! Starting from the bottom, circle the base of the potato mound with the tomato wedges, pulp side down, skin side up. Leave a little space between each, as later you will fill it with beet slices. If you run out of space before all the tomatoes are used, save them. You can spot them here and there after the salad is composed.

6. Circle the cucumber fingers, end to end and evenly spaced, on the *outside* of the tomato wedges to form a base.

7. Place the green pepper rings, evenly spaced around the perimeter of the salad, about half showing above the top of the tomatoes. Press to adhere.

8. Now, working from the top down, place the anchovy slices on the top of the mound, evenly spaced, lengthwise, radiating from the top like the spokes on a wheel.

9. Alternately place and stagger the avocado crescents and the feta cheese around the perimeter, between the ends of

pulp

GREEN BELL PEPPERS
*2 medium, each cut in 8
rings: remove seeds and
pith*

**FLAT ANCHOVY FILLETS
IN OIL** *10 (2-ounce
can), drained*

FETA CHEESE *10 slices, cut
fairly thin*

COOKED SHRIMP *30 to 36
medium, peeled*

PITTED BLACK OLIVES *20*

CANNED, SLICED BEETS
*24 slices, well drained
and patted dry*

**RADISH ROSES (OP-
TIONAL)** *10, page 320*

AVOCADOS *1 medium,
peeled, cut in 10
crescents, and*
SPRINKLED WITH:

LEMON JUICE *1 table-
spoon*

The Dressing

WHITE WINE VINEGAR
¾ cup

**OLIVE OIL (USE PART
SALAD OIL, IF YOU
PREFER)** *½ cup*

DRIED OREGANO LEAVES
A generous sprinkling

The Accompaniment

HERB BREAD, *page 316*
OR TOASTED PITTA BREAD,

the anchovies and the green pepper rings. Press to adhere.

10. Place the shrimp casually here and there to fill in the spaces. Place 3, standing on end, as a plume for the top. Press lightly to adhere.

11. Arrange the olives casually anywhere that you can find space. Press lightly to adhere.

12. Back to the base: put the beet slices standing upright, and at a slight angle, between the tomato wedges. Spot the radish roses on the lettuce leaves, equally spaced around the outer edge of the base, along with any remaining tomato wedges or any other leftover garnish.

13. Sprinkle the ¾ cup of vinegar over all and then the ½ cup of oil. Sprinkle generously with oregano.

14. If you're not in a state of enchantment by now, we give up!

15. Refrigerate until ready to serve.

TO SERVE: Place on the buffet or coffee table with chilled plates and a serving spoon and fork. Put the Herb Bread or Pitta Bread alongside. Let each guest help himself, taking a bit of each garnish and a generous portion of the potato salad.

HOMEMADE, *page 317,*
OR COMMERCIAL

PEGGY'S SALAD

8 SERVINGS

This never fails to make a hit—a happy combination of flavors and texture and a satisfying snack, particularly good for summer evenings.

Must be assembled at least
4 hours ahead.

Serve chilled.

Assemble and prepare all ingredients.

1. In a large bowl, layer one half of the lettuce, onions, peas, and cheese. Sprinkle with 1 tablespoon of the sugar and a few generous grinds of black pepper.

2. Thin the mayonnaise with the vinegar and drizzle one half over the layered ingredients.

3. Repeat the layering, using the other half of the lettuce, onions, peas, cheese, the remaining sugar, and more pepper. Drizzle the rest of the mayonnaise over all. Top with the bacon, evenly distributed.

4. Refrigerate for at least 4 hours.

TO SERVE: Divide among chilled salad plates. Pass the Gougère or bread and butter separately.

LETTUCE *To make 6 cups, when well dried and shredded (1 large head)*

BERMUDA ONIONS *2 medium, peeled and sliced into very thin rounds*

FROZEN GREEN PEAS *2 cups, thawed (do not cook)*

SWISS CHEESE *To make 2 cups when cut in slivers, about 1½ inches long by ⅛ inch wide by ⅛ inch thick*

SUGAR *2 tablespoons*

BLACK PEPPER, GROUND FRESH

MAYONNAISE, PREFERABLY HOMEMADE *(page 296) 2 cups*

WHITE VINEGAR *3 tablespoons*

BACON *1 pound, fried crisp*
  and crumbled

The Accompaniment
GOUGERE, *page 257*
OR HOT CRUSTY FRENCH
  BREAD AND BUTTER

CHEESE

BLUE CHEESE PIE

10 OR MORE WEDGES

The filling is so rich that you will want to serve only a small wedge at first and let your guests ask for more.

The pie shell may be baked a day ahead and refrigerated or it may be frozen, uncooked, and baked just before filling: the completed pie does not freeze well.

Must be completed 6 hours ahead, but can be made up to a day before serving.

Serve chilled.

The Pastry

BAKED PIE SHELL (YOUR OWN RECIPE OR OURS, *page 299*) *One 9-inch*

THE PASTRY: Assemble and prepare all ingredients.

1. Prepare and form the 9-inch pie shell. Freeze unbaked or bake several hours ahead.

2. Cool on a wire rack before filling.

THE FILLING: Assemble and prepare all ingredients.

1. In a small saucepan, sprinkle the gelatin over the ¼ cup of white wine and let it stand 5 minutes to soften.

2. Set over low heat and stir until the gelatin is completely dissolved. Set aside.

3. In a deep bowl, beat the softened blue cheese and cream cheese together until fluffy. This is easiest done with a stationary electric beater. A portable beater

The Filling

UNFLAVORED GELATIN
*1 tablespoon (1
envelope)*

DRY WHITE WINE *¼ cup
plus a little extra for
thinning, if necessary*

BLUE CHEESE *½ pound,
well softened*

CREAM CHEESE
*1 package (3-ounce
size), well softened*

CARAWAY SEEDS *1 teaspoon*

WORCESTERSHIRE SAUCE
2 teaspoons

CAYENNE PEPPER *About
⅛ teaspoon*

HEAVY CREAM *½ cup*

The Garnish

PAPRIKA

The Accompaniment

A BOWL OF FRESH PEARS
OR APPLES, WELL
POLISHED

may be used, but mix the 2 cheeses with a fork first. If the mixture is too stiff, add a tablespoon or two of white wine.

4. Add the gelatin mixture, caraway seeds, Worcestershire sauce, and cayenne pepper. Mix well.

5. Whip the cream and fold it into the cheese mixture. When well blended spoon it into the baked and cooled pie shell. Swirl the top a little so that it looks attractive and sprinkle evenly with a little paprika. Refrigerate for at least 6 hours.

TO SERVE: Cut in small wedges at the table. Put on serving plates, and pass the bowl of fruit.

6 TO 8 SERVINGS

You will need a 1½-quart mold, preferably made of metal.

Must be made 6 hours

CHILLED CHEDDAR CREAM CHEESE

Delicately pretty to look at, cool and pleasant on the tongue, this is a refreshing special for family or guests.

Assemble and prepare all ingredients.
1. Lightly oil the mold and set aside.

ahead, but may be made
a day before serving.

Serve cold.

———————

OIL FOR MOLD
CREAM CHEESE *⅓ cup*
  softened to room
  temperature
MILK OR LIGHT CREAM
  ⅓ cup
DIJON MUSTARD *2 table-*
  spoons
TABASCO SAUCE *½ tea-*
  spoon
SALT *½ teaspoon*
WHITE PEPPER, GROUND
  FRESH *½ teaspoon*
CAYENNE PEPPER *Scant*
  ¼ teaspoon
HEAVY CREAM *1½ cups*
SHARP CHEDDAR CHEESE
To make 2 cups when
  grated coarse (about
  ½ pound)

The Garnish
WATERCRESS
BLACK OLIVES

The Accompaniment
PRETZELS
OR SMALL WATER
  BISCUITS

2. Put the cream cheese into a large bowl. Add the milk a little at a time and beat together until smooth.

3. Add the mustard, Tabasco sauce, salt, white pepper, and cayenne pepper. Mix well and set aside.

4. In a separate bowl, whip the cream until it forms soft peaks.

5. Sprinkle about a third of the grated cheese over the cream cheese mixture. Cover this with about a third of the whipped cream. Repeat layering the Cheddar cheese and the whipped cream until all is used.

6. Fold together, being sure to bring the cream cheese mixture from the bottom of the bowl up and over the whipped cream.

7. Spoon the mixture into the prepared mold, giving it a good tap or two so that there are no air holes. Cover it with plastic wrap or foil and refrigerate for at least 6 hours or up to a day before serving.

TO UNMOLD AND SERVE: 1. Using the tip of a small, thin, sharp knife, loosen the edge of the cheese cream from the mold. Don't go down more than ¼ inch. Dip the bottom and sides of the mold for a second or two in warm but not hot water.

2. Center a serving plate upside down over the mold. Invert plate and mold, holding them firmly together and giving a sharp downward shake. If the cheese won't come out, dip the mold in warm water and invert it again. If necessary, blot up

OR BENNE SEED WAFERS,
page 313

any damp spots with a torn edge of paper toweling.

3. Garnish with sprigs of watercress and black olives. Bring to the table, slice, and serve on chilled plates. Pass the pretzels, biscuits, or wafers separately.

ROYAL CHEESE MOUSSE

1 QUART (12 TO
16 SERVINGS)

Must be made a day ahead.

_____

The aromatic Camembert named by Napoleon and the sharp Roquefort acclaimed the "King of Cheeses" make a royal couple indeed in this velvety mousse.

UNFLAVORED GELATIN
*2 tablespoons (2
envelopes)*
COLD WATER *½ cup*
ROQUEFORT CHEESE
*8 ounces, softened at
room temperature*
CAMEMBERT CHEESE
*6 ounces, softened at
room temperature*
WORCESTERSHIRE SAUCE
2 teaspoons
EGGS *2, separated*
HEAVY CREAM *1 cup*

The Accompaniment
PLAIN CRACKERS OR
ENGLISH WATER
BISCUITS

Assemble and prepare all ingredients.

1. In a small saucepan, sprinkle the gelatin over the cold water and let it stand for 5 minutes to soften. Then put the pan over low heat and stir until the gelatin dissolves completely.

2. Combine the Roquefort cheese and the Camembert cheese with the Worcestershire sauce and the egg yolks. Stir together until smooth. Add the gelatin and mix well.

3. Beat the egg whites until they stand in peaks; then whip the cream until it too stands in peaks. Add both to the cheese mixture and fold them in thoroughly.

4. Pour into a 1-quart mold and refrigerate overnight.

TO UNMOLD: Using the tip of a small, thin knife, loosen the edge of the mousse to a depth of ¼ inch. Dip the bottom and sides of the mold for a few seconds into warm water. Center a platter upside down over the mold. Invert both platter and mold, giving them a sharp downward shake. If the mousse won't come out, dip the mold back into warm water and try again.

TO SERVE: Surround with crackers or biscuits and let guests serve themselves. Wine or beer and a basket of chilled grapes make a perfect snack.

NOTE: This can be a delicious first course when served with crisp radishes.

Sandwiches and Other Filled Snacks

PITTA BREAD WITH A CHOICE OF FILLINGS

EACH FILLING MAKES
ENOUGH FOR 6
SERVINGS

The tuna or sardine filling
may be made up to 2
days ahead: either is
put chilled into the
warmed Pitta loaves.

The skewered beef filling
must be marinated for
from 6 to 24 hours
before serving; the
skewers—you will need
6 or more, about 8
inches long—may be
assembled early in the
day and broiled in the
oven or on a barbecue,
just before serving.

Pitta bread is available,
usually frozen, at most

Either the tuna or the sardine filling is a cinch to make. Just mix and serve. The other delicious beef-and-vegetable filling has to be broiled. We ate the pittas with great pleasure in numerous little Greek restaurants in London, where they are often filled with lamb instead of beef.

THE TUNA FILLING: Assemble and prepare all ingredients.

In a small bowl, break up the tuna with its oil with a fork to about the size of oatmeal flakes. Add the drained garbanzos, *tahini,* lemon juice, and yogurt. Mix well, being careful not to break up the garbanzos. Add salt and pepper to taste. The mixture should be thick but not dry. Add a little more yogurt if necessary. Refrigerate, covered, until ready to use. Instructions for filling the Pitta are at the end of the recipe.

THE SARDINE FILLING: Assemble and prepare all ingredients.

supermarkets; we make our own in Mexico and like it so much we'll always do it, page 317

The Tuna Filling

TUNA IN OIL *1 can (7-ounce size)*

GARBANZOS *1 can (16-ounce size), drained*

TAHINI (SESAME-SEED PASTE) *¼ cup: may be purchased at health-food shops or shops carrying Mediterranean or Middle Eastern foods*

LEMON JUICE *1 tablespoon*

PLAIN YOGURT *½ cup or a little more*

SALT

BLACK PEPPER, GROUND FRESH

The Sardine Filling

BONELESS SARDINES IN OIL *1 can (4¾-ounce size), or an equivalent amount*

ONION *To make ½ cup when peeled and chopped fine*

TOMATO *To make ½ cup when peeled, seeded, and chopped medium-fine*

Mash the sardines and canning oil almost to a paste with a fork in a small bowl. Add the onion, tomato, hard-cooked eggs, feta cheese, oregano, and lemon juice. Mix gently but thoroughly. Add salt and pepper to taste. The mixture should be thick but not dry. Refrigerate, covered, until ready to use. Instructions for filling the Pitta are at the end of the recipe.

THE BEEF-ON-SKEWERS FILLING: Assemble and prepare all ingredients.

1. In a small saucepan, combine the marinade ingredients. Mix well and bring to a boil over medium heat. Reduce the heat and simmer for 5 minutes. Remove from the stove and set aside to cool.

2. Sprinkle each strip of meat with a little of the meat tenderizer, if necessary.

3. Pour the cooled marinade over the beef and let stand for at least 6 hours at room temperature. If longer, refrigerate. More than 24 hours is not recommended.

TO ASSEMBLE THE SKEWERS: 1. Drain the meat and reserve the marinade. Divide the meat into 6 equal parts. Have the onion, tomatoes, green pepper, and mushrooms close by.

2. *To fill 1 skewer:*

a. Take one-sixth of the meat, 2 onion and 2 tomato wedges, 2 green pepper chunks, and 2 mushroom caps. Set aside.

b. Starting with 1 strip of meat, pierce it close to the end with the skewer.

c. Add 1 onion wedge. Turn the

HARD-COOKED EGGS
 2, *peeled and chopped*
 fine
FETA CHEESE (RICOTTA
 CHEESE, DRAINED, MAY
 BE SUBSTITUTED)
 ¼ cup, crumbled
DRIED OREGANO LEAVES
 2 pinches, crumbled
LEMON JUICE *1 table-*
 spoon
SALT
BLACK PEPPER, GROUND
 FRESH

The Beef-on-Skewers Filling

The Marinade
SOY SAUCE *½ cup*
WATER *½ cup*
SCALLIONS *To make ¼*
 cup when peeled and
 sliced thin
SESAME SEEDS *2 table-*
 spoons
GARLIC *2 cloves, peeled*
 and minced with a little
 salt
SUGAR *2 tablespoons*
GROUND GINGER *½ tea-*
 spoon
MONOSODIUM GLUTA-
 MATE *½ teaspoon*
BLACK PEPPER, GROUND
 FRESH *½ teaspoon*

meat toward your left hand, lift it up and pierce it with the skewer to half-encircle the onion tightly and securely. The meat will now be turned toward your right hand.

d. Add 1 tomato wedge and fold the meat back again to the left, piercing it to half-encircle and wrap the tomato securely.

e. In the same manner—serpentining—thread on 1 chunk of green pepper, more meat, 1 mushroom cap, and more meat.

f. Repeat, using the balance of the meat and vegetables. If your strip of meat runs out, start with another. Push down as you fill the skewer. *Do not use more than one-sixth of the meat for each skewer.* If the one-sixth of meat runs out before the vegetables, put the remaining vegetables aside. They will be used later.

3. Repeat steps *a* through *f* with each skewer and refrigerate.

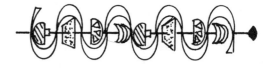

JUST BEFORE SERVING: Arrange the skewers on a rack and brush them with the reserved marinade. If there are any extra vegetables, skewer them and brush them also. Grill under the broiler or on a barbecue for about 5 minutes on each side.

NOTE: Keep the leftover marinade—it's great on chicken or hamburgers.

The Beef and Vegetables

TOP ROUND OR SIRLOIN STEAK *1 pound, cut in strips about 1/4 inch thick, 1 to 1 1/2 inches wide and 4 inches long*

UNSEASONED MEAT TENDERIZER (OPTIONAL)

ONION *1 medium, peeled and cut in 12 wedges: cut vertically from stem to root end to form wedges*

FIRM, FRESH TOMATOES *12 cherry, or 2 medium, cut in 6 wedges each*

GREEN BELL PEPPER *1 medium, seeded, deveined, and cut in 12 chunks of somewhat equal size*

FRESH MUSHROOMS *12, about 1 to 1 1/2 inches in diameter: first wipe with a damp paper towel if necessary and cut off stems even with the base of the caps*

For Any of the Fillings

PITTA (OR ARABIC) BREAD *3 large loaves (6 inches in diameter) or 6 small loaves (less than 6 inches) frozen and defrosted or your own*

TO HEAT AND FILL THE PITTAS: 1. Just before serving, preheat the oven to 400 degrees.

2. Wrap each Pitta individually in aluminum foil. Put in the oven and heat for 10 to 15 minutes or until warmed through.

3. Remove the bread from the oven. Cut large loaves in half crosswise, and make a pocket in each half. For small loaves, cut a slit into one edge of each to make a pocket. Spread a little butter or mayonnaise on the inside of each pocket and stuff with part of either the sardine or tuna filling. If using the meat filling, slide the meat and vegetables from one grilled skewer into each Pitta half or whole. (If you don't like mayonnaise on meat, omit it.)

TO SERVE: Put half a large, or one whole small Pitta on each of 6 individual plates. (Any extra skewers of vegetables can be put on a side plate.) Eat with your hands. Lean over the plate if you wish. Don't forget to have large paper napkins handy. Red wine or beer makes a fine accompaniment.

NOTE: The Tabbouleh salad on page 68 makes another authentic Pitta filling.

homemade Pitta, page
317
SOFTENED BUTTER
OR MAYONNAISE, PREFER-
ABLY HOMEMADE, *page*
296

6 SERVINGS

The Guacamole should be
made no more than 6
hours in advance, but
all the ingredients may
be prepared and cooked
up to a day ahead.

Assemble just before
serving.

Serve cold.

_____

The Tortillas
SALAD OIL *For frying*
tortillas
DAY-OLD OR FROZEN
FLOUR TORTILLAS
(CORN TORTILLAS MAY
BE SUBSTITUTED, BUT
THEY WON'T BE AS
FLAKY WHEN FRIED)
6 (*5 to 5½ inches in*
diameter): *thaw if frozen*

CRABMEAT TOSTADAS
(Mexican Open-Faced Sandwiches)

A tostada *is a fried* tortilla *covered with
anything from simply refried beans with
a bit of hot sauce to this super sophisti-
cated stack we give you here. If there is no
crabmeat to be had, try chicken or ground
beef.*

Assemble and prepare all ingredients.

THE TORTILLAS: 1. Heat about ½ inch of
salad oil in a small skillet (about 7 inches
in diameter) until very hot.

2. Fry one *tortilla* at a time, using a
spatula or tongs to turn frequently. Hold
it under the oil as it crisps and browns very
lightly: this takes less than a minute. The
best method is to put the *tortilla* in the hot
oil, count 1-2-3, turn; count 1-2-3, turn
again; count 1-2-3, turn again. This should
be enough, but count 1 more time if necessary. Strangely, the *tortilla* browns a little as you lift it from the skillet. Drain on
paper towels and store in a dry place until
ready to assemble the *tostadas.*

THE FILLING: 1. Heat 1 tablespoon of the

The Filling

BACON DRIPPINGS, OIL
OR LARD *1 or 2 table-
spoons*

REFRIED BEANS *1 can
(1 pound 4-ounce size)*

CANNED EVAPORATED
MILK *3 tablespoons or
more*

CANNED CALIFORNIA
DICED GREEN CHILIES
*3 tablespoons (half of a
4-ounce can)*

OIL FOR DOUBLE BOILER

MONTEREY JACK CHEESE
*To make 1 cup when
shredded (¼ pound)*

ICEBERG OR BOSTON
LETTUCE *To make 2
cups when shredded fine
lengthwise and then cut
into 1-inch lengths: wrap
in a towel to crisp*

CRABMEAT, FRESH OR
FROZEN, THOROUGHLY
DEFROSTED AND
DRAINED *¾ to 1 pound,
shredded fine: discard
any bits of cartilage or
shell*

SEASONED WITH:

SALT AND BLACK PEPPER,
GROUND FRESH

GUACAMOLE *Full recipe,
page 320*

COMMERCIAL SOUR
CREAM

bacon drippings in a skillet. Add the re-fried beans. Mix well and cook over medium heat, stirring constantly. Be careful, they burn easily. Add a little more drippings, if necessary. Add 3 tablespoons of the evaporated milk. Stir and cook until the drippings and milk are absorbed and you have a creamy, heavy, quite dry paste.

2. Add the diced chilies and mix well. If the filling seems a little too dry, add a bit more milk, combining well.

3. Divide the mixture into 4 parts. Lightly oil the upper section of a double boiler. Spoon and spread a quarter of the seasoned beans into it. Sprinkle with about a third of the cheese. Repeat layering and spreading a quarter of the beans and a third of the cheese, ending with the beans. Do not stir. The heat from the beans will melt the cheese just enough.

4. Place a piece of plastic wrap, folded to fit the top of the beans, directly on top of them. Leave in the top section of the double boiler and put in the refrigerator until ready to rewarm it and assemble the *tostadas*. Refrigerate the rest of the ingredients, wrapped separately, up to a day ahead, but remember not to prepare the Guacamole more than 6 hours in advance.

TO ASSEMBLE (*about 20 minutes before serving*):

1. Put the upper section of the double boiler containing the beans over simmering water. Cover and heat for about 10 minutes, or until warmed through.

2. On a counter or pastry board, line up

The Garnish
RIPE OLIVES
RADISHES *Trimmed,*
cleaned, and crisped

the 6 *tortillas.* Spread each with equal parts of the refried beans, bringing the mixture to the edges to cover the *tortilla.*

3. Pat the top of each with about ⅓ cup of the shredded lettuce, mounding it to about ½ inch of the edge.

4. Mound a sixth of the crabmeat on top of each, not quite covering the lettuce.

5. Top each with 3 or 4 heaping table-spoons of Guacamole—more if you have any left—spooning it on in blobs.

6. Top each with 2 or 3 generous dol-lops of sour cream.

TO SERVE: Put on individual serving plates and surround with a few olives and rad-ishes. We advise a knife and fork for each guest. Most of our Mexican friends are able to eat, out of hand, a 5-inch *tortilla* stacked high with good things, without a major disaster. We can't. We cut it into wedges and use fingers and a fork!

Cold beer, dry white wine or alternating sips of tequila and *sangrita* make a fine accompaniment. *Sangrita* may be pur-chased at many well-stocked liquor stores. Do not confuse it with *Sangria*—a drink made of sweetened red wine with orange juice, lemon juice, and other fruit added.

CHICKEN SALAD IN PUFFS

8 SERVINGS

Freshly made *pâte à choux* paste is a must.

Another winner made with pâte à choux. *The filling is a different chicken salad, created by Sergeant Cox at the Stuttgart*

The puffs may be baked early in the day, or they may be baked in advance and frozen.

If frozen, thaw the puffs, warm them in a hot oven to crisp, and then cool them.

The filling may be made a day ahead.

Serve the puffs at room temperature and the salad chilled.

The Puffs
OIL FOR BAKING SHEET
PATE A CHOUX PASTE,
  MADE FRESH *1 recipe,*
  page 304

The Chicken Salad
COOKED CHICKEN, PREF-
  ERABLY BOILED
  To make 3 cups when
  diced
BACON *To make 1 cup*
  when fried crisp and
  crumbled into coarse
  pieces (about 10 slices)
PITTED BLACK OLIVES
  To make ½ cup when
  chopped

Officers' Club. Also a hit for luncheon, served in orange shell baskets.

THE PUFFS: 1. Preheat the oven to 375 degrees, and oil a baking sheet.

2. Using a large spoon and a spatula or knife, place 8 large mounds of the paste, each about 2½ to 3 inches in diameter, spaced well apart on the baking sheet. Make them as round and as equal in size as possible.

3. Bake on the middle rack of the pre-heated oven for 25 minutes. Do not open the oven door. Reduce the heat to 300 degrees and bake for another 15 minutes. Turn the oven off.

4. Remove the puffs, large, golden and firm, cut a slit in the side of each—turn the knife a little for a wider opening to let out the steam.

5. Return the puffs to the turned-off oven for 10 minutes more to dry out and crisp. Remove and cool them. At this point, they may be kept at room temperature for several hours, or they may be frozen. If frozen, see note at end of recipe.

THE CHICKEN SALAD: Assemble and prepare all ingredients. Put into a bowl and mix well. Refrigerate until ready to assemble and serve.

TO ASSEMBLE AND SERVE: Slice the tops off the puffs about one-third of the way down. Remove any bits of unbaked pastry from the insides. Fill each with part of the chicken salad and replace the tops.

SHELLED MIXED NUTS
*To make ½ cup when
chopped coarse*
CANNED PINEAPPLE
CHUNKS *To make 1 cup
when drained*
CELERY *To make 1 cup
when peeled and
chopped coarse*
MONOSODIUM GLUTA-
MATE *1 teaspoon*
GARLIC SALT *1 teaspoon*
MAYONNAISE, PREFER-
ABLY HOMEMADE
(*page 296*) *1⅓ cups*

6 TO 8 SERVINGS

A 7-inch *crêpe* pan or
skillet is required, and a
large flat-bottomed
serving plate.

The *crêpes* may be made
up to a day ahead and
refrigerated, or they
may be frozen until
needed: thaw before
using.

Assemble several hours
before serving.

Serve cold.

_____

NOTE: To use frozen baked puffs, thaw
them first and then heat them in a 350-
degree oven for about 10 minutes, or until
crisp.

SPRING TORTE

This recipe, adapted from The Family
Cookbook: Italian, *by Charlotte Adams
and Alvin Kerr, published by Holt, Rine-
hart and Winston, is beautiful to look at
and better to eat.*

Assemble and prepare all ingredients.

1. Arrange the Spring Torte directly on
the plate from which it is to be served, pro-
ceeding as follows: spread each *crêpe,* on 1
side only, with a rounded ½ teaspoon of
the mayonnaise.

2. Place 1 *crêpe,* mayonnaise side up,
on the plate and cover it evenly with 2 of
the lettuce leaves, overlapping them if necessary.

3. When you layer the torte, spread the
edges a little thicker than the center so
that the completed torte will be as level as

CREPES 15 (7 *inches in diameter*) *page 306*

MAYONNAISE, PREFER-
ABLY HOMEMADE (*page 296*) *About 2 cups*

ROMAINE OR BOSTON
LETTUCE 4 *leaves or more, trimmed of heavy ribs and flattened*

MORTADELLA SAUSAGE
8 *thin slices*

PROVOLONE CHEESE 8 *thin slices*

FRESH OR FROZEN
CHOPPED SPINACH
To make ½ cup when cooked, well drained and cooled

COOKED CHICKEN
BREAST 4 *to* 6 *thin slices*

FIRM, RIPE TOMATO
5 *thin slices, peeled*

SALAMI 6 *thin slices*

COOKED HAM 4 *thin slices*

COOKED VEAL OR PORK
3 *thin slices*

CANNED PIMIENTOS
2, *split lengthwise, drained, dried between paper towels, and flattened*

UNFLAVORED GELATIN
1 *tablespoon* (1 *envelope*)

CHICKEN BROTH ½ *cup*

DRY WHITE WINE 1 *table-spoon*

possible and will not sag toward the edges.

4. On top of the lettuce, stack 13 more of the *crêpes,* also with spread sides up, interspersing them evenly with, in the following order:

4 slices of the mortadella
4 slices of the cheese
¼ cup of the spinach
The chicken
The tomato slices
The salami
The remaining spinach
The ham
The veal or pork
The pimientos
The remaining slices of cheese
The remaining slices of mortadella
The remaining lettuce

5. Place the remaining *crêpe* on top, mayonnaise side down. Even up the stack, tucking in any loose ends.

6. In a small saucepan, sprinkle the gelatin over the chicken broth. Let stand 5 minutes to soften, then put on low heat. Stir until the gelatin is dissolved. Cool to room temperature.

7. Combine the gelatin and broth with the remaining mayonnaise. Stir the white wine into the mixture. Spread the stack of filled *crêpes* with half of the mayonnaise mixture, coating the top and sides like a cake.

8. Secure the stack by inserting 4 skewers down through it at even intervals. Refrigerate until the glaze is set.

9. Remove the skewers and coat the torte again on all sides with the remaining

The Garnish

PIMIENTO-STUFFED
   GREEN OLIVES *4 large,*
   sliced crosswise
PARSLEY SPRIGS

mayonnaise mixture. Refrigerate until the glaze is set.

10. Decorate the outside edges of the top with the slices of olives and put a few sprigs of parsley in the center.

11. Arrange more sprigs of parsley around the base of the torte. Chill for several hours.

TO SERVE: Cut in wedges at the table. A skewer inserted downward through the center will help anchor it while you cut.

SWEETS

CANTALOUPE SPOOM BALLS

12 TO 14 BALLS, USING A SCOOP 2½ INCHES IN DIAMETER (1 PER GUEST)

A blender is a must.

Must be made and frozen at least 1 day ahead, but may be frozen for up to 2 weeks.

VERY RIPE CANTALOUPES *About 3 medium, halved: remove seeds and scoop out the flesh with a spoon*
LIME JUICE ¼ *cup*
WATER *1 cup*
SUPERFINE GRANULATED SUGAR *1½ cups*
EGG WHITES ¾ *cup* (*about 6*) *at room temperature*

This one takes a little time and attention, but it is refreshingly different. A "spoom" is a sherbet made with Italian meringue.

Assemble and prepare all ingredients.

1. Put the cantaloupe and lime juice into a blender and purée until it is almost smooth. A little pulp will show. You should have about 5 cups. Set aside.

2. Put the water and sugar into a saucepan and bring it to a boil. Swirl the pan slowly, but do not stir, until the sugar has dissolved and the liquid is clear.

3. Reduce the heat to a simmer and stop swirling. Let the liquid simmer until it reaches the soft-ball stage—240 degrees on a candy thermometer—or until it makes a firm-soft mass that flattens out when dropped into cold water and worked with your fingers. Check this frequently as soon as the bubbles start to thicken.

4. A few minutes before the syrup is finished, put the egg whites, cream of tar-

CREAM OF TARTAR
½ teaspoon
SALT *Big pinch*
HEAVY CREAM *1 cup*

The Garnish
FRESH MINT SPRIGS

The Accompaniment
A NOT-TOO-SWEET
  COOKIE SUCH AS
  LADY FINGERS
  OR SHORTBREAD
  OR MADELEINES

tar, and salt into a mixing bowl and beat with an electric or rotary beater until it forms soft peaks. Still beating, add the hot syrup in a very thin stream. Continue beating until the mixture becomes thick, smooth, and shiny and forms stiff peaks when it is lifted with the blades of the beater.

5. Whip the cream and fold it into the cantaloupe purée. Then fold the beaten egg whites into the mixture until it is well combined.

6. Divide the mixture between 2 metal pans about 9 by 5 by 3 inches deep. They should be equally filled so that they will freeze evenly. Place them in the freezer and freeze for about 1 hour, or until the mixture is mushy.

7. Transfer the spoom to a large, chilled bowl and beat it rapidly until it is smooth. Put it back in the pans and freeze it again until it is mushy.

8. Again transfer it to a large, chilled bowl and beat it rapidly until it is smooth. Put it back in the pans and freeze until it is firm.

9. Using an ice-cream scoop, scoop out full balls and put them in a single layer on a Teflon or waxed-paper-lined baking sheet. Freeze until ready to serve. Remove from the freezer at least 15 minutes before serving.

TO SERVE: Place 1 ball per guest into an individual, small, shallow crystal bowl, stemmed sherbet glass, or martini glass. Top each with a sprig of mint and serve at once. Accompany with a not-too-sweet cookie.

CHOCOLATE MOUSSE BOMBE

16 TO 18 SERVINGS

You will need a 3-quart mold, preferably a deep, decorated one, and a blender.

Must be prepared at least a day ahead.

May be kept for several months in the freezer.

The chocolate sauce may be made up to 5 days ahead and refrigerated separately.

_____

VANILLA ICE CREAM
1 quart

The Chocolate Mousse
COCOA ½ *cup*
SUGAR *1 cup*
PREPARED COFFEE ⅓ *cup*
EGG YOLKS 6
SALT ¼ *teaspoon*
GRAND MARNIER OR ANY
ORANGE-FLAVORED
LIQUEUR 2 *tablespoons*

After you have tried one bombe, *you'll find them irresistible. The combinations are without limit—try the chocolate mousse inside a mint-green ice cream; or another mousse, coffee-flavored. You've already guessed that the chocolate mousse is perfectly delicious all by itself, without the ice cream. In this case, it need not be frozen.*

Assemble and prepare all ingredients.

Chill the mold in the freezer and line with the vanilla ice cream, pressing it against the sides and leaving the center hollow. Put the mold into the freezer to harden the ice cream again.

THE CHOCOLATE MOUSSE: 1. In a saucepan combine the cocoa, sugar, and coffee until well mixed. Bring to a boil over medium heat and cook slowly, without stirring, until the sugar reaches the softball stage (236 degrees) when a drop is tested in cold water. This takes only about 5 minutes. Remove from heat.

2. With an electric beater, beat the egg yolks with the salt until they are thick and pale yellow. Continue beating while you add the chocolate mixture in a slow, steady stream. Beat until the mixture thickens.

HEAVY CREAM *3 cups*

The Chocolate Sauce
MILK *1 cup*
UNSWEETENED BAKING
    CHOCOLATE *6 ounces,*
    broken into small pieces
SUGAR *1½ cups*
VANILLA *2 teaspoons*

Refrigerate until thoroughly chilled. Mix in the Grand Marnier.

3. Whip the cream until it stands in peaks. Fold it into the chilled chocolate mixture, scraping the bottom and sides of the bowl to incorporate all of the chocolate.

4. Pour the chocolate mousse into the hollow center of the ice cream–lined mold. Freeze at least 6 hours.

THE CHOCOLATE SAUCE: 1. Heat the milk to the boiling point.

2. Put the chocolate pieces into the blender, add the hot milk, sugar, and vanilla.

3. Blend at high speed for a few seconds. Stop and scrape down the sides with a rubber spatula. Blend again until the sauce has no lumps. May be refrigerated, covered, at this point, for up to 5 days.

AT LEAST 1 HOUR BEFORE SERVING: Loosen the edges of the frozen *bombe* to a depth of about ½ inch with a sharp, pointed knife. Immerse the mold in warm water to within ½ inch of the top. Place a serving platter over the mold and invert both quickly. If the *bombe* doesn't come out, repeat the warm-water bath. Put the platter and *bombe* back into the freezer.

20 MINUTES BEFORE SERVING: Heat the chocolate sauce in the top of a double boiler, over simmering water. Remove the *bombe* from the freezer to soften a little.

TO SERVE: Slice in wedges, put on chilled plates, and top with warm chocolate sauce.

THE ANGEL GABRIEL'S FRESH COCONUT ANGEL PIE

A seraphic dish, relayed directly from Headquarters.

Assemble and prepare all ingredients.

THE PIE SHELL: 1. Lightly coat a 10-inch pie pan with butter and set aside.

2. Preheat the oven to 350 degrees.

3. In a bowl combine the graham cracker crumbs, sugar, and nutmeg. Using your fingers, rub in the ¼ cup of butter until it is well combined.

4. Press the mixture evenly and firmly into the prepared pan. Don't make the sides too high—about three-quarters of the way up is just right.

5. Place on the middle rack of the preheated oven and bake for 8 to 10 minutes. Set aside to cool.

THE FILLING: 1. Preheat the oven to 250 degrees.

2. Put the egg whites, cream of tartar, corn syrup, and sugar into the upper section of a 2-quart double boiler. Using an an electric beater, beat for about 1 minute to combine the ingredients.

3. Then place over rapidly boiling water (the water in the bottom should not touch the upper section). Beat constantly

---

8 TO 10 SERVINGS

Fresh coconut is a must: see note at end of recipe.

You will need a portable electric beater and a 10-inch pie pan, preferably made of heatproof glass, or one pretty enough to come to the table.

The pie shell may be made a day ahead.

Must be completed and chilled at least 3 hours before serving.

The Pie Shell

BUTTER ¼ *cup, softened, plus enough extra for the pie pan*

GRAHAM CRACKERS *To make 1¼ cups when rolled to a powder*

SUPERFINE GRANULATED SUGAR ¼ *cup*

NUTMEG, GRATED FRESH
¼ teaspoon

The Filling
EGG WHITES 5, at room
temperature
CREAM OF TARTAR ½ tea-
spoon
LIGHT CORN SYRUP
2 tablespoons
SUPERFINE GRANULATED
SUGAR 1 cup, plus 2
tablespoons

The Topping
HEAVY CREAM 1 cup,
chilled at least 2 hours
VANILLA 1 teaspoon
CONFECTIONERS' SUGAR
3 tablespoons
FRESH COCONUT To make
1¾ cups when grated
on the coarsest side of
a 4-sided grater (about
1 medium)
SALTED PECANS To make
¼ cup when slivered:
to salt, warm them in the
oven, remove, sprinkle
immediately with a little
salt and turn to coat
evenly

7 to 10 minutes, or until stiff peaks form when the beater is raised slowly.

4. Spoon the mixture lightly into the prepared pie shell. Fill it to the top, but don't cover the rim. Smooth the filling out so that there are no peaks. Place on the middle rack of the preheated oven and bake for 1 hour. Then turn the oven off, and with the door slightly ajar, let it cool in the oven for 1 hour.

THE TOPPING: 1. Put the cream into a bowl, preferably chilled, and with the beater at medium speed, whip until it starts to froth; then add the vanilla and confectioners' sugar. Continue to whip until it forms soft peaks when the beater is raised.

2. Fold in the coconut and spread the mixture over the pie. Sprinkle evenly with the salted pecans and refrigerate for at least 3 hours before serving. For easier serving, dip a knife into warm water before cutting each slice.

HOW TO OPEN A COCONUT: We find it easiest to open the shell with heat. Preheat the oven to 350 degrees. Using a long, fat nail or screwdriver, puncture the 3 eyes, or indentations, at the end. Drain the milk through these holes. If you wish, save the milk for another use. Place the coconut in a shallow pan and bake it for 15 to 20 minutes, no longer. Too much heat will destroy the flavor. When it is cool enough to handle, wrap it in a heavy cloth to prevent the pieces from flying all over. Crack it by tapping with a hammer.

The husk should come off easily. If not, pry it off with a small, pointed knife. Peel off the thin brown skin with a swivel-bladed vegetable peeler. Wash the meat under cold running water.

CAFÉ MYSTIQUE

A blender is a must.

The mixture may be made ahead and the ice added just before serving.

_____

Per Person
PREPARED COFFEE *⅓ cup*
KAHLUA OR COFFEE-
    FLAVORED LIQUEUR
    3 ounces
CHOCOLATE DRINK MIX
    OR MALTED MILK
    DRINK MIX *1 rounded
    tablespoon*
CRUSHED ICE *⅓ cup*
ICE CUBES *2*
HEAVY CREAM *½ cup
    whipped (will serve
    6 to 8)*

A most surprising and refreshing drink for late evening, popular in Texas and served to us by friends there.

Assemble and prepare all ingredients.
    Mix the coffee, Kahlua, and chocolate drink mix. Combine thoroughly, to dissolve the mix. This may be done hours or a day before and the mixture refrigerated.

JUST BEFORE SERVING: 1. Put into a blender, add the crushed ice, and blend until the ice is a slush and the mixture is foamy and frothy.
    2. Pour into a large wineglass over 2 ice cubes. Top with a large dollop of whipped cream and serve with a straw.

After Dinner: Evening Snacks

HOT

Soups

BLACK BEAN SOUP WITH RUM

10 TO 12 SERVINGS
(3½ QUARTS)

A blender is a must.

Must be started the night
before.

Allow at least 4 hours
cooking time before
serving.

May be made up to 2 or 3
days in advance and
refrigerated, or it may
be frozen.

DRIED BLACK (TURTLE)
BEANS 2 *cups* (*about 1
pound*)
WATER 2 *quarts, plus up to
2 cups more if necessary*
SMOKED HAM HOCK *1*

*A rich, hearty soup laced with rum, this
might have been the dish that inspired
Robert Browning to write, "What most
moved him was a certain meal on beans."*

The night before serving, wash the beans
and put them into a 4- or 5-quart saucepan
or soup pot. Add 1 quart of the water.
Cover and let soak overnight.

The next day assemble and prepare all
other ingredients.

1. Add 1 quart more water to the beans
—allow any water in which the beans
soaked to remain. Add the ham hock or
smoked pork chops, onions, celery, garlic,
carrots, and the *bouquet garni.*

2. Bring to a simmer, cover, and cook
for 2 to 2½ hours, or until the beans are
very soft. Stir frequently, as the beans are
inclined to stick. Add up to 2 cups more
water if the soup becomes too thick.

3. Remove the meat. Discard any

OR SMOKED PORK CHOPS 2
ONIONS *1 large, peeled and chopped coarse*
CELERY *3 stalks, chopped coarse*
GARLIC *2 cloves, peeled and minced*
CARROTS *1 large, peeled and chopped coarse*
BOUQUET GARNI:
  PARSLEY, *1 sprig*
  BAY LEAF, *1*
  DRIED MARJORAM LEAVES *¼ teaspoon*
  WHOLE CLOVES, *6*
  Wrap and tie the bouquet garni in cheesecloth bag
DARK RUM *¼ cup*
MILK TO THIN, IF NECESSARY *Up to 1 cup*
SALT
BLACK PEPPER, GROUND FRESH

The Accompaniment
TINY PITCHERS OR JIGGERS OF DARK RUM (NOT MORE THAN 1 OUNCE) FOR EACH PERSON
CORN MUFFINS (OP-TIONAL)

gristle, fat, or bones and return the meat to the pot. Remove and discard the *bouquet garni*.

4. In a blender purée the mixture about 2 cups at a time. Stop the motor and scrape down the sides of the bowl as necessary. Remove to a large bowl as the mixture is puréed. At this point the soup may be frozen if desired: thaw before continuing with the recipe.

5. When all is puréed, add the rum and blend. The soup should be thick but drop easily from a spoon. If necessary, add up to 1 cup of milk, a tablespoon at a time, until it is to your liking. Add salt and pepper to taste and refrigerate.

6. Just before serving heat to the boiling point, stirring frequently so that it does not stick.

TO SERVE: Put the soup in warm cups or small bowls. At each place have a tiny pitcher or jigger (not more than 1 ounce) of dark rum, for each person to add to his taste. Serve with hot corn muffins.

PROVINCIAL ONION SOUP

8 SERVINGS

You will need a wide-topped ovenproof casserole or terrine of about 3-to-4-quart capacity: if not available, use 2 smaller ones of equal total capacity.

The onions and mashed potatoes may be cooked a day ahead, covered, and refrigerated separately.

The soup may be partially assembled and the *croûtes* prepared 6 to 8 hours ahead, or the *croûtes* may be prepared and frozen: bring to room temperature before using.

Complete about 30 minutes before serving.

BUTTER ¾ *cup, plus enough to butter the cooking pan and the* croûtes

A thicker, heartier version of the French classic, made so by the addition of egg yolks and potatoes.

Assemble and prepare all ingredients.

1. Put the ¾ cup of butter into a large saucepan or skillet that has a cover, and place over medium heat. When it is hot, add the onions, cover, and cook for several minutes. Then lower the heat and continue cooking, uncovered, until the onions are an even, deep gold. Stir frequently and do not let them brown. This will take at least 30 minutes. Set aside, or refrigerate.

2. When ready to continue, generously butter the bottom and about 2 inches up the sides of the casserole or terrine. If using 2 casseroles, divide all the following ingredients between them.

3. Spread the beaten egg yolks on the bottom and then sprinkle them with 1½ cups of the grated cheese. (The balance will be used for the topping.)

4. Spread the mashed potatoes over the cheese and set aside. Steps 2 through 4 may be done up to 8 hours ahead.

THE CROUTES: 1. Butter each bread round on 1 side only and place them, buttered side up, on a baking sheet.

2. Light and set the oven at 400 degrees. After 5 *minutes only,* place the *croûtes* on the lowest rack, and continue

ONIONS, PREFERABLY
   YELLOW *To make 11
   or 12 cups when peeled,
   cut into halves from root
   to stem end and sliced
   fine into half circles
   (about 10 large)*
EGG YOLKS 5, *beaten*
GRUYERE CHEESE (SWISS
   OR PARMESAN MAY BE
   SUBSTITUTED) *To make
   3 cups when grated
   medium-fine (about ¾
   pound)*
POTATOES *3 medium,
   peeled, diced, cooked,
   and mashed*
OR PACKAGED MASHED
   POTATOES *To make 2
   cups when prepared
   according to package
   directions*
FRENCH BREAD FOR
   CROUTES *16 slices cut
   into rounds about ⅝
   inch thick*
CANNED BEEF BROTH,
   UNDILUTED, OR FULL-
   FLAVORED BEEF
   BROTH *(page 291)*
   2 quarts
DRY WHITE WINE *2 cups*
SALT
BLACK PEPPER, GROUND
   FRESH

baking at the same setting for 10 to 15 minutes, or until they are brown. They will brown on both sides as they bake. Watch them carefully. Set aside, or freeze. Bring to room temperature before using.

ABOUT 30 MINUTES BEFORE SERVING: 1. Preheat the oven to 450 degrees.

2. In a large saucepan, mix the broth and wine and bring to a boil on top of the stove.

3. Spread the reserved onions in the casserole on top of the potatoes and add the boiling broth-and-wine mixture to within 2 inches of the top of the casserole. Add salt and pepper to taste. If there is too much broth, put it back on the stove to keep hot.

4. Float the *croûtes* in a single layer on top. Sprinkle the top thick with the remaining cheese.

5. Put in the oven for 15 minutes or more, until the cheese has melted and is bubbly and slightly brown.

6. Heat any remaining broth and put in a separate bowl or pitcher, to be added to the soup as needed.

TO SERVE: Ladle into 8 warmed soup bowls, spooning to the bottom to give each guest part of the onions and cheese and two *croûtes* each. Pass any remaining broth separately.

DON FELIPE'S TARASCAN SOUP

6 SERVINGS

You will need a blender.

The *chiles* must be softened in boiling water for about 45 minutes before cooking the soup.

The soup may be made and the *tortillas* fried up to 2 days ahead.

Freezing is not recommended.

DRIED CHILES ANCHOS, DRIED CHILES PASILLAS, OR DRIED CHILES MULATOS (*See note at end of recipe for purchasing and substitutions*), 4 (*1 for the soup and 3 for garnish*)

HOT WATER

OIL 2 *tablespoons*

ONION *To make ½ cup when chopped fine* (*1 medium*)

GARLIC 2 *large cloves, peeled and minced with a little salt*

In Patzcuaro, 7,000 feet high in green mountains surrounding a sparkling lake, Don Felipe Oseguera Iturbide, owner of the charming Hosteria de San Felipe, created this fragrant, aromatic soup. Unusual for a dignified Spanish Don, he enjoys cooking for family and friends. Whenever we have had his Tarascan Soup, we have asked for a second bowl and agreed with Sidney Smith, when he said, "Serenely full, the epicure would say, 'Fate cannot harm me—I have dined today.'"

Assemble and prepare all ingredients.

1. Put the *chiles* into a small bowl and pour enough very hot water over them to cover. Set aside to soften for about 45 minutes, turning once or twice so that they will soften evenly.

2. Heat the 2 tablespoons of oil in a 1½- or 2-quart saucepan. When it is quite hot, add the onions and sauté until they are soft but not colored. Add the garlic and sauté for 2 minutes more.

3. Sprinkle with the flour and continue sautéeing for a minute or so longer, turning frequently. Remove from the heat.

4. Remove the largest of the softened *chiles* from the water and pull off and discard the stem. Then break it open and remove and discard the seeds by washing it quickly under running water. Cut the *chile* into chunks and put it into a blender with

FLOUR 2 *tablespoons*

HOMEMADE CHICKEN
  BROTH, YOUR OWN
  OR OUR RECIPE (*page
  293*) 6 *cups*

TOMATO PASTE *⅓ cup*

DRIED THYME LEAVES
  ½ teaspoon, crumbled

DRIED MARJORAM LEAVES
  ½ teaspoon, crumbled

BAY LEAF *1, crumbled*

GROUND SAFFRON
  2 pinches

PARSLEY *To make 2 table-
  spoons when minced*

SALT

BLACK PEPPER, GROUND
  FRESH

OIL FOR FRYING
  TORTILLAS

DAY-OLD TORTILLAS OR
  FROZEN TORTILLAS,
  DEFROSTED *8 (5½ to 6
  inches in diameter) cut
  into 1-inch squares*

MOZZARELLA CHEESE
  (MONTEREY JACK
  CHEESE MAY BE SUB-
  STITUTED) *To make 1
  cup when grated (about
  ¼ pound)*

COMMERCIAL SOUR
  CREAM *About ½ cup*

The Garnish
REMAINING SOFTENED
  CHILES *3*

a little of the chicken broth. Blend until smooth, and pour into the onion mixture along with the remaining chicken broth, the tomato paste, thyme, marjoram, bay leaf, saffron, and parsley. Mix well.

5. Return the soup to the heat, cover, and simmer gently for ½ hour. The full flavor will develop as it cooks. Add salt and pepper to taste and correct the seasonings if necessary. Set aside.

6. Pour about 1 inch of oil into a heavy-bottomed skillet or saucepan. When it is very hot and a haze begins to form, add a few of the cut *tortillas* and fry them until crisp and golden. This will take only a minute or so. Do not let them brown. Remove from the oil and let them drain on paper toweling while you fry the remaining squares.

7. Drain the remaining *chiles,* discarding the liquid. Pull off and discard the stems, break them open, and discard the seeds by washing them quickly under running water. Break or cut them into rough-shaped chunks about 2½ or 3 inches square. You will need 6 chunks. Wrap them tightly and reserve for the garnish. At this point you may refrigerate the soup, *tortilla* squares, and garnish separately for up to 2 days.

ABOUT 15 MINUTES BEFORE SERVING: 1. Warm 6 small bowls. Reheat the soup until it comes to a boil and add the *tortilla* squares. Lower the heat and simmer together for 2 or 3 minutes. The *tortillas* will puff, deflate, and soften.

2. Divide the cheese among the bowls.

Pour the boiling soup over the cheese and spoon equal portions of the *tortillas* into each. Add one *chile* square to each bowl and top with a tablespoon of sour cream. Serve hot. Don Felipe says do not eat the *chile* squares!

NOTE: The *chiles* may usually be purchased in shops carrying Mexican foodstuffs. If you find it impossible to find 1 of the 3 recommended dried *chiles*, try for the powdered form of any 1 of them—use 1 tablespoon of powder in the soup and forget about the garnish. The flavor will be approximately the same—without the flare.

Seafood

SHRIMP TOAST

6 SERVINGS

Dong and Helena Kingman, famed as artist and photographer, have equal talent in the kitchen. They gave us this favorite recipe of theirs, itself a work of art in color, design, and taste. Also good as a first course, and with cocktails, too.

The paste for the shrimp toast may be prepared up to 1 day ahead and refrigerated.

It may be spread on the bread several hours before serving.

At its best fried just before serving, but may be fried ahead, frozen, and reheated without thawing.

Assemble and prepare all ingredients.

In a bowl combine the shrimp, parsley, scallions, soy sauce, egg white, sherry, cornstarch, salt, and pepper. This mixture may be refrigerated up to a day ahead.

UP TO SEVERAL HOURS AHEAD: Spread each bread triangle with part of the mixture until all is used. Be sure to cover the edges and corners, but not the sides. Press the mixture well into the bread. The surface should be smooth. Refrigerate until ready to fry.

FRESH OR FROZEN
SHRIMP *1 pound, shelled and chopped* very *fine: deveined only if you wish*
PARSLEY *To make 1 tablespoon when minced*

JUST BEFORE SERVING: 1. Put a 10-to-12-inch skillet over high heat. Pour in the oil

SCALLIONS 2, *minced:*
include about 2 inches
of the pale-green stem
SOY SAUCE ½ *teaspoon*
EGG WHITE 1, *lightly*
beaten
DRY SHERRY 1 *teaspoon*
CORNSTARCH ½ *teaspoon*
SALT ½ *teaspoon*
BLACK PEPPER, GROUND
FRESH ⅛ *teaspoon*
SANDWICH BREAD, PREF-
ERABLY DAY-OLD
9 *slices, about ⅜ inch*
thick, cut diagonally to
make 18 triangles: do
not remove crusts
PEANUT OIL OR COOKING
OIL

The Garnish (*optional*)
RADISH ROSES, *page 320*

to a depth of 1 inch or more. Heat to 330 degrees on a deep-frying thermometer, or use an automatic deep fryer.

2. Put a triangle of the prepared bread *shrimp side down* on a slotted spoon. Place in the oil and let the bread float off the spoon while pulling the spoon out. Fry a few pieces at a time until the edges start to turn a light golden-brown. Turn each piece and fry on the other side until golden.

3. Remove from the pan with a slotted spoon, drain on paper towels, and keep warm in the oven on very low heat until all the pieces are fried. Serve hot, the sooner the better.

TO SERVE: Arrange the shrimp toast and radishes on a platter. Pass small warm plates separately. If you wish, accompany them with a glass of chilled, dry white wine.

NOTE: If the shrimp toast has been fried ahead and frozen, preheat the oven to 400 degrees. Place the unthawed shrimp toast in a single layer on an ungreased baking sheet. Heat for 4 to 6 minutes, or until warmed through and crisp. Drain on paper towels.

6 SERVINGS

The beer batter and the bacon may be done several hours ahead.

HANGTOWN FRY

Another San Francisco favorite that will become one of yours. In the Gold Rush days, eggs and oysters were precious, and it is said that this was the requested last

ALL-PURPOSE FLOUR
 1 cup, unsifted
PAPRIKA *½ teaspoon*
SALT *1 teaspoon*
BEER *1 cup*
BACON *12 slices*
SHUCKED OYSTERS
 18 medium, or about 1⅓
 cups when well drained
EGGS *9*
SALT
BLACK PEPPER, GROUND
 FRESH

The Accompaniment
SLICES OF FRESH FRENCH
 BREAD AND BUTTER
CHILLED ROSE WINE
OR COLD BEER

meal of many condemned to the gallows. The oysters are normally dipped in flour, egg, and bread crumbs, but we offer our own variation, beer batter, which is different and good.

Assemble and prepare all ingredients.

1. Put the flour, paprika, and the 1 teaspoon of salt into a bowl. Add the beer and beat with a wire whisk until the batter is smooth and light. It should stand, if possible, for half an hour, but you may use it right away if you must. Stir it from time to time as it stands and again before using.

2. Put the bacon into a large, cold skillet, preferably one made of iron, and fry slowly on both sides over medium heat. This takes more time but produces tender, straight, evenly cooked slices. (If you prefer, broil the bacon or cook it in the oven, spread on a rack over a rimmed baking sheet to catch the fat.) Fry until crisp. Remove and drain on paper towels. Whatever way you do it, reserve the fat. You may now reserve the batter and bacon at room temperature or continue with the recipe.

ABOUT 15 MINUTES BEFORE SERVING: 1. Remove all but about ¼ cup of bacon fat from the skillet and set over medium heat. When quite hot place the oysters into the batter, remove each with a slotted spoon, and put into the skillet. If the oysters are small, scoop up several at a time. Fry the oysters until they are golden-brown underneath, then turn them and fry on the other

side, a little less brown. The bottom of the pan will be almost covered with the oysters.

2. Lay the browned bacon slices evenly over the top of the oysters.

3. Lightly beat the eggs, salt, and pepper to taste, and pour over all. Lower the heat and cook slowly until the eggs are set. Lift the cooked portions of eggs occasionally to allow the uncooked eggs to run underneath. In order not to overcook or burn the oysters, cover the pan during the last several minutes to cook the eggs on top.

TO SERVE: Serve from the skillet, accompanied with fresh French bread and butter and a chilled rosé wine or ice-cold beer.

NOTE: Served with a crisp salad or lettuce with an oil-and-vinegar dressing, or fried onions and green peppers, this makes a full supper instead of a late-evening snack.

BAKED SARDINES WITH WALNUTS

8 SERVINGS

May be partially prepared 6 to 8 hours ahead.

Fry the croutons and bake just before serving.

_____

Admittedly, sardine and onion sandwiches are great, but how about trying this near-exotic treatment of the sardine, with walnuts and pimientos.

Assemble and prepare all ingredients.

1. Pour the oil from the sardines into a flat, shallow, oblong baking dish, about 13 by 9 by 2 inches. (You could also use two

BRISLING SARDINES IN
   OLIVE OIL *4 cans (3¾*
   ounces each): pour off
   and reserve the oil, plus
   a little extra olive oil
   if necessary
SHALLOTS OR SCALLIONS
   To make ½ cup when
   chopped fine
PIMIENTOS *1 can (5-to-6-*
   ounce size), cut in strips
   ⅛ inch wide and 1½ to
   2 inches long
GROUND WALNUTS *½ cup*
LEMON JUICE *2 table-*
   spoons
SALT
BLACK PEPPER, GROUND
   FRESH
SALAD OIL
DAY-OLD FIRM WHITE
   BREAD *16 slices, ½ to*
   ¾ inch thick, cut in
   3-inch rounds
PARSLEY *To make about*
   ⅓ cup when chopped
   fine

The Garnish
LEMON WEDGES

8-inch square baking pans or two or three 9-inch cake pans.) If there is not enough oil to cover the bottom of the pan generously, add a little extra olive oil.

2. Using a spatula and taking 3 or 4 sardines at a time, place them in a single layer in the pan. Handle them carefully so that they won't break.

3. Sprinkle the shallots or scallions over all. Then place the pimiento strips on top, parallel to the sardines, spacing them evenly.

4. Sprinkle with the ground walnuts and the lemon juice. Season lightly with salt and fairly heavily with pepper. At this point you may cover and refrigerate the dish or keep it at room temperature to be baked later.

ABOUT 30 MINUTES BEFORE SERVING: 1. Preheat the oven to 375 degrees.

2. Bake the sardines on the middle rack for 10 to 15 minutes or until heated through and bubbly.

3. In the meantime heat enough salad oil in a heavy skillet to cover the bottom about ⅛ inch deep. When it is very hot and a haze is just visible, put in the bread rounds, 3 or 4 at a time, and fry quickly on both sides until golden. Do not let them get dark or too crisp. It will only take seconds. Drain them on paper toweling.

TO ASSEMBLE AND SERVE: 1. Put 2 croutons on each of 8 warm plates. Carefully lift the sardines and pimiento strips from the baking dish and place them on the croutons, again in a single layer, covering the bread as well as possible.

2. Sprinkle some of the parsley over each and garnish each plate with 1 or 2 lemon wedges. Serve at once, accompanied with a glass of beer or dry red wine.

OYSTER LOAF WITH ISH'S BEER BATTER

The well-known "peacemaker" brought home by New Orleans night-wandering husbands to their waiting wives. To make it different, we've used a batter on the oysters rather than egg and bread crumbs.

Assemble and prepare all ingredients.

1. In a 2-quart bowl, put the 1 cup of flour, salt, 1 tablespoon of oil, beer, and egg yolk. Beat with a wire whisk or hand beater until smooth. Let stand at room temperature for from 2 to 6 hours.

2. Cut off the tops of the rolls, slicing them lengthwise about ¾ inch down. Pull out and discard the inside dough from both pieces, leaving about ½ inch of bread all around to form a hollow shell and lid. Refrigerate, well covered, until ready to assemble and cook.

ABOUT 45 MINUTES BEFORE SERVING: 1. Preheat the oven to 350 degrees.

2. Using a pastry brush, spread the melted butter evenly and generously inside both the bottom shells and the lids. Place, hollow side up, on a baking sheet

6 SERVINGS

The batter must be partially prepared 2 to 6 hours ahead.

The rolls may be prepared several hours ahead.

———

ALL-PURPOSE FLOUR
  1 cup, unsifted
SALT *½ teaspoon*
OIL *1 tablespoon*
LIGHT BEER *1 cup*
EGG YOLK *1*
FRENCH BREAD ROLLS
  6, about 5 inches long
MELTED BUTTER *For the rolls*
VEGETABLE OIL FOR FRYING
EGG WHITES *2, at room temperature*
MILK *About 1 cup*
FLOUR, FOR COATING OYSTERS *About 1½*

cups, unsifted
MIXED WITH:
BLACK PEPPER, GROUND
   FRESH *½ teaspoon*
SHUCKED OYSTERS
   *24 medium or 36 small,
   drained*

The Garnish
PICKLE SLICES

and bake on the middle rack of the oven for 10 to 15 minutes, or until the rolls are crisp and lightly toasted. Remove and keep warm until you complete the batter and fry the oysters.

3. Pour about 3 inches or more of vegetable oil into a deep fryer or heavy, large saucepan and heat to 375 degrees.

4. Then beat the egg whites until they hold soft peaks. Spoon about a fourth of them into the batter and mix well. Fold in the remaining beaten whites lightly and carefully. Set aside.

5. Put the milk into a shallow bowl and the 1½ cups of flour, mixed with the pepper, into a separate dinner plate or soup bowl. Dip 2 to 3 oysters at a time into the milk and then roll them in the flour. When they are evenly covered, dip them one by one into the batter, and remove them with a slotted spoon, letting the excess batter run off.

6. Immediately place them in the heated oil and fry, browning on both sides. (You may fry several at a time.) This should take only 2 or 3 minutes. As they brown transfer them to paper towels to drain, and put in a low oven to keep warm. Remove any specks of batter that are left in the oil. Repeat until you have fried all the oysters.

TO ASSEMBLE AND SERVE: Divide the oysters into 6 parts and pile a part into the toasted bottom shell of each roll. Top with the lids and put on a large, warm platter garnished with pickle slices. Serve hot.

JAMBALAYA

8 SERVINGS

May be prepared in the
morning and finished
just before serving.

———————

BUTTER ¼ *cup*

CELERY 2 *stalks, chopped*
fine: do not use the
leaves or tops

ONIONS 2 *medium, peeled*
and chopped fine

GREEN BELL PEPPER
To make ½ cup when
seeded, deveined, and
chopped fine

GARLIC 4 *cloves, peeled*
and chopped fine

COOKED HAM *To make*
2½ cups when cut in
½-inch dice (about 1
pound)

CANNED TOMATOES
2 cups (1 can, 16-ounce
size), with their juice

BAY LEAF 1 *whole*

GROUND THYME ¼ *tea-*
spoon

CHICKEN BROTH OR
WATER 3½ *cups, plus*
a little more if necessary

UNCOOKED LONG-GRAIN
RICE 1½ *cups*

FRESH SHRIMP 2 *pounds:*

If you have not lived in the bayou country
of Louisiana, there is a possibility that you
may have missed jambalaya. Such an omis-
sion must be corrected. The dish is made
in many ways, with chicken, sausage, craw-
fish, or shrimp alone. Our shrimp-and-ham
version is full-flavored and may make you
believe the story of the Cajun who left
Heaven because those responsible in the
kitchen had forgotten to provide jamba-
laya.

Assemble and prepare all ingredients.

1. In a heavy-bottomed 12-inch skillet
or 3-to-4-quart casserole, melt the butter
over low heat. Add the celery, onions,
green pepper, and garlic. Sauté until the
vegetables are tender but still a bit crisp.

2. Add the ham and continue to cook
for 5 minutes more.

3. Add the tomatoes and their juice, the
bay leaf, and thyme. Mash the tomatoes
with a fork, and mix well. Simmer, covered, for 10 minutes.

4. Add the 3½ cups of broth and the
rice, mix well, then raise the heat and
bring to a boil. Cover the pot and turn the
heat to very low. Simmer for about 25
minutes or until all the liquid has been
absorbed by the rice and the grains are
tender but not too soft. Add a little more
broth if necessary. May be made several
hours ahead to this point.

peel but do not cook
PARSLEY *To make 1 table-*
  spoon when minced
CAYENNE PEPPER ⅛ *tea-*
  spoon or more
SALT

ABOUT 15 MINUTES BEFORE SERVING:
1. Add the shrimp, parsley, and ⅛ teaspoon of cayenne pepper, or more to taste. We use ¼ teaspoon—we enjoy this dish piquant. Add salt to taste.

2. Mix lightly with a fork to combine and fluff the rice. Put on low heat, uncovered, until warmed through. Fluff with a fork from time to time. The mixture should be moist but not souplike, and the grains of rice should be separated. Add a little more broth if necessary. Serve immediately.

TO SERVE: Serve directly from the skillet (if it's an attractive one) or mound in a large, heated bowl. Spoon into warmed, small bowls for individual servings. Accompany with a glass of dry red wine or coffee for those who wish it.

KEDGEREE

6 SERVINGS

The fish-and-rice mixture may be prepared ahead and reheated in a double boiler.

The sauce may be prepared ahead and rewarmed over low heat.

———

COOKED RICE 3 *to 4 cups*
  (*1 cup uncooked*)

Kedgeree is a favorite English breakfast, but we have become fond of it for a late snack or supper. A small amount of cooked, peeled, and cut-up shrimp will add flair and flavor.

Assemble and prepare all ingredients.
1. Gently but thoroughly combine the cooked rice, fish, eggs, parsley, curry powder (if desired), and ½ cup of light cream. Add salt and pepper to taste. Heat in the top section of a double boiler over simmering water.

COOKED FISH (SEA BASS,
    HALIBUT, SNAPPER OR
    ANOTHER FIRM, LEAN
    FISH) *To make 2 cups
    when flaked (about 1
    pound uncooked)*
HARD-COOKED EGGS
    3, chopped coarse
PARSLEY *To make 3 table-
    spoons when chopped
    fine*
CURRY POWDER (OP-
    TIONAL) *1 teaspoon*
LIGHT CREAM *½ cup*
SALT
BLACK PEPPER, GROUND
    FRESH
BUTTER OR MARGARINE
    4 tablespoons
ALL-PURPOSE FLOUR
    4 tablespoons
MILK *1 cup*
LIGHT CREAM *1 cup*

The Accompaniment
TOASTED ENGLISH
    MUFFINS

2. Melt the butter or margarine in a saucepan over medium heat. Add the flour and cook for several minutes, stirring constantly. Do not brown.

3. Remove from the heat, add the milk and 1 cup of light cream. Return to the heat and stir with a wire whisk until the mixture becomes thick. Let it boil gently for 2 or 3 minutes. Add salt and pepper to taste. The sauce should be of medium thickness, not too heavy.

TO SERVE: Pile the hot kedgeree in a mound on a platter and pour the cream sauce over it. Let guests serve themselves. Pass the English muffins.

CHUPE—A SEAFOOD CASSEROLE

8 SERVINGS

May be prepared a day ahead and baked just before serving.

Or may be frozen, thawed,

In Chile a chupe *is a popular hodgepodge dish. Ours came to us by way of Ruth Netherton, a resident of Chile for some years.*

Assemble and prepare all ingredients.

and then baked.

———————

BUTTER FOR BAKING PAN

SCALLOPS, FRESH OR
   FROZEN *1 pound*

SHRIMP, FRESH OR
   FROZEN *1 pound, shelled*

CRABMEAT, FRESH OR
   FROZEN *1 pound, or, if
   canned, 2 cans (7½
   ounces each): shred,
   removing all bits of shell
   and cartilage*

DRIED BREAD CRUMBS
   2 cups

MILK *2 cups*

TABASCO SAUCE *5 shakes*

SALT

BLACK PEPPER, GROUND
   FRESH

RESERVED BROTH *About 1
   cup*

BUTTER *4 tablespoons*

ONION *1 medium, peeled
   and chopped fine*

MOZZARELLA CHEESE
   *⅓ pound, cut into thin
   slices*

HARD-COOKED EGGS
   2, sliced

FRESH GRATED PARMESAN
   CHEESE *⅓ cup*

The Accompaniment
HERB BREAD, *page 316*

1. Butter a shallow baking dish, about 8 by 14 inches, and set aside.

2. Cook the scallops in slowly boiling water to cover for 2 minutes. Drain and reserve the broth.

3. Cook the shrimp in slowly boiling water to cover for 3 minutes. Drain and reserve the broth.

4. In a bowl combine the scallops, shrimp, and crabmeat.

5. In a saucepan cook the bread crumbs in the milk for about 3 minutes. The mixture will form a thick paste. Add the Tabasco sauce, salt, and pepper to taste, and up to 1 cup of the combined reserved cooking broth from the scallops and shrimp to thin the paste to a spreadable consistency.

6. In a small skillet, heat 2 tablespoons of the butter. Add the onions and sauté until soft and golden but not brown, stirring frequently. Stir into the bread-crumb paste.

7. Divide the seafood mixture into 2 parts, and spread 1 part in the bottom of the prepared pan. Cover with half the slices of mozzarella cheese. Spread with half the bread-crumb paste.

8. Repeat with the remaining seafood, cheese, and paste. Arrange the slices of hard-cooked eggs on top, dot with the remaining 2 tablespoons of butter, and sprinkle with the Parmesan cheese. At this point the dish may be refrigerated for up to a day or frozen.

TO BAKE AND SERVE: 1. Preheat the oven to 400 degrees.

2. Bake on the middle rack for about

30 to 40 minutes or until lightly browned and thoroughly hot.

3. Serve at the table from the baking dish, along with Herb Bread and a dry, chilled white wine—Chilean, if available.

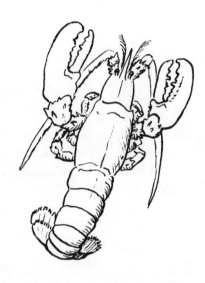

Meat and Poultry

8 SERVINGS, USUALLY

A table-top heating unit is
helpful but not
essential.

May be made up to 2 days
ahead and refrigerated,
or may be frozen.

LEAN PORK *1 pound, cut
in 1½-inch cubes*
LEAN BEEF *1 pound, cut in
1½-inch cubes*
COLD WATER *To cover*
SALT *1 teaspoon*
COOKING OIL *3 table-
spoons*
ONION *1 large, peeled and
chopped fine*
GARLIC *2 cloves, peeled
and minced with a little
salt*
TOMATOES *4 large, peeled*

ROPA VIEJA (Old Clothes)

*This is a spicy and enticing old Mex-
ican dish, never found in restaurants but
popular in homes of all classes. We always
double the recipe, to have some in the
freezer as a special for surprise visitors.*

Assemble and prepare all ingredients.

1. Put the pork and beef into a large
saucepan, about 2-quart size. Add cold
water, to cover, and salt; bring to a simmer.
Remove any scum that comes to the top.
Cover and cook gently for about 2 hours,
or until very tender. If you have a pressure
cooker, this can be done in half an hour.

2. Strain the broth, reserve it, and let
the meat cool.

3. Put the broth back into the saucepan
and reduce it by boiling rapidly, uncovered, until about ¾ cup remains. Reserve.

4. Heat the oil in a 3-quart saucepan,
add the onion, and sauté until it is soft and
transparent, but not brown. Stir frequently.
Add the garlic and sauté a minute or two
more.

and chopped coarse:
include the juice and
seeds

GREEN BELL PEPPER
1 large: remove and dis-
card top, core, seeds, and
pith—then cut in very
thin strips, about 2 inches
long and 1/8 inch wide

TOMATO CATSUP *1 cup*

RESERVED MEAT BROTH
3/4 cup

CANNED JALAPENO
PEPPERS *To make 1/2*
cup when cut into very
thin strips, about 1 inch
long and 1/8 inch wide:
discard any seeds, but
reserve the canning
liquid

LIQUID FROM JALAPENO
PEPPERS *2 tablespoons*
or more to taste

WINE VINEGAR *1 table-*
spoon

MONOSODIUM GLUTA-
MATE *1 teaspoon*

FRESH CORN TORTILLAS
OR DEFROSTED FROZEN
24

5. Add the tomatoes and green peppers, mix well, and sauté 10 minutes.

6. Add the catsup, reserved and reduced meat broth, *jalapeño* peppers, 2 tablespoons of the *jalapeño* canning liquid, vinegar, and monosodium glutamate. Simmer uncovered for about 1 hour or until the mixture is very thick but still moist. Taste it now and then. You may want to add more *jalapeño* liquid if you like it a little more piquant.

7. While the mixture is simmering, tear the cooked meat into fine shreds ("old clothes") and reserve.

8. About 10 minutes before the tomato sauce is finished, add the meat, which will thicken it somewhat. It should drop in large blobs from a spoon, and be thick enough so that it does not drip from the *tortilla* when eaten. At this point it may be refrigerated for up to 2 days or frozen.

ABOUT 30 MINUTES BEFORE SERVING:
1. Preheat the oven to 350 degrees and reheat the meat on top of the stove.

2. Separate the *tortillas* into stacks of 12 or 14. Put each stack on a piece of aluminum foil about 12 inches square, or large enough to make a covered package. Sprinkle a little cold water on the foil. Wrap, not too tightly, and put in the oven for at least 20 minutes. If necessary, you can turn the oven off, or to very low, and keep them hot for another 30 minutes.

TO SERVE: Put the warm Ropa Vieja in a heatproof serving bowl—one of Mexican earthenware would be very attractive. Put it on a food warmer or over a table-top heating unit to keep hot. Put the *tortillas* into a bowl or basket lined with a gay napkin. Place on a table or sideboard, along with a serving spoon and a plate and napkin for each guest—no forks!

TO EAT: Put a generous tablespoonful in the center of a *tortilla,* held in the left hand or on a plate. Then roll the *tortilla* and eat, holding it with your fingers. You may want to lean over your plate—it just may drip! Serve with red wine or cold beer.

MOCTEZUMA'S PIE

8 SERVINGS

You will need a 2½- or 3-quart casserole, preferably oval or round.

May be prepared up to a day ahead.

Bake just before serving.

_____

SALAD OIL *For oiling casserole and frying* tortillas, *plus 2 tablespoons more for sautéeing onions*
CORN TORTILLAS *18*
ONION *To make ½ cup when peeled and chopped fine*

Of the many tasty Mexican tortilla *combinations, this one, with meat, cream, and* chiles, *is our favorite.*

Assemble and prepare all ingredients.

1. Oil the casserole and set aside.

2. Put enough oil in a large skillet to cover the bottom about ¼ inch deep. Place over medium heat and, when the oil is very hot, lightly fry 1 or 2 *tortillas* at a time. They will soften almost immediately. Using a spatula, turn them quickly. Do not allow them to become crisp. As they are softened, drain them on paper towels. Repeat until all are fried.

3. Cut each *tortilla* into quarters and set aside.

4. Discard the oil in the pan, retaining about 2 tablespoons, or add more oil if necessary. Turn the heat to medium-low

FRESH TOMATOES *To make 2½ cups when peeled and chopped coarse (about 1½ pounds)*: *retain the seeds and juice*

SALT *½ teaspoon*

COOKED CHICKEN *To make 2½ cups when torn into bite-sized pieces*

CANNED WHOLE GREEN CHILES *1 can (7-ounce size), split and seeded*

HEAVY CREAM *1 cup*

MONTEREY JACK CHEESE *To make 4 cups when shredded on the coarse side of a 4-sided grater (about 1 pound)*

and add the onions. Sauté, turning frequently, until they just begin to soften. Do not let them color.

5. Add the tomatoes and their juice and cook until they are warmed through but still a little firm. Remove from the heat, mix in the salt, and set aside.

6. Into the prepared casserole, layer:
   24 *tortilla* quarters
   A third of the tomato mixture
   A third of the chicken
   A third of the *chiles*
   A third of the cream
   A third of the grated cheese

Repeat twice more, ending with a layer of cheese. Cover and refrigerate until ready to bake.

TO BAKE: About 45 minutes before serving, preheat the oven to 350 degrees. Put the casserole on the middle rack and bake for 20 to 25 minutes, or until it is heated through, bubbles around the edges, and shows a little color on the cheese. Do not let it dry out. Serve hot, accompanied by a glass of beer or dry red wine.

NOTE: This also makes a fine buffet dish. For a crowd, it's best to use 2 casseroles and double the recipe. Serve with a mixed green salad.

JOE'S SPECIAL

4 SERVINGS

Cook just before serving.

May be partially cooked in
the kitchen and finished
at the table on a table-
top burner.

_____

OLIVE OIL OR SALAD OIL
    2 tablespoons
GROUND BEEF 1 pound,
    crumbled
SCALLIONS To make ½
    cup when chopped
DRIED OREGANO LEAVES
    ½ teaspoon, crumbled
FROZEN CHOPPED
    SPINACH To make 1 cup
    when thawed and very
    well drained
EGGS 4, lightly beaten
SALT
BLACK PEPPER, GROUND
    FRESH

The Accompaniment
CRUSTY FRENCH BREAD,
    TOASTED AND
    BUTTERED

*This is a late-night San Francisco favorite,
invented in one of the restaurants, so they
say, when the chef had nothing left in the
kitchen but these ingredients. It is popular
even with spinach-haters, quick to prepare, full of flavor, and satisfying, whether
you are very hungry or want just a snack.
Great after a party with the nightcap you
invited everyone to stop by for.*

Assemble and prepare all ingredients.

1. Heat the oil in a skillet over high
heat. Add the ground beef and stir until it
is well browned.

2. Add the scallions and oregano. Sauté,
stirring, until the scallions are almost soft,
about 3 minutes.

3. Add the chopped spinach and sauté,
stirring, another 3 minutes.

4. Lower the heat to medium, add the
beaten eggs, and stir until the eggs are just
set but not dry. Add salt and pepper to
taste.

5. Serve immediately from the frying
pan, accompanied with toasted and buttered slices of crusty French bread and a
glass of hearty red wine.

If you wish to cook it partially at the table:
In the kitchen brown the beef and add the
scallions and oregano as directed above.
Put the spinach and eggs on a pretty tray.
Put the skillet with the cooked meat–and–

scallion mixture over a table-top burner. Add the spinach and eggs and cook as directed above.

"BONES"

4 TO 6 SERVINGS

You will need a large roasting pan and rack, maybe 2.

The sauce must be prepared a day ahead, to blend with the flavors, but it may be prepared up to several days in advance.

The ribs may be baked the day before serving, but they must be baked at least 3 to 4 hours ahead.

They may be frozen after baking and thawed before broiling.

Broil just before serving.

———————

The Sauce

TOMATO CATSUP 2 *cups*
SUGAR 1½ *teaspoons*
BAY LEAVES 3, *whirled in a blender until they are*

Served at Carlos O'Willy's restaurant in Guadalajara, these barbecued spareribs are so good that we brought some sauce home and spent many happy hours of experiment duplicating it. Make plenty—they are quite irresistible.

THE SAUCE: A day ahead, assemble and prepare all ingredients for the sauce and mix together well. Cover and refrigerate until ready to marinate the spareribs.

THE SPARERIBS: 1. Preheat the oven to 250 degrees.

2. Place the spareribs on a rack, fatty side up, in a single layer over a large roasting pan, or use 2 racks and 2 pans. If necessary to make them fit, cut the ribs into 2 or 3 sections, but not into serving portions.

3. Sprinkle with a few grinds of the pepper mill and coat each piece well with some of the reserved sauce. Keep the rest for the final coating and serving.

4. Put about ¼ inch of water in the roasting pan to catch the drippings and to give out moisture to keep the ribs from getting dry. Do not let the ribs touch the water.

5. Roast on the middle rack of the preheated oven for 3 to 4 hours, depending

*in tiny pieces, or mashed
in a mortar*
SALAD OIL ⅓ *cup*
VINEGAR ¼ *cup*
GARLIC 5 *medium cloves,
minced almost to a paste
with a little salt*
BLACK PEPPER, GROUND
FRESH ¾ *teaspoon*

The Spareribs

BABY PORK SPARERIBS,
THE BEST QUALITY
AVAILABLE 3 *to 4
pounds: cut away any
breastbone or gristle that
may be attached to the
ribs, but do not cut them
into serving portions
(this will be done later)*
BLACK PEPPER, GROUND
FRESH

upon the thickness of the ribs. From time to time, you may have to add a little more water to the pan.

6. Turn the ribs when they are three-quarters done, to brown the other side. They should be cooked through but not brown, and they should be so tender that the meat pulls off the bones easily and leaves the bones clean. Test one.

7. Remove them from the oven and discard the fat and liquid at the bottom of the pan.

8. When they are cool enough to handle, cut them into 2-rib sections. At this point they may be refrigerated, very tightly covered, for a day, or frozen. If frozen, thaw before broiling.

ABOUT 15 MINUTES BEFORE SERVING: 1. Preheat the broiler and warm the reserved sauce on the top of the stove.

2. Place the ribs on the broiler rack, about 3 inches from the heat, and broil for 3 to 5 minutes, or until they are a lovely dark mahogany color, but not dry. It is not necessary to turn them.

3. Brush them generously on both sides with part of the warmed sauce.

TO SERVE: Put on a warmed platter and serve on heated plates. Be sure to have plenty of large paper napkins handy. Fingers are allowed! Pass the remaining sauce separately. Why not follow the "Bones" with a small glass of Kahlua and milk and a plate of hard candies and lollipops like they do at Carlos O'Willy's?

KAHLUA AND MILK: For each person put several ice cubes into an Old Fashioned glass. Pour 1½ ounces of Kahlua and ½ ounces of evaporated milk over the ice. Put a short straw in each glass.

HOISIN CHICKEN WINGS

6 TO 8 SERVINGS

The *hoisin* sauce and plum sauce are musts, and may be purchased at Chinese food shops, or at some shops carrying imported or specialty foods: they will keep indefinitely in the refrigerator.

Must marinate 2 hours or up to a day before broiling.

Serve warm.

_____

The Marinade
SOY SAUCE *½ cup*
DRY WHITE WINE *¼ cup*
HOISIN SAUCE *¼ cup*
PLUM SAUCE *2 tablespoons*
HONEY *3 tablespoons*
GINGER *To make 1 teaspoon, minced, if fresh, or, if dried, ¼ teaspoon, ground*

Teriyaki sauce is good—we have made it even better by adding hoisin sauce and plum sauce. These are wonderful for a special cocktail party, too.

THE MARINADE: Assemble and prepare all ingredients.

Put all the ingredients for the marinade into a bowl. Mix thoroughly until the *hoisin* sauce, plum sauce, and the honey are incorporated.

THE CHICKEN WINGS: Put the chicken wings into the marinade in a large baking pan. Turn so that they are well coated. Let them remain at room temperature for 2 hours or in the refrigerator for up to 24 hours. Turn occasionally.

2 HOURS BEFORE SERVING: 1. Preheat the broiler.

2. Using tongs or your fingers, arrange the chicken pieces in a single layer on the broiler pan and brush with the marinade. Reserve the marinade remaining in the baking pan for later.

3. Broil 3 or 4 inches from the heat for 12 to 15 minutes or until they color evenly

GARLIC 2 *cloves, peeled
and minced*

SCALLIONS 4 *to 6, minced:
include about 2 inches of
the pale-green stems*

The Chicken Wings

CHICKEN WINGS
*30, washed, dried, and
cut through the joints
to make 3 parts: discard
the tips or save for the
soup pot*

WATER ½ *cup*

and are a deep mahogany. Watch them
closely, they burn easily.

4. Remove them from the broiler, turn
each over, and brush again with the marinade.

5. Return to the broiler for 10 to 12
minutes more, or until they are colored
evenly. Again take care not to burn them.
You may have to broil a second batch.

6. Put the broiled wings back into the
marinade in the baking pan. Add ½ cup
of water. Seal with aluminum foil and
bake at 250 degrees for 1 hour. Keep warm
until ready to serve.

TO SERVE: Put the wings on a platter and
pour the remaining marinade from the
baking pan over them. A nice thoughtful
touch, borrowed from the Chinese, is to
put a warm, dampened, small towel or
napkin on a plate beside each diner for
finger-wiping; or plenty of paper napkins.
The wings are picked up in the fingers and
eaten out of hand—definitely messy, but
so good!

NOTE: Any leftover sauce is good for marinating a steak, chicken, or even hamburgers.

8 SERVINGS

May be made a day ahead
and reheated before
serving.

CHICKEN AND LONG RICE

*A popular Hawaiian recipe, refreshingly
light yet fully satisfying. Long rice (pro-
nounced with the accent on "long," to
distinguish from "short rice") is a translu-*

The broth and chicken may be frozen separately: prepare and add the long rice up to a day ahead.

The Chicken and Broth

CHICKEN *About 3 pounds, cut in pieces*

WATER *4 cups*

CHICKEN BROTH *4 cups*

GARLIC *3 cloves, peeled and minced*

GROUND GINGER *½ teaspoon*

ONION *1 medium, peeled and sliced into thin rounds: cut each round in half*

DRIED CHINESE BLACK MUSHROOMS *About 2 ounces: soak in boiling water to cover for 15 to 30 minutes before using, then drain and cut in ⅛-inch strips*

SHRIMP *½ cup, if dried, or, if fresh, or frozen 15 medium: peel but do not cook*

SOY SAUCE *1 tablespoon*

MONOSODIUM GLUTA-MATE *1 teaspoon*

SALT *1 teaspoon: omit if dried shrimp are used*

cent, vermicelli-like product that may be purchased in Chinese or Japanese food shops or in the Oriental food section of many supermarkets. They are sometimes called bean threads or transparent noodles. Vermicelli may be substituted, but we hope not—it won't be the real thing.

THE CHICKEN AND BROTH: Assemble and prepare all ingredients.

1. Put the chicken, water, and broth into a stockpot or stewpot. Bring to a boil and remove the scum. Wipe the inside edge of the pot with a damp piece of paper toweling to remove any bits of scum clinging to it.

2. Add the garlic, ginger, onion, mushrooms, shrimp, if dried (if using fresh shrimp, they will be added later), soy sauce, monosodium glutamate, salt (optional), and 5 or 6 grinds of the pepper mill.

3. Bring to a simmer and cook gently, uncovered, for 45 minutes to 1 hour, or until the chicken is tender when pierced with a fork. If using fresh shrimp, add them 10 minutes before the end of the cooking time.

4. Remove the chicken from the broth and take the meat from the bones, discarding bones, skin, and any fat. Cut the meat in 1-inch pieces. At this point you may freeze the broth and chicken separately or continue with the recipe.

THE LONG RICE: Cover the long rice with warm water, soak at least 1 hour, and

BLACK PEPPER, GROUND FRESH

The Long Rice
LONG RICE (BEAN THREADS OR TRANS-PARENT NOODLES)
1 package (8-ounce size)
WARM WATER

The Garnish
SCALLIONS *To make 1 cup when chopped: include some of the green stems*

8 SERVINGS

You will need a baking dish pretty enough to come to the table and just large enough to hold 8 *crêpes* in a single layer.

The sauce may be prepared up to a day ahead and refrigerated separately.

drain. May be prepared up to 24 hours ahead and refrigerated, well covered.

UP TO A DAY AHEAD OR JUST BEFORE SERVING: 1. Bring the broth to a boil and add the drained long rice. Boil gently for about 15 minutes or until the rice becomes translucent. Surprisingly, it will absorb almost all the broth. To make the rice more manageable, use a large knife to cut it through several times in each direction in pot.

2. Add the chicken and combine. The mixture should be very moist, but not liquid, like soup.

TO SERVE: Divide among 8 warm bowls and sprinkle the top of each serving with some of the chopped scallions. No accompaniment is needed, but you might serve tea.

HAM AND BANANAS IN CREPES

This exceptional dish was born of a happy combination of circumstances—a rapidly ripening stalk of bananas hanging in the garage, some extra crêpes *in the freezer, leftover slices of ham, and an affinity for Mornay sauce. It will henceforth be a family "staple."*

Assemble and prepare all ingredients.

THE CHEESE SAUCE: 1. Put the butter in a heavy-bottomed saucepan and place it over

The *crêpes* may be
prepared and
assembled, ready for the
oven, in the morning.

Finish and bake just before
serving.

The Crepes
*Full recipe, page 306, use
a* crêpe *or omelette pan
about 7½ inches in
diameter at the bottom,
and use a scant ¼ cup
of batter for each: this
will make more crêpes
than you need, but freeze
the balance for another
use*

The Cheese Sauce
BUTTER ¼ *cup*
ALL-PURPOSE FLOUR
   ¼ *cup*
MILK 2 *cups*
DRY SHERRY 2 *tablespoons*
SWISS OR MONTEREY
   JACK CHEESE *To make
   ⅓ cup when grated*
SALT
WHITE PEPPER, GROUND
   FRESH

The Filling
COOKED HAM 8 *slices,
about 5 inches wide, 6*

low heat. When it is bubbling, add the
flour, blend, and cook slowly, stirring, until
the butter and flour froth together for 1 or
2 minutes. Do not let the mixture color.

2. Remove from the heat and add the
milk. Immediately beat vigorously with a
wire whisk to blend.

3. Place the saucepan over moderate
heat and continue stirring with the whisk
to remove all lumps, until the sauce thickens to about the consistency of a very heavy
syrup and coats the whisk well.

4. Remove from the heat and add
the sherry and grated cheese. Stir until the
cheese melts. Add salt and pepper to taste.
At this point the sauce may be refrigerated
for up to a day with a piece of plastic wrap
folded to fit and pressed on the surface.

TO ASSEMBLE AND FILL: 1. Cover the bottom of a baking dish with about ⅓ cup of
the cheese sauce and reserve the rest. The
pan should be just large enough to accom-
modate 8 filled and rolled *crêpes* in a single layer, close together.

2. Spread each slice of ham generously
with the mustard, covering to the edges.
Turn each slice with the narrow end toward you.

3. Peel the bananas and place 1 along
the narrow end of each ham slice, centering them. Roll each banana in a slice of
ham. The bananas will probably extend a
bit on either end; it's more attractive this
way.

4. Now roll each in a *crêpe,* centering
it. Place in the prepared baking dish, open

*inches long, and ⅛ inch
thick: if it is sliced too
thin, you won't get a
nice taste of ham, and if
it is too thick, it won't
roll properly*
DIJON MUSTARD
FIRM RIPE BANANAS
*8, about 7 or 8 inches
long, peeled*

The Topping
RESERVED CHEESE SAUCE
PARMESAN CHEESE,
     GRATED FRESH

side down. You may now refrigerate the
crêpes, lightly covered, until ready to bake
and serve.

TO BAKE AND SERVE: 1. Preheat the oven
to 350 degrees.

2. Pour the remaining cheese sauce over
the rolls, spreading it to cover and letting
it run down the sides.

3. Sprinkle each roll generously with
the grated Parmesan cheese.

4. Place on the center rack of the oven
and bake for 30 minutes, or until the
crêpes are heated all the way through, and
the bananas are soft. Bring to the table immediately and divide among individual
warm plates. These are so rich and good
that we don't feel an accompaniment is
needed, but if you wish, serve a small glass
of sherry with it.

Eggs

QUICHE PROVENÇALE

A variation on a classic, but we couldn't leave it out.

You will need a 10-inch *quiche* pan or a false-bottomed 10-inch straight-sided cake pan, no more than 1½ inches deep, or a 10-inch pie pan.

The pastry shell may be made several days ahead, tightly wrapped and refrigerated, then partially bake several hours ahead.

The filling, except for the eggs and cream, may be made up to a day ahead, covered, and refrigerated.

Serve warm.

Assemble and prepare all ingredients.

1. Brush the bottom and sides of the pastry shell with the slightly beaten egg white and prick it at ½-inch intervals with a fork. Refrigerate until very firm before baking.

2. Preheat the oven to 375 degrees. To keep the sides of the pastry shell from collapsing, line it with a large piece of buttered lightweight foil, buttered side down. Press the foil against the sides of the shell and fill it with dried beans. Put it on the middle rack of the oven for 12 to 15 minutes or until the pastry is set, partially baked and very lightly colored, and just beginning to shrink from the sides of the mold.

3. Remove from the oven, remove the beans and foil, and let the pastry cool until ready to fill and finish baking.

UNBAKED PASTRY SHELL
   FOR QUICHE *1, page
   299*
EGG WHITE *1, slightly
   beaten*
DRIED BEANS *for weighting
   pastry shell*

The Filling

OIL *2 tablespoons*
ONIONS *To make 1 cup
   when chopped fine*
GARLIC *4 cloves, peeled
   and minced with a little
   salt*
FRESH TOMATOES
   *To make 1 cup when
   chopped medium-fine:
   first peel them, then cut
   them in half crosswise
   and squeeze them gently
   to extract the liquid and
   seeds*
PITTED BLACK OLIVES
   *To make 2 tablespoons
   when chopped medium-
   fine*
PARSLEY *To make 1 table-
   spoon minced*
GROUND THYME *⅛ tea-
   spoon*
SALT *½ teaspoon*
WHITE PEPPER, GROUND
   FRESH *¼ teaspoon*
EGGS *2 whole, plus 2 yolks*
LIGHT CREAM *1½ cups*

THE FILLING: 1. Put the oil in a medium skillet. When it is very hot and a haze is starting to form, add the onions. Turn the heat to medium-low and sauté until they are limp and just starting to turn golden. Turn and toss frequently, so they do not burn.

2. Add the garlic and sauté for a minute more. Then add the tomatoes, turn the heat to medium-high, and sauté, stirring occasionally, until the juice has evaporated, the mixture looks like a thick, moist purée, and there is a film of oil on the bottom of the pan.

3. Add the olives, parsley, thyme, salt, and pepper. Mix well and sauté a minute or two more. Set aside and cool or refrigerate until you are ready to bake the *quiche*.

TO ASSEMBLE, BAKE, AND SERVE: 1. About 45 minutes before you are ready to serve, preheat the oven to 350 degrees.

2. Put the eggs, cream, and salt and pepper to taste in a medium bowl. Beat together until slightly foamy. Then stir in the cooled tomato mixture. Pour into the cooled, partially baked pastry shell, being sure the mixture does not come to within more than ⅛ inch of the rim of the shell. Bake in the upper third of the oven for about 25 to 30 minutes, or until it is puffed and golden, and a knife inserted in the center comes out clean.

3. Let the *quiche* cool briefly. If you are using a false-bottomed *quiche* or cake pan, set the pan on a large jar or coffee can and slip down the outside rim. Now either

SALT
WHITE PEPPER, GROUND
  FRESH

slide the *quiche* onto a serving platter or leave it in place, using the bottom of the pan as a platter. If using a pie pan, just bring it to the table in the pan. Cut and serve warm. A glass of white or rosé wine is a nice accompaniment.

GATEAU DE SIX OMELETTES

4 SERVINGS

You will need a *crêpe* or omelette pan 5 inches or 5 ½ inches in diameter at the bottom.

The fillings may be made up to 24 hours and refrigerated.

The omelettes must be made just before serving, but they take just a minute or two each.

The Fillings

First Filling
BUTTER 2 *tablespoons*
FROZEN CHOPPED
  SPINACH *To make* ⅓
  cup when defrosted and
  very well drained by
  pressing against a sieve
FLOUR ½ *tablespoon*

We had this in Paris and it's as good to eat as to look at. It's composed of 6 flat, unfolded omelettes, arranged one on top of the other, like a layer cake, with a different filling between each, then topped with chives and nuts.

THE FILLINGS: Assemble and prepare the fillings and refrigerate.

First Filling: Creamed Spinach
  1. Melt the butter in a small skillet or saucepan. Add the drained spinach and stir thoroughly with a fork until it has absorbed the butter.
  2. Sprinkle with the flour and stir for a minute longer. Add the cream and nutmeg and blend thoroughly.
  3. When the spinach has absorbed the cream and is the consistency of a purée, add salt and pepper to taste. Put in a small bowl and refrigerate, covered, until ready to rewarm and use.

Second Filling: Boiled, Diced Ham
  Put in a small bowl and refrigerate, covered, until ready to use.

LIGHT CREAM *⅓ cup*
NUTMEG GRATED FRESH
  Generous pinch
SALT
BLACK PEPPER, GROUND
  FRESH

Second Filling
BOILED HAM *To make ⅓*
  cup when cut into
  ¼-inch dice

Third Filling
SWISS CHEESE *To make ¾*
  cup when grated

Fourth Filling
COOKED CHICKEN
  To make ½ cup when
  shredded or cut into
  ¼-inch cubes

Fifth Filling
BUTTER *2 tablespoons*
FRESH MUSHROOMS
  To make 1 cup when
  sliced (about ¼ pound):
  wipe clean with a damp
  paper towel, if necessary;
  trim stems even with base
  of the caps and save
  stems for another use
  (cut large mushrooms in
  half crosswise before
  slicing)

Third Filling: Grated Cheese

Put in a small bowl and refrigerate, covered, until ready to use.

Fourth Filling: Cooked Chicken

Put in a small bowl and refrigerate, covered, until ready to use.

Fifth Filling: Mushrooms

Put the butter in a small skillet and, when it is very hot, add the mushrooms. Stir until golden and soft. Put in a small bowl and refrigerate, covered, until ready to rewarm and use.

THE TOPPING: Put the mixed walnuts and chives in a small bowl and refrigerate, covered, until ready to use.

Before starting the omelettes, assemble the fillings and topping close to the stove and reheat the spinach and mushrooms. Heat the lemon butter accompaniment until tepid. Put the potato chips in a baking pan and warm in the oven at 350 degrees for 10 minutes.

THE OMELETTES: Assemble and make just before serving. Each will cook in a minute or two.

1. Put the 12 eggs, the water, Tabasco sauce, and salt in a medium bowl. Beat quickly with a whisk or rotary beater until all is well mixed and the yolks are broken up but look "stringy" when the beater is lifted. Now measure them. You should have 3 cups. If not, beat 1 more egg separately and add it to the mixture.

The Topping

WALNUTS *To make ¼*
cup when chopped fine
MIXED WITH:
SNIPPED CHIVES *2 table-*
spoons

The Omelettes

LARGE EGGS *12 at room*
temperature, plus 1 extra
egg if necessary
COLD WATER *¼ cup*
TABASCO SAUCE *Scant ⅛*
teaspoon
SALT *½ teaspoon*
BUTTER *6 tablespoons*
(¾ stick)

The Accompaniment
(optional)

MELTED BUTTER *½ cup*
(1 stick)
MIXED WITH:
FRESH LEMON JUICE
1 tablespoon
WARMED POTATO CHIPS
(OPTIONAL)

2. Make the first omelette: put the *crêpe* or omelette pan over medium heat until hot. When a few drops of water sprinkled in the pan jump and dance around, it is ready.

3. Add 1 tablespoon of the butter to the pan and swish it around as it melts so that the sides of the pan are buttered about a third of the way up.

4. Using a ½-cup measure, pour ½ cup of the beaten eggs into the hot pan.

5. Now, very quickly, using the back of a fork in your right hand, immediately make circular motions around the bottom of the pan. At the same time, grasp the handle of the pan with your left hand and shake it back and forth to keep the eggs loose.

6. After 3 or 4 seconds of stirring and shaking, pause briefly to allow the eggs to set. Prick and push aside the eggs in several places with a fork to allow some of the liquid in the center to run under and cook.

7. When the eggs have thickened, but the top is still soft, creamy, and very moist, lift the omelette with the help of a spatula and slide it onto a serving plate.

8. Spread it with the spinach filling all the way to the edges.

9. Proceed making 5 more omelettes, spreading each filling to the edges and stacking each filled omelette on top of the other like a layer cake, in the following order:

a. Make the second omelette, stack it on top of the spinach, and spread it with the ham.

b. Make the third omelette, stack it on top of the ham, and spread it with the cheese.

c. Make the fourth omelette, stack it on top of the cheese, and spread it with the chicken.

d. Make the fifth omelette, stack it on top of the chicken, and spread it with the mushrooms.

e. Make the sixth omelette, stack it on top of the mushrooms, and top it with the nuts and chives.

TO SERVE: Cut into quarters at the table and put on individual plates, accompanied by a glass of dry red or rosé wine. Pass the lemon butter and potato chips separately.

SOUFFLEED TOASTS WITH CHOICE OF FILLINGS

6 SERVINGS

Either filling may be prepared ahead, except for the avocado in the ham and avocado, which should be sliced fresh.

The toast may be prepared ahead.

Assemble, prepare the soufflé topping, and bake just before serving.

_____

An exceptional recipe. After you have tried these 2 fillings, create your own. Use asparagus instead of avocado, chicken instead of ham, add some mustard to the topping and use it without any filling. You can't go wrong.

Assemble and prepare all ingredients.

THE MUSHROOM FILLING: 1. Put the mushrooms in a heavy medium skillet with no liquid or fat. Cover the skillet and place it over medium heat. Cook until all the liquid has evaporated and the mushrooms almost begin to stick to the pan. Stir frequently.

The Mushroom Filling

MUSHROOMS ¾ *pound:*
first wipe with a damp
paper towel if necessary,
then cut them in thin
slices lengthwise, with
the stems on
BUTTER 2 *tablespoons*
FLOUR 2 *tablespoons*
LIGHT CREAM ¾ *cup*

The Toast

FIRM WHITE BREAD,
  PREFERABLY A DAY OLD
  6 *slices, with crusts*
SOFTENED BUTTER *About*
  3 *tablespoons*
DIJON MUSTARD

The Souffle Topping

EGG YOLKS 4, *at room*
  temperature
WORCESTERSHIRE SAUCE
  ½ *teaspoon*
CAYENNE PEPPER 2 *or 3*
  dashes
SALT ½ *teaspoon*
SHARP CHEDDAR CHEESE
  To make 1 cup when
  grated (*about* ¼ *pound*)
EGG WHITES 4, *at room*
  temperature

Ham and Avocado Filling

COOKED HAM 6 *slices, cut*
  ⅛ *inch thick and*
  trimmed to the same size
  as the bread

2. Remove the cover and add the butter. Stir until the butter melts and continue to cook, uncovered, a minute or two more.

3. Sprinkle the mushrooms with the flour and mix well. Continue to sauté, for 2 or 3 minutes.

4. Add the cream and cook until the mixture is thick but moist, with no visible liquid showing at the bottom of the skillet. Remove from the heat and reserve or refrigerate.

5. Next, prepare the toasts: spread 1 side of the bread lightly with the softened butter. Put on a broiler rack, buttered side up.

6. Toast them on this side only until light gold. Watch carefully, it will take just a minute or so.

7. Remove the toasts from the broiler and place them, well separated, on a buttered baking sheet, *toasted side down.*

8. Spread the untoasted sides lightly with the mustard. At this point you may refrigerate them, tightly wrapped.

ABOUT 25 MINUTES BEFORE SERVING:
1. Preheat the oven to 375 degrees.

2. Cover each piece of toast with part of the reserved mushroom filling, but don't spread it quite to the edge.

3. In a medium bowl, beat the egg yolks, Worcestershire sauce, cayenne pepper, and salt, until the eggs are light and lemon-colored. Stir in the grated cheese.

4. In a separate bowl, beat the egg whites until they are stiff enough to hold firm peaks, but not dry.

5. Mix about a fourth of the beaten egg

FIRM RIPE AVOCADOS
  2 medium, cut length-
  wise: remove the seed
  and peel the halves, then
  cut lengthwise into
  ⅛-inch slices

white into the cheese mixture to lighten it. Then spoon the remaining whites on top. Fold together gently but thoroughly. However, don't overdo this; it doesn't matter if the mixture is a little lumpy.

6. Heap each toast with part of the soufflé mixture, covering the filling.

7. Bake on the center rack of the preheated oven for 10 to 15 minutes or until puffed and lightly brown. Serve at once.

THE HAM AND AVOCADO FILLING: Assemble and prepare all ingredients.

1. Follow the steps for toasting the bread as given above.

2. Cover each piece of toast with a slice of ham and top the ham with enough avocado slices to cover.

3. Follow all instructions under "About 25 Minutes Before Serving" above.

STUFFED EGGS IN SOUBISE SAUCE

8 SERVINGS

You will need two 8-by-
  8-by-2-inch baking pans
  or 1 pan about 7½ by
  11½ by 2 inches and
  a blender.

May be prepared up to a
  day ahead and
  refrigerated.

Bake just before serving.

_____

Soubise *is a velvety-smooth onion purée, sometimes made with rice and onions, used in France as an accompaniment to meats, particularly grilled. The onion flavor is enticing, especially as we have used it here with eggs.*

THE STUFFED EGGS: Assemble and prepare all ingredients.

1. Lightly butter the baking pans and set aside.

2. Cut the eggs in half lengthwise. Carefully remove the yolks to a small

The Stuffed Eggs

HARD-COOKED EGGS
  12, cooled and peeled
MAYONNAISE, PREFER-
  ABLY HOMEMADE,
  *page 296 (About 3
  tablespoons)*
DIJON MUSTARD *1 tea-
  spoon*
SALT
BLACK PEPPER, GROUND
  FRESH

The Sauce

BUTTER *¼ cup, plus a
  little more for buttering
  the pan and dotting the
  top*
ONIONS *To make 4 cups
  when peeled and
  chopped medium-fine
  (about 4 large)*
FLOUR *3 tablespoons*
POWDERED CHICKEN-
  STOCK BASE *2 teaspoons*
MILK *1½ cups, heated but
  not boiling*
HEAVY CREAM *About ½
  cup*
NUTMEG, GRATED FRESH
  ⅛ teaspoon
SALT
WHITE PEPPER, GROUND
  FRESH
DRY BREAD CRUMBS
  2 tablespoons
  MIXED WITH:

bowl, keeping the whites intact. Put the whites aside.

3. Using a fork, mash the yolks against the sides of the bowl. Add the 3 table-spoons of mayonnaise, the mustard, and salt and pepper to taste. The mixture should be moist and slightly creamy. Add a little more mayonnaise if it seems dry.

4. Spoon the mixture into the hollows of the reserved egg whites, place them, yolk side up, in a single layer in the pre-pared baking pans, and set aside.

THE SAUCE: Assemble and prepare all in-gredients.

1. Heat the butter in a large, heavy-bottomed skillet or saucepan. Add the on-ions and cook slowly for 20 to 30 minutes, or until the onions are very tender but not browned. Stir and toss frequently.

2. Sprinkle with the flour and the pow-dered chicken-stock base and stir over low heat for 2 or 3 minutes.

3. Add the heated milk and combine. Raise the heat slightly and simmer slowly for about 15 minutes.

4. Transfer the sauce to a blender and purée it until very smooth. You will have to do this in 2 or 3 batches, stopping the motor and pushing down the mixture with a rubber spatula if necessary.

5. Return the mixture to the saucepan or skillet and heat to a simmer. *Add the cream by spoonfuls,* stirring well after each addition, until the sauce is quite thick and not runny. You may use more or less than the amount specified.

ROMANO OR PARMESAN
    CHEESE, GRATED FRESH
    2 tablespoons

The Accompaniment
TOASTED AND BUTTERED
    FRENCH BREAD
    OR GARLIC BREAD

6. Add the nutmeg and salt and pepper to taste.

7. Spoon the sauce over and around the eggs, dividing it as evenly as possible. At this point you may refrigerate the dish, well covered, up to a day ahead. To prevent a "skin" from forming, press a piece of plastic wrap directly onto the eggs and sauce.

TO BAKE: 1. About ½ hour before serving, preheat the oven to 375 degrees.

2. Sprinkle the eggs with the breadcrumbs–and–cheese mixture and dot with a little butter.

3. Bake on the middle rack of the oven for about 15 minutes or until the edges are bubbly and the top is just starting to turn a light brown. Do not overbake.

TO SERVE: Spoon 2 or 3 egg halves and some sauce on each warm service plate. Accompany with toasted and buttered French bread or garlic bread and a glass of chilled, dry white wine.

8 SERVINGS

The eggs may be prepared up to a day ahead, but they must be chilled at least 1 hour before frying.

Fry just before serving.

MAC DOUGALL'S SCOTCH EGGS

No pub counter in Scotland or England is without a platter of these tasty eggs—a grand little snack with ale or beer. We prefer ours hot, but they are good at room temperature, too.

THE EGGS: Assemble and prepare all ingredients.

The sauce may be made
several hours in advance
and reheated.

WELL-SEASONED BULK
  SAUSAGE MEAT 2 *cups*
  (*about 1 pound*)
LARGE HARD-COOKED
  EGGS 8, *cooled and
  shelled*
DIJON MUSTARD OR
  OTHER PREPARED
  MUSTARD
FLOUR ¼ *cup, or a little
  more*
EGGS 2, *beaten*
UNSEASONED DRY BREAD
  CRUMBS *1 cup or more,
  depending on the size of
  of the eggs*
OIL OR VEGETABLE
  SHORTENING FOR
  FRYING

The Sauce
MORNAY SAUCE
(WITHOUT THE CHEESE)
  Full recipe, page 98

The Accompaniment
TOASTED OATMEAL BREAD

1. Divide the sausage meat into 8 parts (a scant ⅓ cup each). Form each into a flattened, rough-shaped circle.

2. Put 1 part on a piece of waxed paper and cover it with another piece of waxed paper. Using a rolling pin and your fingers, press the sausage meat into a rough-shaped oval about 6 inches long and 5 inches wide, or large enough to completely enclose the egg. If there are any thin spots, pinch them together or patch them with a little trimming from the edges.

3. Remove the top piece of waxed paper and, starting at the long end of the oval nearest you, roll the egg in the sausage meat and fold the ends over. Pick up the sausage-enclosed egg in your hand and press it all smoothly together so that the sausage meat adheres to the egg. Save the bottom piece of waxed paper for subsequent rolling. Repeat with each egg and sausage patty.

4. Spread each covered egg lightly, all over, with mustard, and roll or dip each gently in flour, then in beaten egg, and lastly in the bread crumbs, again pressing the bread crumbs into the sausage meat.

5. Refrigerate in a single layer, well covered, for at least 1 hour, or up to a day ahead.

THE SAUCE: Several hours before serving, prepare the sauce, page 98, omitting the cheese.

JUST BEFORE SERVING: 1. Reheat the sauce in the upper section of a double

boiler, adding a little milk, if necessary, to bring it back to the original consistency.

2. Heat the oil or shortening at least 3 inches deep in a pot or deep fryer until it is very hot—about 375 degrees.

3. Fry the eggs 1 or 2 at a time until the outside is golden-brown. Remove and drain them on paper towels. Place them in a very low oven to keep warm until all are fried.

TO SERVE: Put about ¼ cup of the sauce on the bottom of each of 8 small, warm plates. Place 1 egg on each and accompany with the toasted oatmeal bread and a glass of ale.

ARTICHOKE FRITTATA

Every time we have been in Florence, Italy, we have had artichoke frittata *at a small outdoor café in the shadow of Michelangelo's magnificent David in the Piazza della Signora. A perfect setting, but the* frittata *is good at home, too.*

Assemble and prepare all ingredients.

THE ARTICHOKES: 1. Put the frozen artichokes in a saucepan with the water and the salt. Bring to a full boil over medium heat, separating the artichokes with a fork. As soon as they are separated, remove them them from the heat, drain, and cool.

2. When cool enough to handle, take the artichokes, 1 at a time, and cut them in

6 TO 8 SERVINGS

You will need 2 skillets, one of them 10 inches in diameter and pretty enough to come to the table.

The artichokes may be prepared and fried several hours ahead.

Add the eggs and cook just before serving.

_____

The Artichokes
FROZEN ARTICHOKE

HEARTS *1 package (9-ounce size)*

WATER *1/4 cup*

SALT *Pinch*

OLIVE OIL *1/4 cup*

ALL-PURPOSE FLOUR *About 1/2 cup*

The Eggs

LARGE EGGS 7, *at room temperature*

COLD WATER 3 *tablespoons*

DRIED OREGANO LEAVES *Generous pinch, crumbled*

MONOSODIUM GLUTA-MATE *1/4 teaspoon*

SALT *1/2 teaspoon*

BLACK PEPPER, GROUND FRESH

OLIVE OIL FOR SKILLET *3 tablespoons*

PARSLEY *To make 2 tablespoons when minced*

MIXED WITH:

PARMESAN CHEESE, GRATED FRESH *3 tablespoons*

The Accompaniment

BREAD STICKS AND BUTTER OR HERB BREAD, *page 316*

half lengthwise, keeping the halves intact. To do this you will need a very sharp knife. As they are halved, put them, cut side down, on paper toweling to drain.

3. Put the 1/4 cup of olive oil in a skillet. Turn the heat to medium-high and heat until a haze begins to form.

4. Sprinkle the drained artichoke halves on all sides with the flour. Place them in a single layer in the hot oil and fry until just golden-brown on 1 side. Turn them and fry on the other side until golden. Carefully remove them from the skillet, keeping them intact, and drain on paper toweling. At this point the artichokes may be kept at room temperature until ready to finish cooking the *frittata.*

ABOUT 15 MINUTES BEFORE SERVING:

1. In a medium bowl, combine the eggs, water, oregano, monosodium glutamate, salt, and a few grinds of the pepper mill. Beat until well mixed but not frothy. Set aside.

2. Put the 3 tablespoons of olive oil in a 10-inch skillet pretty enough to come to the table, and heat. When it is quite hot, turn the heat to the lowest possible point and add the previously fried artichoke hearts, arranging them in a single layer as evenly spaced as possible. Pour the beaten eggs over them.

3. As the eggs set, run a spatula under the edge to loosen them, and tilt the pan to let the uncooked portion run underneath. If the top is runny, prick it with a fork so that the eggs will cook evenly. Neither the

top nor the bottom should be brown.

4. When the *frittata* is set but still soft, remove it from the heat, sprinkle it all over with the parsley-and-cheese mixture, and run it under the broiler for several minutes to brown a little.

TO SERVE: Bring to the table in the skillet, along with warm plates. Cut into pie-shaped wedges and accompany with bread sticks and butter or hot Herb Bread and a glass of medium-dry white wine.

BAKED EGGS AND SAUSAGES WITH CHEDDAR CAKES

8 SERVINGS OF SAUSAGES AND EGGS AND 36 TO 40 CHEDDAR CAKES

You will need 8 custard cups or ramekins and a shallow baking pan.

The Cheddar Cakes may be kept in an airtight container for several days, or frozen.

Cook the eggs and sausages just before serving.

The Cheddar Cakes
BUTTER *1 cup* (*2 sticks*), *softened, plus enough*

A way to glorify eggs—the Cheddar Cakes have a smooth, tangy filling.

THE CHEDDAR CAKES: Assemble and prepare all ingredients.

1. Put the 1 cup of softened butter into a bowl, and, using an electric mixer, beat until creamed. Add the cheese and continue beating until it is well combined but not oily.

2. Mix the flour with the cayenne pepper. Add gradually to the butter mixture, working it in first with the beater and then by hand until you have a fairly smooth dough.

3. Wrap tightly in waxed paper or foil and refrigerate for 1 hour.

WHEN READY TO BAKE AND FILL: 1. Preheat the oven to 350 degrees.

*extra for the baking
sheet*

SHARP CHEDDAR CHEESE
*To make 2 cups when
grated (8 ounces)*

ALL-PURPOSE FLOUR *To
make 2 cups when sifted,
plus extra for rolling*

CAYENE PEPPER *Generous
pinch*

The Filling

BUTTER *½ cup (1 stick),
softened*

SHARP CHEDDAR CHEESE
*To make 1½ cups when
grated (6 ounces)*

HOT MUSTARD *1½ tea-
spoons*

BRANDY *1 tablespoon*

WORCESTERSHIRE SAUCE
½ teaspoon

CAYENNE PEPPER *2
shakes*

The Sausages and Eggs

PORK SAUSAGES *16*

BUTTER *For custard cups,
plus extra for dotting
eggs*

FRESH EGGS *8*

LIGHT CREAM *½ cup*

SIMMERING WATER

SALT

**BLACK PEPPER, GROUND
FRESH**

2. Butter 1 or 2 baking sheets and set aside.

3. Lightly flour a pastry board or marble slab. Roll out the dough to ¼ inch thick. If necessary, lift the dough and sprinkle underneath with a little flour to keep it free-moving at all times.

4. Using a 2-inch round cookie cutter, cut in circles and place on baking sheets about ½ inch apart. Press the trimmings together, roll and cut out as many as you can. Place on the middle rack of the preheated oven. If your oven is small, refrigerate 1 batch while you bake the other. Bake for about 15 minutes or until golden.

5. Remove the cakes from the baking sheet and cool on racks.

6. Combine all the filling ingredients and cream together until well mixed.

7. When the cakes are cool, spread half of them with the filling and top each with 1 of the remaining rounds. Press together. If not used immediately, store in an airtight container for 2 or 3 days, or freeze. Bring to room temperature before serving. Cheese just doesn't taste as good cold!

THE SAUSAGES AND EGGS: Assemble all ingredients.

1. Pan-fry the sausages according to the package directions. Keep warm while you bake the eggs.

2. Preheat the oven to 350 degrees.

3. Butter the custard cups. Break 1 egg into each, top with 1 tablespoon of cream, and then dot each generously with butter.

4. Pour enough of the simmering water into a baking pan to reach about two-thirds of the height of the custard cups. Place the cups in the water and bake uncovered for 15 to 20 minutes. The eggs will be done when they are just set but still slightly trembly.

5. Remove from the water. Add salt and pepper to taste and serve at once.

TO SERVE: Put each custard cup on a small plate, about the size of a salad plate, along with 2 sausages. Put the Cheddar Cakes on a platter or in a basket and pass separately. A dry white wine is good with this.

FARMER'S BREAKFAST
(Bauernfruhstuck)

Our first Bauernfrühstück *was at a German inn high on the mountainside overlooking the meeting of the Moselle and the Rhine rivers. It went from late breakfast through a lazy afternoon full of the heady scent of the near-harvest vineyards in the late September sun. And all of this golden pleasure soothed by a number of bottles of Bernkasteler Riesling. But the dish is good in any setting—just don't forget the Rhine or Moselle wine!*

6 TO 8 SERVINGS

All the ingredients may be prepared ahead.

Begin cooking about 20 to 30 minutes before serving and warm the Herb Bread.

───────────

BACON 10 *medium-thick slices, cut in 1-inch pieces*

BACON FAT

POTATOES 4 *large, peeled, cut in half lengthwise, and then cut in slices*

Assemble and prepare all ingredients.

NOTE: If preparing ahead, the bacon may be cooked and crisped, the potatoes sliced and covered with water to which you have

crosswise, about ⅛ inch
thick (about 2 pounds)
ONIONS *To make 2 cups*
when peeled, cut in
quarters lengthwise, and
then sliced thin crosswise
(about 2 medium)
EGGS *10*
WATER *3 tablespoons*
SALT
BLACK PEPPER, GROUND
   FRESH

The Accompaniment
HERB BREAD, *page 316*

added a little lemon juice, and the onions
sliced and wrapped in plastic.

1. Put the bacon, part at a time, into a
cold skillet, and cook over low heat until it
is brown and crisp.

2. Using a slotted spoon, transfer the
pieces as they are done to paper towels to
drain. Reserve the bacon and bacon fat.

3. In the same skillet, heat the bacon
fat until a haze forms. Add the potato
slices, 1 at a time, layering them. (If they
have been soaking in water, drain and dry
them well first.)

4. Cook over moderate heat, lifting and
turning occasionally with a large spatula,
until they start to color a light gold.

5. Turn the heat to medium-high and
add the onions, lifting and turning occasionally until the onions are tender and
most of the potatoes are a light brown but
not mushy.

6. Break the eggs into a medium bowl.
Add the water, salt to taste, and a few
grindings of pepper. Beat very lightly—
just enough to break the yolks.

7. Sprinkle the reserved bacon pieces
evenly over the potatoes and pour in the
eggs evenly.

8. Reduce the heat to low and cook,
lifting the edges now and then and piercing the center with a fork so that the eggs
cook evenly.

9. The Bauernfrühstück is done when
the eggs are set but still creamy and moist.

TO SERVE: Bring the skillet to the table.

Cut into wedges to serve, pass the warm Herb Bread separately, and a Rhine or Moselle wine, well chilled.

MYSTERY SAVORY

8 SERVINGS

The ingredients may be chopped early in the day and refrigerated separately.

Warm the savory and toast the bread just before serving.

Serve warm.

————————

BUTTER *¼ cup*
ONIONS *To make 1½ cups when minced very fine (about 2 medium)*
FLAT ANCHOVY FILLETS IN OIL *1½ cans (2 ounces each), chopped to a paste, plus the oil from 1 can*
HARD-COOKED EGGS *6, chopped very fine*
BLACK PEPPER, GROUND FRESH
FIRM WHITE BREAD *8 slices, cut about ½ inch thick: do not remove the crusts*

The idea for this savory came from a very old English cookbook. If you chop the ingredients fine enough, so their texture does not give them away, the indefinable flavor will have your guests completely mystified. Make them guess. They'll enjoy the game and the savory.

Assemble and prepare all ingredients.

1. Melt the butter in a large saucepan or skillet over moderate heat. When it stops bubbling, add the chopped onions and sauté, turning frequently until soft and golden but not brown.

2. Take off the heat and add the anchovy fillets, the oil from the can, and the chopped eggs. Blend thoroughly.

3. Return to the heat and stir until just warmed through. Season with 3 or 4 grinds of the pepper mill. You won't need salt. Keep warm while you toast the slices of bread.

4. Toast the bread on 1 side only. Place the slices toasted side down on a counter or breadboard. Divide the mixture and mound it on the toast. Then cut each slice into quarters diagonally.

TO SERVE: Put four quarter pieces on each small individual plate. Garnish each plate

The Garnish
PARSLEY OR WATERCRESS
SPRIGS

with a sprig of parsley or watercress. This may also be served from a tray or platter and eaten out of hand.

Vegetables

BAGNA CAUDA (HOT BATH)

One of the finest contributions of Italian cooking. The secret of perfection is in using only the very freshest of vegetables.

THE VEGETABLES: Assemble and prepare all ingredients.

If prepared a day ahead, wrap each vegetable separately in plastic wrap and refrigerate to crisp. If prepared the same day, soak in a bowl of ice cubes for an hour to crisp, dry thoroughly, wrap each vegetable separately in plastic wrap, and refrigerate.

THE SAUCE: Assemble and prepare all ingredients.

Put the butter and olive oil in a small saucepan over low heat until the butter is melted. Add the garlic and sauté very briefly, keeping the heat low. Add the mashed anchovies, stirring vigorously to blend. Cook a minute or two longer; do not let the mixture color. If the sauce is made ahead, refrigerate, or keep at room

6 SERVINGS

You will need a 1½- or 2-cup heatproof earthenware or enamel crock or a 6-inch skillet that will fit over a candle warmer, spirit lamp, or electric hot tray, and 6 skewers.

May be prepared a day ahead, but rewarm the sauce before serving.

If increasing the recipe, you will need 2 crocks and 2 warmers.

Serve the sauce hot and the vegetables cold.

The Vegetables

WHOLE, FRESH MUSH-
ROOMS *12 medium,
stems cut off evenly with
the base of the caps:
wipe with a damp towel*

FRESH, CRISP RED
RADISHES *12, cleaned
but not peeled: cut off
the root but leave 2 or
2½ inches of the stem
end and a few of the
green leaves, if there are
any, to hold for dipping*

SCALLIONS *12, cut in 3-to-
4-inch lengths: wash
thoroughly, trim off the
root ends and the tough
outer skin*

GREEN OR RED BELL
PEPPER *1 medium, cut
in 1-inch squares: first
remove veins and seeds*

YOUNG, FRESH ASPARAGUS
WITH TIGHT TIPS *12,
cut in 4-inch lengths
measuring from the tip
(discard the lower part):
use a swivel-bladed
peeler to trim off the
tough outer fibers*

CARROTS *2 medium, cut in
¼-inch rounds*

YOUNG, FRESH ZUCCHINI
*3, the smallest you can
find (no more than 4
inches long): wash well,*

temperature for a few hours. Rewarm just before serving.

TO SERVE: 1. Take 1 or 2 large platters or plates, or 2 sectioned plates. Arrange the vegetables attractively in them—each variety in its own little group.

2. Rewarm the sauce and put it in a serving crock or skillet. Set on a tray over a candle warmer or other source of heat.

3. Slice the bread and put it in a basket.

4. Put the tray in the center of the table and place the breadbasket and vegetables nearby.

TO EAT: Pick up a vegetable piece in the fingers of your right hand or impale it on a skewer. In your left hand, pick up a slice of bread. Swirl the vegetable in the sauce. As you lift it from the sauce, hold the slice of bread under it to catch any drips. Eventually the bread soaks up enough sauce to become a delicious morsel. Eat both, and take more vegetables and bread. Keep eating until you or the vegetables give out.

At the very end, when everyone has had his fill, there will be a few hearty souls, including us, who will take a piece of bread, or 2, or 3, or 4—and mop up the saucepan. Our friends have been known to fight politely over who gets the last swipe!

Break the rhythm only for a sip of dry red wine.

*dry, and cut lengthwise
in quarters*

YOUNG, TENDER SPINACH
*A handful of the smallest
leaves, thoroughly
washed and dried: leave
the stems on to hold for
dipping*

**BROCCOLI FLOWERETS
WITH TIGHT BUDS**
*12, washed, dried, and cut
off where the stem joins
the main stalk; trim the
stems with a swivel-
bladed peeler*

**CAULIFLOWER FLOWER-
ETS WITH TIGHT BUDS**
*12, washed and dried:
leave about 1 inch of
stem on to hold for
dipping*

The Sauce
BUTTER *½ cup (1 stick)*
OLIVE OIL *½ cup*
GARLIC *4 large cloves,
peeled and minced*
**FLAT ANCHOVY FILLETS
IN OIL** *10 to 12 (2-
ounce can), drained and
mashed to a paste*

The Accompaniment
**FRENCH OR ITALIAN
BREAD** *1 or 2 loaves, the
smallest diameter possi-
ble, cut in ¼-inch slices
just before serving*

STUFFED LETTUCE LEAVES

6 TO 8 SERVINGS
(2 ROLLS EACH)

The filling may be made up to a day ahead and reheated before serving.

The same amount of diced, cooked pork or turkey may be substituted.

Serve the filling hot and the lettuce icy cold and crisp.

FIRM ICEBERG LETTUCE *1 large head*

OIL *¼ cup*

ONIONS *To make ¾ cup when chopped fine (about 1 medium)*

CHINESE DRIED MUSH-ROOMS *8, soaked in hot water for 15 minutes, then drained and chopped fine: remove the stems*

OR CANNED SLICED MUSHROOMS *To make ½ cup when drained and sautéed in a little butter*

CANNED WATER CHEST-NUTS *12, chopped fine*

COOKED CHICKEN *To*

The contrast between the hot filling and the icy cold lettuce leaves is surprisingly delicious!

Assemble and prepare all ingredients.

1. Several hours ahead wash and split the head of lettuce in half vertically with a long, sharp knife. Remove and discard the triangular-shaped hard center core. Discard the outside leaves and peel away 16 or 20 of the largest leaf halves. Pat them dry and wrap them in a damp towel. Reserve in the refrigerator.

2. Put the oil in a large skillet and when it is hot, add the onions and sauté them over moderate heat until they are soft but not brown.

3. Add the dried or canned mushrooms, water chestnuts, chicken, and ¾ cup of the chicken broth. Mix well and heat, stirring frequently.

4. While the broth heats, combine the cornstarch, soy sauce, sugar, and monosodium glutamate in a small bowl. Add it, stirring, to the chicken mixture.

5. Cook, stirring rapidly, for about 15 seconds. The mixture should be thick and hold together. If it is too juicy, mix together a little more soy sauce and cornstarch and add it, stirring, until you achieve the right consistency. If it is too dry, add a little more chicken broth. Add salt and pepper to taste. The mixture should be moist but not soupy. At this

make 2 cups when diced

CHICKEN BROTH ¾ cup,
plus a little more if
necessary

CORNSTARCH 1 tablespoon,
plus a little more if
necessary

SOY SAUCE 1 tablespoon,
plus a little more if
necessary

SUGAR ½ teaspoon

MONOSODIUM GLUTA-
MATE 1 teaspoon

SALT

BLACK PEPPER, GROUND
FRESH

WALNUTS OR CASHEW
NUTS To make ½ cup
when cut in medium-
small dice: do not use a
nut grinder

point it may be refrigerated up to a day
ahead.

JUST BEFORE SERVING: Reheat the
chicken mixture and blend in the walnuts
or cashews. Add a little more chicken
broth if necessary to bring it back to the
original consistency.

TO SERVE: Put the chicken into a warm
bowl and accompany it with a platter of
icy cold, crisp lettuce leaves. Let each
guest help himself to a lettuce leaf and
spoon a generous tablespoon of the
chicken into it, roll up with his fingers,
and eat while the chicken is hot. This is
so good it deserves champagne.

TOMATO AND AVOCADO PIE

8 SERVINGS

The biscuit crust may be
made up to 3 hours
ahead.

Assemble and bake just
before serving.

———————

BUTTER FOR PAN

ALL-PURPOSE FLOUR To
make 2 cups when sifted

*Our pie has garden-fresh flavors, lightly
herbed and pleasantly enhanced with
cheese.*

Assemble and prepare all ingredients except the avocados.

1. Butter a 9- or 10-inch pie pan well
and set aside.

2. Sift the 2 cups of flour, baking
powder, and salt together into a medium
bowl.

3. Add the chunks of butter to the

*before measuring, plus
extra for rolling*
BAKING POWDER *4 tea-
spoons*
SALT *1 teaspoon*
BUTTER *¼ cup, cut into
chunks*
PARSLEY *To make ¼ cup
when minced*
BLACK PEPPER, GROUND
FRESH *½ teaspoon*
MILK *⅔ cup, plus a little
more if necessary*
DIJON MUSTARD
AVOCADOS *2 medium,
peeled, pitted, and sliced
about ¼ inch thick*
FIRM RIPE TOMATOES *4
or 5 (about 3 inches in
diameter), cut in slices
about ⅜ to ½ inch
thick: first remove the
stem and blossom ends
and peel them, then cut
in half crosswise and
squeeze and shake to
discard the liquid and
seeds, then slice (you will
get about 4 slices from
each tomato)*
CHIVES *To make 2 table-
spoons when snipped*
BASIL *1½ teaspoons,
crumbled, if dried, or, if
fresh, to make 1½
tablespoons when
chopped*

mixture. Using the tips of your fingers, a large fork, or 2 knives, scissors-fashion, work the butter into the flour until the mixture resembles coarse oatmeal. Don't worry if you have a few larger pieces, they will blend in the next steps.

4. Add the parsley and pepper and combine.

5. Make a well in the center of the mixture and pour in ⅔ cup of milk all at once. Using a fork, stir slowly around the bowl to scrape the flour into the liquid. If the mixture seems dry, add a little more milk, but just enough to form a dough that leaves the sides of the bowl and forms a ball. It should be moist but not wet.

6. Put the dough on a lightly floured board or marble slab and knead about 10 times. If the dough is sticky, sprinkle with a little more flour, but the less the better.

7. Gently roll out from the center, alternating directions, to form a circle about ⅛ inch thick and 2 inches larger than the diameter of the pie pan. Be sure the dough is free-moving at all times. If it starts to stick, use a spatula to loosen it and sprinkle a little flour underneath. If the rolling pin sticks, pat a little flour on the top surface too.

8. Gently and loosely roll about half of the circle of dough onto the rolling pin. Center it over the prepared pie pan and unroll. Then ease the dough into the pan lightly, pressing it gently onto the bottom and sides.

SALT

BLACK PEPPER, GROUND
    FRESH

MAYONNAISE, PREFER-
    ABLY HOMEMADE
    (*page 296*) *1 cup*

SHARP CHEDDAR CHEESE
    *To make 1 cup when
    grated (about ¼ pound)*

The Accompaniment
FRESH FRUIT (OPTIONAL)

9. Fold the overhanging dough under and bring it up over the rim of the pie pan. Pinch all around to flute and form a high edge.

10. Spread the bottom and sides, but not the fluted edge, generously with mustard. At this point you may refrigerate the crust for up to 3 hours.

ABOUT 45 MINUTES BEFORE SERVING:
1. Preheat the oven to 400 degrees.

2. Slice the avocados and set aside.

3. Remove the biscuit crust from the refrigerator, and using about half of the tomato slices, place a generous layer of them on it, then a layer of the sliced avocados. Sprinkle with the chives, and finish with another layer of tomatoes.

4. Sprinkle the top with the basil and add salt and pepper to taste.

5. Thoroughly blend the mayonnaise with the cheese and spread evenly over the top, like the frosting on a cake.

6. Bake on the middle rack of the preheated oven for from 25 to 35 minutes, or until the edges of the crust are a light brown and the top is beautifully golden. Serve hot.

TO SERVE: Bring the pie to the table, cut in wedges, and serve on warm plates. Accompany with a bowl of fresh fruit and a glass of rosé wine, if you wish.

Sandwiches and Breads

PUPUSAS
("Sandwiches" from Central America)

The Pupusas may be made
and filled a day ahead
and refrigerated.

A *tortilla* press is helpful
but not essential.

Cook just before serving.

The Filling

OIL *2 tablespoons*

ONION *To make ½ cup
when peeled and chopped
fine*

GREEN BELL PEPPER *To
make ¼ cup when
chopped fine: first re-
move the core, seeds,
and white veins*

LEAN GROUND BEEF OR

*These "sandwiches" are filled with a tasty
meat mixture and are very substantial.
One per person is plenty.* Masa harina *is
a dry form of the fresh corn mixture used
in the Latin countries for* tortillas *and in
many other dishes. It is readily available
in the West, Southwest and Texas, Chi-
cago and New York. In other areas check
specialty markets and gourmet shops.*

Assemble and prepare all ingredients.

THE FILLING: 1. Heat a medium skillet.
Add the oil and, when a haze starts to
form, add the onions and green peppers.
Turn the heat to low and sauté them,
stirring frequently, until the onions start
to soften but do not color.

2. Add the ground beef or pork, break-
ing it apart with a fork. Continue to sauté,
stirring frequently, until the meat loses its
color. Do not let it brown.

PORK *1 pound*

TOMATO SAUCE *1 can*
(*10-ounce size*)

GARLIC *2 cloves, peeled*
and minced with a little
salt

CHILE POWDER *2 tea-*
spoons

DRIED OREGANO LEAVES
½ teaspoon, crumbled

GROUND CUMIN *¼ tea-*
spoon

GROUND CORIANDER *1*
teaspoon

MONTEREY JACK CHEESE
To make 2 cups when
grated

SALT

The Fresh Masa
Tortillas

MASA HARINA (QUAKER
BRAND) *4 cups, plus a*
little more for rolling

SALT *1½ teaspoons*

PAPRIKA *½ teaspoon*

GROUND CUMIN *½*
teaspoon

COLD WATER *2⅔ cups,*
plus a little more if
necessary

WAXED PAPER *48 pieces*
cut about 6 inches square

The Accompaniment

LETTUCE *To make 3 cups*
when shredded

3. Add the tomato sauce, garlic, *chile* powder, oregano, the ¼ teaspoon of cumin, and the coriander. Stir well. Increase the heat and bring it to a simmer. Continue simmering, uncovered, until the liquid in the bottom of the pan has evaporated, but the mixture is still slightly moist.

4. Remove it from the heat, and let it cool to room temperature. Then stir in the cheese until it is well blended. Add salt to taste. Set aside.

THE MASA TORTILLAS: 1. In a large bowl, combine the *masa harina,* salt, paprika, and the ½ teaspoon of cumin. Stir in the water and knead and press together by hand to blend well. If necessary, add a little more water to make the dough stick together. It should be damp and silky but not sticky.

2. Divide the dough into quarters. From each quarter form 6 balls, each about 1½ inches in diameter. You will have a total of 24 balls.

3. Take 24 squares of waxed paper, put a ball on each square, and sprinkle each lightly with a little dry *masa harina.* Cover each ball with 1 of the remaining 24 squares of waxed paper. Using a rolling pin, the palm of your hand, or a *tortilla* press, gently press each into a 5-inch circle.

TO ASSEMBLE AND COOK THE PUPUSAS:
1. For each Papusa, peel the top paper from one circle, letting the bottom paper re-

RADISHES *To make 1 cup*
   when sliced thin
COMMERCIAL SOUR CREAM
   About ¾ cup, or enough
   to bind the lettuce and
   radishes
SALT
BLACK PEPPER, GROUND
   FRESH

main. Spread a slightly rounded ¼ cup of the reserved filling on it, bringing it to within ½ inch of the edge.

2. Peel the top paper from a second circle and invert the *tortilla* over the filling like a sandwich. Then carefully peel off the remaining top paper. (Tear the paper into strips if necessary for easier removal.) Don't worry if the dough tears a little—just press the torn edges together. Repeat until all the *tortillas* are filled.

3. Taking 1 at a time, carefully hold the edges with 2 fingers of the left hand and with the forefinger of the right hand, gently push and flute the edges together to seal. Don't press so hard that the edges get thin. Let the bottom piece of wax paper remain. At this point the sandwiches may be refrigerated up to a day ahead. Put them in a single layer on a baking sheet and cover lightly with plastic wrap or foil.

ABOUT ½ HOUR BEFORE SERVING: 1. Heat an ungreased griddle or skillet, Teflon preferred, over low heat. Taking 2 or 3 Pupusas at a time, depending upon the size of your griddle, invert them on it, top side down. The waxed-paper side will be up. They should be well separated. Pull off the remaining waxed paper.

2. Cook them for 7 or 8 minutes, or until the bottom is lightly browned. Turn them over and cook for 7 or 8 minutes more until the second side is lightly browned and the Pupusas are heated through.

3. Keep them warm in a very low oven

until all are cooked. Serve hot.

4. While they cook mix the lettuce and radishes with enough sour cream to bind them together. Add salt and pepper to taste.

TO SERVE: Put the Pupusas on individual plates. Put the lettuce mixture into a bowl to pass. To eat, each guest will gently squeeze the Pupusa to open it about half-way and spoon a little of the lettuce-and-radish mixture inside. Eat with a knife and fork.

CROQUE MONSIEUR

This delicious sandwich has an obscure French past but a brilliant present. Cut in half to serve as a first course and in bite-sized portions as a cocktail hors d'oeuvre, it is irresistible in any size.

2 SANDWICHES

The sandwiches may be assembled hours ahead.

At its best fried just before serving, but may be fried in advance and reheated in a 375-degree oven for 5 minutes.

SANDWICH BREAD, THE
 BEST FIRM, HOME-
 MADE-TYPE AVAILABLE
 *4 slices, cut about ⅜
 inch thick*
SOFTENED BUTTER
DIJON MUSTARD
MOZZARELLA OR SWISS
 CHEESE *To make ⅔ cup*

Assemble and prepare all ingredients.

1. Lay out the 4 slices of bread and lightly spread 1 side of each with butter and then with mustard.

2. Sprinkle 2 of the slices with half of the grated cheese, pressing it down.

3. Cover the cheese with 1 slice of ham.

4. Sprinkle each ham slice with part of the remaining cheese.

5. Take the remaining bread and lay it, buttered side down, on top of each sandwich. Press firmly together with the palm of your hand. At this point the sandwiches may be covered tightly with plastic wrap and set aside.

when grated (*a scant ¼
pound*)

COOKED HAM *2 slices, cut
⅛ inch thick and
trimmed to the exact
dimensions of the bread*

SALAD OIL *3 tablespoons,
or a little more if necessary*

EGG *1, well beaten until it
is light and extremely
fluffy*

MIXED WITH:

MILK *2 tablespoons*

AND

SALT *⅛ teaspoon*

JUST BEFORE SERVING: 1. Put about 3
tablespoons of oil in a frying pan and heat.

2. In the meantime dip the sandwiches
in the beaten egg, milk, and salt mixture,
turning them carefully so that both sides
are soaked.

3. Fry them slowly on each side so that
the cheese will melt and they will become
golden-brown and crisp. Add more oil as
needed.

TO SERVE: Cut each sandwich into 2 sections and serve hot to 2 guests. Accompany with a bottle of dry white wine.

REUBEN SANDWICH

*If Arnold Reuben of New York restaurant
fame doesn't enter the Gates of Heaven
because of his generosity to starving actors,
this sandwich, his creation, will certainly
get him in.*

6 SANDWICHES

You will need toothpicks
to secure the sand-
wiches.

The ingredients may be
prepared ahead, but
should be assembled
just before serving.

RYE BREAD, PREFERABLY
DARK *18 slices, cut ⅛
inch thick*

RUSSIAN DRESSING *1
recipe, page 298*

SWISS CHEESE *12 thin
slices, trimmed to fit the
bread*

Assemble and prepare all ingredients.

1. Just before serving, line up 18 slices
of bread on a flat surface. Spread each slice
generously with part of the Russian Dressing, bringing it all the way out to the
edges. Proceed as follows:

FIRST: Take 6 of the bread slices and
place them near you, dressing side up.

SECOND: Put 1 slice of cheese on each.

THIRD: Spoon 2 tablespoons of sauerkraut on top of each slice of cheese, spreading it to the edges.

COLD COOKED SAUER-
KRAUT *To make about
1½ cups when well
drained by pressing
against the edge of a
sieve and chopped in
½-to-1-inch strands: see
note at end of recipe for
improving flavor*
COOKED CORNED BEEF 24
*thin slices, trimmed to fit
the bread*
BUTTER *Softened to room
temperature*
OIL FOR GRILLING

The Accompaniment
DILL PICKLES 3 *or 4, cut in
quarters lengthwise*
OLIVES

FOURTH: Cover each with 2 slices of the corned beef.

FIFTH: Take 6 more bread slices and put 1 on each sandwich, dressing side down.

SIXTH: Spread each top slice of bread generously with more dressing, bringing it to the edges.

SEVENTH: Spoon 2 more tablespoons of sauerkraut over it, spreading it to the edges.

EIGHTH: Top each with 2 more slices of corned beef.

NINTH: Top each with 1 more slice of cheese.

TENTH: Cover each with the remaining slices of bread, dressing side down.

2. Spread the outside surfaces of each sandwich with softened butter and secure them with toothpicks.

3. Put a little oil on a grill or into a large skillet. When it is very hot, grill the sandwiches in it until they are a light golden-brown on one side and the cheese has melted slightly. Then turn and grill on the other side.

TO SERVE: Bring to the table on individual plates, each garnished with 3 or 4 pickle wedges and a few olives. You'll probably want to use a knife and fork. Warn your guests of the hidden toothpicks. Accompany with icy cold beer.

TO IMPROVE CANNED SAUERKRAUT: Drain off the canning liquid and rinse under cold running water. Drain. Chop and cook in ½-to-⅔-cup of dry white wine. Drain for use in the sandwich.

QUICK PISSALADIERES WITH THREE FILLINGS

6 TO 8 SERVINGS

All the fillings may be made up to a day in advance, but the shrimp filling must be made at least 6 hours ahead.

The English muffins may be toasted several hours ahead.

Assemble, garnish, and warm in the oven just before serving.

The Shrimp Filling

WINE VINEGAR 2 *tablespoons*

DIJON MUSTARD *1 teaspoon*

SALT ⅛ teaspoon

BLACK PEPPER, GROUND FRESH

OLIVE OIL ¼ *cup*

SALAD OIL ¼ *cup*

GARLIC *1 large clove, peeled and minced with a little salt*

Easier than it looks. We use split and scooped-out English muffins as a base. Then we fill part of them with the classic onion, anchovy, and black olive combination. We fill the rest with sautéed mushrooms and marinated shrimp—but not mixed! The marinated shrimp was inspired by Elizabeth David in her book French Provincial Cooking.

Assemble and prepare all fillings.

THE SHRIMP FILLING: 1. In a medium bowl, put the vinegar, mustard, salt, and a few grinds of pepper. Mix well. Then beat in the olive and salad oils, a little at a time. Add the garlic and oregano and combine.

2. Add the cooked, cut shrimp and the 8 whole shrimp reserved for garnish.

3. Toss together until the shrimp are well coated with the marinade. It may be necessary to press them down a little. Cover tightly and refrigerate at least 6 hours, or up to a day ahead. Stir occasionally.

THE ONION FILLING: 1. In a 10- or 12-inch skillet, put the water, olive oil, salt, and pepper to taste. Add the quartered

DRIED OREGANO LEAVES
¼ teaspoon, crumbled

COOKED MEDIUM SHRIMP,
OR CANNED TINY
SHRIMP *To make 1½*
cups when simmered,
peeled, and cut in ¼-
inch chunks (about 1¼
pounds uncooked):
reserve 8 of the prettiest
whole ones for garnish;
if using canned tiny
shrimp, it is not necessary
to cut them

The Garnish

RESERVED WHOLE SHRIMP
8

PITTED GREEN OLIVES *8,*
halved lengthwise

The Onion Filling

WATER *¾ cup*

OLIVE OIL *¼ cup*

SALT *½ teaspoon: be*
cautious about adding
more, the anchovies will
be salty

BLACK PEPPER, GROUND
FRESH

ONIONS *To make 4 cups*
when peeled and sliced
into thin rounds, then
each round cut in quarters
(about 1¼ pounds)

GARLIC *3 or 4 cloves,*
peeled and minced with

onion rounds, mix thoroughly, and bring the liquid to a boil.

2. Continue to boil, uncovered, over high heat until most of the liquid has evaporated. Stir frequently.

3. Turn the heat to medium and continue to cook until the onions are a light gold, but no darker. Stir frequently. Remove from the heat, stir in the garlic and refrigerate, covered, up to a day ahead.

THE MUSHROOM FILLING: 1. Heat the olive oil in a large skillet. When it is hot, add the mushrooms and sauté over medium heat until they are soft and all the liquid has evaporated, leaving just a trace of oil at the bottom of the pan. Add salt and pepper to taste.

2. In a small separate bowl, mix together the tomato paste and sugar.

3. Refrigerate the mushrooms and tomato paste separately, covered, up to a day ahead.

THE ENGLISH MUFFINS: 1. Split each muffin into 2 rounds.

2. Insert the point of a small, sharp knife about ³⁄₁₆ inch between the crust and the soft part of each half; then carefully saw all around, not more than ¼ inch deep.

3. Pull or scoop out the soft center to form a shell with the bottom and side wall about ³⁄₁₆ inch thick. Work carefully and slowly so as not to break the shell, but still have it scooped out enough to hold a generous amount of the filling.

a little salt

The Garnish

FLAT ANCHOVY FILLETS
  IN OIL *1 can (2-ounce*
  size): *if they are very*
  salty, drain them, soak in
  cold water for no more
  than an hour, and dry on
  paper towels before
  using; reserve the can-
  ning oil
PITTED BLACK OLIVES *8,*
  cut lengthwise into
  quarters

The Mushroom Filling

OLIVE OIL *3 tablespoons*
FRESH MUSHROOMS *To*
  make 4 cups when sliced
  thin lengthwise, retaining
  the stems (¾ to 1
  pound): *first wipe with*
  a damp paper towel
SALT
BLACK PEPPER, GROUND
  FRESH
TOMATO PASTE *¼ cup*
SUGAR *¼ teaspoon*

ENGLISH MUFFINS,
  PREFERABLY MADE OF
  SOURDOUGH *12*
RESERVED MARINATING
  OIL FROM THE SHRIMP
RESERVED CANNING OIL
  FROM THE ANCHOVIES

4. Put the shells under the broiler and toast them very lightly. Reserve until ready to fill. This may be done several hours ahead.

TO ASSEMBLE AND FILL: 1. About 30 minutes before serving, preheat the oven to 350 degrees.

2. Assemble all the prepared fillings, and the prepared green olives, anchovy canning oil, anchovies, black olives, tomato paste, and extra olive oil.

THE SHRIMP PISSALADIERES: 1. Drain the shrimp filling and reserve the marinade and the whole shrimp.

2. Take 8 of the toasted muffin halves and drizzle about ½ teaspoon of the marinade on the inside bottom of each.

3. Divide the shrimp filling among them.

4. Garnish each with a whole shrimp and 2 green olive halves.

5. Drizzle about ¼ teaspoon more marinade over each and place on a baking sheet.

THE ONION PISSALADIERES: 1. Take 8 more of the toasted muffin halves and drizzle about ¼ teaspoon of the reserved anchovy canning oil on the inside bottom of each. (If you do not have enough, use a little olive oil.)

2. Divide the onion filling among them.

3. Separate the anchovies. (If you have soaked them in water, drain and dry them well.) Taking 2 fillets at a time, place

OLIVE OIL, FOR DRIZZLING

them on top of the onions at right angles to each other to form a cross. If necessary, split the anchovies in half or patch pieces to have a sufficient number.

4. Place a black olive slice between each section of the cross. Place on the baking sheet.

THE MUSHROOM PISSALADIERES: 1. Take the remaining 8 toasted muffin halves and spread the inside of each with part of the tomato paste.

2. Divide the mushroom filling among them, and drizzle each with about ¼ teaspoon of olive oil. Place on the baking sheet.

TO HEAT AND SERVE: 1. Place the baking sheet on the center rack of the preheated oven and bake for 10 to 15 minutes or until heated through.

2. Arrange the Pissaladières on a heated platter or hot tray. Give a warm plate and a knife and fork to each guest. Fingers are allowed. Each will help himself. Accompany with a dry red or white wine or beer.

AZTEC CORN BREAD WITH A BIG BOWL OF FRUIT

12 SERVINGS

You will need an iron skillet about 11 inches wide at the top, or a flat-bottomed 2-quart casserole, or 2 bread

The creamed corn adds moisture, the seasonings add zip, to a new improved corn bread that will surprise you.

THE CORN BREAD: Assemble and prepare all ingredients.

pans, each about 8 by 4½ by 3 inches.

The bread may be made a day ahead, tightly wrapped in foil, and refrigerated, or it may be frozen: bring to room temperature and reheat before serving.

The fruit may be prepared in the morning.

Serve the corn bread warm and the fruit chilled.

The Corn Bread

OIL OR BACON GREASE FOR PAN

ALL-PURPOSE FLOUR *1½ cups, unsifted*

YELLOW CORN MEAL *1½ cups*

BAKING POWDER *4 teaspoons*

SUGAR *3 tablespoons*

SALT *2 teaspoons*

MILK *2½ cups*

EGGS *3, beaten*

SALAD OIL *½ cup*

BACON *8 thin slices, fried crisp and then crumbled (you may use the bacon drippings to grease the baking pan)*

1. Preheat the oven to 425 degrees.

2. Generously oil or grease the baking pan and set aside.

3. Sift together into a large bowl the flour, corn meal, baking powder, sugar, and salt.

4. In a separate bowl, combine the milk, eggs, and salad oil. Pour the wet into the dry ingredients, combining them thoroughly with a few rapid strokes.

5. Add the crumbled bacon, onion, garlic, *jalapeño* peppers, pimientos, corn, and cheese. Combine well. The mixture will be quite thin.

6. Pour the batter into the prepared pan and bake it on the middle rack of the preheated oven for 35 to 40 minutes, or until a skewer inserted in the center comes out clean.

7. Remove from the oven, place on a rack, and let it cool in the pan. You may either refrigerate it up to a day ahead or freeze it. Either way, reheat it well, covered with foil, in a hot oven before serving.

A BIG BOWL OF FRUIT: Assemble and prepare all the ingredients except the bananas and ice early in the day.

The oranges: Peel and cut into sections. Insert a skewer in each section.

The pineapple: Peel and cut in quarters lengthwise. Remove the eyes and core. Slice in 1-inch or 1½-inch sections. Insert a bamboo skewer in each.

The strawberries: Wash but do not stem them.

The fresh coconut: Crack and break

GRATED ONION *To make 3½ tablespoons of juice and pulp*

GARLIC *4 cloves, peeled and minced with a little salt*

CANNED JALAPENO PEPPERS *To make ½ cup when drained and chopped fine: remove any seeds and veins*

CANNED PIMIENTOS *To make ½ cup when drained and chopped fine*

CANNED CREAM-STYLE CORN *1 cup*

SHARP YELLOW OR CHEDDAR CHEESE *To make 1½ cups when grated (about 6 ounces)*

The Fruit Bowl

The fruits, except for the bananas, may be prepared early in the day.

You will need 2 large bowls, one to fit inside the other, cracked and cubed ice, and bamboo skewers.

CHOOSE AS MANY AS YOU WISH OF THE FOLLOWING, BUT AT LEAST 4: THE LIMES ARE A MUST

NAVEL ORANGES

away the outer husk. Remove the brown skin, and break into chunks. See page 182 for instructions on opening a coconut.

Melon or papaya: Peel and cut in wedges about 3 inches long. Insert a skewer in each.

At this point you may cover the fruit tightly with plastic wrap and refrigerate until ready to serve.

JUST BEFORE SERVING: 1. Reheat the corn bread, well covered with foil, in a hot oven.

2. Prepare the bananas by peeling them halfway down and rolling back the skin or tucking it in.

3. Put a large bowl into a larger bowl of cracked ice. Place the fruit of your choice in the inner bowl. Add the prepared bananas and arrange attractively. Squeeze the juice of 1 or 2 limes over all and add plenty of ice cubes here and there.

TO SERVE: Cut the corn bread in wedges and bring it to the table in its pan. Put on individual plates. A fork for each guest may be necessary. Pass the bowl of fruit and have plenty of paper napkins handy.

FRESH PINEAPPLE

LARGE STRAWBERRIES

FRESH COCONUT

MELON

PAPAYA

BANANAS: THE SMALLEST
   YOU CAN FIND

LIMES

GOUGERE

8 SERVINGS

Fresh-made Pâte à Choux
   paste is a must.

May be baked early in the
   day and reheated or not
   as you wish.

Or it may be baked and
   frozen: bring to room
   temperature and reheat
   until crisp.

Serve warm or cold.

—————

OIL FOR BAKING SHEET

DIJON MUSTARD *1½*
   teaspoons

TABASCO SAUCE *3 or 4*
   dashes

SWISS OR GRUYERE
   CHEESE *To make 1½*
   cups when grated fresh:
   reserve ¼ cup for

A cheese bread frequently served at wine tastings in France, to "cleanse the palate." Everyone enjoys it—you'll find yourself looking for reasons to make and serve it.

Assemble and prepare all ingredients.

1. Lightly oil a baking sheet and set aside.

2. Preheat the oven to 375 degrees.

3. Beat the mustard, Tabasco sauce, and 1¼ cups of the cheese into the Pâte à Choux paste.

4. Using about three-quarters of the paste and a serving spoon or large soup spoon, scoop up heaping ½ spoonfuls of the paste, and place, one mound just touching the next one, on the baking sheet to form a ring with an empty center. Push each off the spoon with a spatula. You should have 12 equal-size mounds, each about 1½ to 2 inches across. To form a circle more easily, follow the numbers on the diagram below: first place mound 1, then opposite mound 2, then midway,

sprinkling the top (about 6 ounces)

PATE A CHOUX PASTE, FRESH-MADE *1 recipe, page 304*

MILK FOR PAINTING TOP

mound 3 and opposite mound 4. Then fill in mounds 5 through 12.

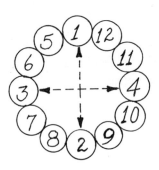

5. Using a teaspoon and the remaining paste, place a small mound on top of each larger mound. With a pastry brush, paint the top but not the sides lightly with a little milk. Pat lightly so that there are no "peaks" to the paste. Be sure that the milk doesn't drip down the sides or it will prevent the puffs from rising properly.

6. Take the remaining ¼ cup of cheese, place a dab on each mound, and wipe up any spills on the sheet.

7. Bake on the center rack of the preheated oven for 45 to 50 minutes, or until the ring becomes puffed, crusty, and a deep golden-brown. Do not open the door while the Gougère is rising, and resist the temptation to remove it from the oven too soon. It must be dry, with only an occasional bubble of butter showing.

8. Remove from the oven and slide the Gougère onto a wire rack. Use a small, sharp knife and twist it to make a circular hole about ½ inch in diameter near the bottom of each puff, to release the steam and dry any dampness inside. Turn off the

oven and return the Gougère to it for 5 to 10 minutes more, to dry thoroughly.

TO SERVE: Put on a large plate and bring to the table. Break in serving-size wedges and accompany with a glass of rosé or red wine. Serve warm or cold.

NOTE: To reheat the baked pastry, place on a baking sheet in a 350-degree oven for about 15 minutes.

CHEESE

CHEESE IN CAPTIVITY

8 SERVINGS

The sauce may be cooked a day ahead.

The cheese may be coated in the morning, but must be chilled 1 hour before frying.

OLIVE OIL *⅓ cup*
ONION *To make ¾ cup when chopped fine (1 medium)*
TOMATOES *To make 4½ cups when peeled and cut in medium chunks: retain seeds and juice (5 or 6 large)*
DRIED BASIL LEAVES *1½ teaspoons, crumbled*
GROUND THYME *⅛ teaspoon*

Unless you have tasted a warm, soft cheese not yet at the liquid stage, you can't imagine how delicious it can be. The slightly tangy sauce complements but doesn't overwhelm. Try it and then attempt to describe the taste sensation to a friend.

Assemble and prepare all ingredients.

1. Heat the ⅓ cup of olive oil in a large skillet or a 2- or 3-quart heavy-bottomed saucepan.

2. When the oil is hot, add the onions and sauté them over medium heat, stirring frequently, until they are soft and translucent but not brown.

3. Add the tomatoes, their juice and seeds, the basil, thyme, and sugar.

4. Raise the heat and bring the mixture to a boil, then lower the heat to moderate and cook fairly briskly. While cooking, mash and break up the tomatoes with the back of a large spoon or fork.

5. Continue to cook for 45 to 60 min-

SUGAR *½ teaspoon*

SALT

BLACK PEPPER, GROUND
   FRESH

FLOUR *⅓ cup*

MILK *¼ cup*
   MIXED WITH:

EGG *1, whole, lightly beaten*

DRY BREAD CRUMBS,
   GROUND FINE *⅓ cup*
   MIXED WITH:

PAPRIKA *1 teaspoon*

MONTEREY JACK CHEESE
   (TELEME OR ANY
   OTHER SOFTLY MELT-
   ING UNPROCESSED
   CHEESE MAY BE
   SUBSTITUTED) *8
   oblongs, 3 inches long by
   1½ inches wide by ½
   inch thick*

OIL (EITHER OLIVE OIL
   OR SALAD OIL, OR A
   MIXTURE OF THE TWO)
   *Enough to fill the bot-
   tom of a small skillet to
   a depth of about 1 inch*

utes, or until the sauce becomes a coarse purée that will hold its shape on a spoon, and most of the liquid has evaporated. Scrape the bottom of the pan from time to time so that it does not burn. Lower the heat if necessary.

6. Add salt and pepper to taste and set aside at room temperature, or refrigerate.

7. In the meantime put the flour, the egg-milk mixture and the bread-crumb–paprika mixture into 3 separate small, shallow bowls.

8. Taking 1 cheese oblong at a time, dip it into the flour, then into the egg-milk mixture and then into the bread-crumb mixture, coating well with each. As each oblong is finished, put it on a small rack that will fit into the refrigerator. Chill for at least 1 hour or until ready to fry.

ABOUT 15 MINUTES BEFORE SERVING:

1. Warm the tomato sauce in a saucepan.

2. In a skillet large enough for 2 pieces of cheese, put enough oil to cover the bottom to a depth of about 1 inch. Heat to 375 degrees.

3. Line up 8 small, warm plates. Divide the warm sauce among them.

4. Fry the oblongs, 1 or 2 at a time, for about a minute, or until they turn golden, are crisp outside, and soft inside. As they are fried, remove them with a slotted spoon, and put each on a plate on top of the tomato sauce. Serve hot.

MEXICAN GRILLED CHEESE WITH GUACAMOLE
(Queso Asado)

6 SERVINGS

The pimiento topping may be made up to 2 days ahead.

The Guacamole may be made several hours in advance.

Grill and serve in individual 5- or 6-inch shallow pottery or heatproof plates: the French or Mexican earthenware ones are excellent, or use a small heatproof platter, *gratin* dish, or pie pan.

Grill just before serving.

You will need 2 forks for each diner.

The Pimiento Topping
CANNED PIMIENTOS *1 can (8 ounces, about 5 pimientos) drained, split, dried on paper towels and chopped fine*

This is one of the most popular antojitos *("little whims") in Mexico. A Mexican gentleman of sophistication will order it with tequila, served in a small, slim, straight glass, and another matching glass of well-chilled* sangrita—*a delicious non-alcoholic mixture of orange juice, chiles, and spices. The formality of partaking of this is quite stringent. First a sip of tequila. Then, slowly, without swallowing, a sip of* sangrita. *The mixture is held in the mouth a moment or two, then swallowed. Next a bit of cheese and Guacamole are rolled in a* tortilla *and eaten. The whole procedure is repeated as long as the supply or appetite lasts.*

Assemble and prepare all ingredients.

THE PIMIENTO TOPPING: Put the chopped pimientos into a small bowl. Add the minced *chiles,* mix well, and taste. Then wait a minute. If you detect a small "bite," the amount is just right for you. If not, add a little more *chile* until it's just a little piquant. Add salt to taste. Cover with plastic wrap and refrigerate until ready to assemble and grill.

ABOUT 15 MINUTES BEFORE SERVING:
1. Preheat the broiler. While it heats wrap

CANNED SERRANO CHILES
3, drained, rinsed, par-
tially deseeded, and
minced (about 1 table-
spoon), or more to taste:
be cautious—they are
hot!;
or *an equal amount of*
jalapeño chiles *or any*
other canned hot
chiles;
or *an equal amount of*
green bell peppers plus
a dash or two of
Tabasco sauce
SALT

The Tortillas and Cheese

CORN TORTILLAS *12 or*
more (3 inches to 4
inches in diameter),
fresh or frozen and
defrosted: canned
tortillas *are not rec-*
ommended for this
recipe
MUENSTER, WHITE
CHEDDAR, MONTEREY
JACK, OR ANY OTHER
MILD, EASILY MELTING
CHEESE *¾ pound,*
grated coarse

The Guacamole

1 recipe, page 320

the *tortillas* in a dampened cloth or napkin and finally in foil. Place them in the top section of a double boiler over hot but not boiling water. Cover and let them warm and soften for about 10 to 15 minutes. Turn the packet over once during this time.

2. Divide the grated cheese evenly among 6 individual heatproof plates or spread it evenly on one plate. Drain off any liquid that may have accumulated under the pimiento topping. Dot the topping on each plate, dividing it evenly.

3. Place the plates under the broiler about 3 inches from the heat. Broil for a minute or two until the cheese melts and bubbles. Watch carefully and remove before it browns.

TO SERVE: 1. Put the *tortillas* in a bowl or basket lined with a large, gay napkin. Put the Guacamole with its seed in an attractive small bowl. Pass these separately.

2. Each diner will shred his cheese with 2 forks, and place a portion of the cheese along the near half of a *tortilla* (a Mexican will hold the *tortilla* in the cupped palm of his hand), then top it with a bit of Guacamole. Roll the *tortilla* like a cigar and eat. Serve with beer, or with tequila, as suggested in the introduction.

NEVIN'S FONDUE

4 SERVINGS

A fondue pot is preferable, but a small earthenware or heavy enameled cast-iron pot or a chafing dish may be substituted.

You must have a controllable source of heat at the table, like an alcohol flame, an electrical hot plate, or a table-top butane cooking unit.

Fondue forks are necessary.

If increasing the recipe, it would be better to make 2 pots, for easier dipping.

Make just before serving.

———————

FRENCH BREAD *1 long, thin loaf, cut in 1-inch cubes, with a piece of crust on each cube (small hard rolls may be substituted)*
CRISP GREEN APPLES *3 or 4, peeled, cored, and cut in 1-inch chunks*

We particularly enjoy the crunchy apples dipped in this well-flavored cheese fondue.

Assemble and prepare all ingredients.

1. Put the bread cubes in a pretty bowl or basket. Cover with foil or a napkin and set aside.

2. Put the apple chunks into a bowl that may be taken to the table. Sprinkle them with the lime juice, mixing them so that they are well coated. Refrigerate until ready to serve.

3. Sprinkle the Cheddar cheese with the cornstarch, mixing until it is evenly coated. Reserve.

4. Put the cream cheese into a small bowl and beat until it is very soft and creamy. Reserve.

5. Put the 1 cup of wine into the top section of a double boiler. Warm directly over moderate heat until a few small bubbles start slowly rising to the surface. Do not let it boil.

6. In the meantime heat water in the bottom section of the double boiler until it is simmering.

7. When the wine is hot, put the top section over the bottom section and add the butter.

8. When the butter has melted, add the reserved Cheddar cheese by handfuls. Using a wooden spoon or rubber spatula, blend in thoroughly before adding the next handful. Lower the heat to keep the water

LIMES *Juice of 2 medium*

SHARP AGED CHEDDAR
    CHEESE *To make 2 cups*
    when cut in small dice
    (about ½ pound), at
    room temperature

CORNSTARCH *1½ table-*
    spoons

CREAM CHEESE *1 package*
    (3 ounces), at room
    temperature

DRY WHITE WINE *1 cup,*
    plus a little more for
    thinning the fondue, if
    necessary

BUTTER *2 tablespoons*

BRANDY *½ cup*
    MIXED WITH:

GRAND MARNIER *½ cup*

NUTMEG, GRATED FRESH
    ¼ teaspoon

CAYENNE PEPPER *¼ tea-*
    spoon

SALT

in the bottom section at a slow simmer. The cheese should not melt too fast.

9. When all the cheese has melted and is almost free of lumps, put about ½ cup of it into the softened cream cheese and beat together until well blended.

10. Return the mixture to the melted Cheddar cheese. Stir well until it has no lumps.

11. Stir in the brandy and Grand Marnier, a little at a time. Sprinkle with the nutmeg and cayenne, stirring until the mixture is smooth and creamy. Add salt to taste.

12. Put the fondue pot on a tray and light the heat source. Pour the fondue into the fondue pot and bring to the table along with the fondue forks, the bread, and the apple chunks.

13. Regulate the flame of the warmer. The fondue must be kept at a slow simmer —no lower, and certainly no higher.

TO SERVE AND EAT: Give each guest a fondue fork. Spear a bread cube through the soft side into the crust, or, if you prefer, an apple cube. Dunk the bread or apple into the fondue with a stirring motion. (The stirring helps the cheese to stay blended and smooth.) Raise the fondue fork and twirl to remove any excess cheese.

A chilled dry wine or champagne is a nice accompaniment.

NOTE: If the fondue should become too thick while eating, stir in a little warm wine.

BREAD AND CHEESE ON SKEWERS
(*Spiedini alla Romano*)

8 SERVINGS

You will need 8 skewers, each about 7 inches long.

The sauce may be made ahead.

The bread and cheese may be prepared and spread with the sauce early in the day and refrigerated.

Bake just before serving.

———————

UNSLICED, FIRM DAY-OLD
HOME-STYLE WHITE
BREAD *1 loaf, 8 by 4 by
4 inches: if not available,
use long loaves of French
bread*
MOZZARELLA CHEESE 32
*slices about 1 by 1 by ¼
inch (about 1 pound):
save the scraps for
another use*
MELTED BUTTER *⅓ cup*
OLIVE OIL *⅓ cup*
ANCHOVY PASTE 2 *level
tablespoons*

Spiedini are skewers, and this unusual bread, cheese, and anchovy recipe is from northern Italy. Cutting the bread may be tricky, but don't worry about being too precise. The flavor will be the same, regardless of the dimensions.

Assemble and prepare all ingredients.

1. Remove the 2 side and end crusts from the loaf of bread. Cut the loaf in half lengthwise, then across, and, last, horizontally through the center.

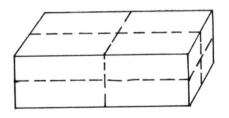

You will have 8 pieces, each one approximately 3¾ by 1¾ by 1¾ inches, each with crust on 1 side. If the square loaf is not available, cut as many pieces of the same approximate size out of a long loaf of French bread. You will probably need 2 loaves. Be flexible—if it is more convenient to have 5-inch pieces because of the size of your loaf, adapt the slits and amount of cheese to your bread.

2. Put the 8 pieces of bread, crust-side down, on a work surface. Make 4 cuts in

PARSLEY *To make 2 table-*
spoons when minced
GARLIC 2 *cloves, peeled and*
minced almost to a
paste

The Accompaniment
PEELED COLD MELON
SLICES
DRY WHITE OR ROSE WINE

each, about ¾ inch apart; cut down to the crust but *not through* it.

3. Place 1 slice of mozzarella into each slit, pressing each one down a bit so that they fit into each slit as smoothly as possible.

4. Skewer each bar horizontally, through bread and cheese gently but tightly. Put each bar almost to the end of the skewer, for easier handling.

5. In a small bowl, put the butter, olive oil, anchovy paste, parsley, and garlic. Mix and mash together so that the anchovy paste is evenly distributed and there are no lumps.

6. Brush each bar on all sides except the crust with the anchovy mixture, stirring before each brushing—the anchovy paste has a tendency to settle at the bottom. (If you are making the *spiedini* ahead of time, wrap them in foil and either refrigerate or freeze them. If frozen, bring to room temperature before baking.)

ABOUT 25 MINUTES BEFORE SERVING:
1. Preheat the oven to 450 degrees.

2. Line a baking sheet with foil. Arrange the skewers on it, crust side down, separating them. Bake for about 5 to 7 minutes, or until the cheese starts to melt and the bread is light gold.

3. Remove them from the oven and slide the baking sheet under the broiler, cheese side up, for 30 seconds or until the top is slightly crisp and a little brown.

TO SERVE: Put a skewer on each of 8 small,

warm plates. Place a slice of melon on each plate and serve the *spiedini* hot, accompanied, if you wish, by a glass of dry white or rosé wine.

SWEETS

OVEN PUFF PANCAKE

Make this with either the sausage or the fresh strawberry topping. Both are delicious.

THE PUFF PANCAKE WITH KIELBASA TOPPING: Set the prepared *kielbasa* sausage aside. Assemble but do not mix the rest of the ingredients.

ABOUT 45 MINUTES BEFORE SERVING:
1. Preheat the oven to 425 degrees.

2. Thoroughly butter the bottom and sides of the skillet and set aside.

3. Put the eggs and the mustard into a bowl and beat them with a wire whisk until blended.

4. Slowly add the flour, beating constantly.

5. Stir in the salt, milk, and melted butter until well blended.

6. Pour the batter into the cold prepared skillet and put the reserved *kielbasa*

4 TO 6 SERVINGS

The sausage or strawberries may be prepared ahead.

Mix and bake just before serving.

Best baked in a 9- or 10-inch iron skillet, but any other ovenproof skillet, baking pan, or cake pan of about the same dimensions may be used.

The Puff Pancake with Kielbasa Topping
KIELBASA OR POLISH
SAUSAGE 1, *cooked in boiling water for about*

*10 minutes: slice 7 or 8
inches of it thin (do not
remove the skin; save
the rest of the sausage for
another use)*

The Pancake Batter

SOFTENED BUTTER *For
skillet or pan*

EGGS *4*

DIJON MUSTARD *½ tea-
spoon*

ALL-PURPOSE FLOUR *⅔
cup, unsifted*

SALT *¼ teaspoon*

MILK *⅔ cup*

MELTED BUTTER *3 table-
spoons*

KIELBASA SLICES *Prepared
as described above*

The Puff Pancake with Fresh Strawberry Topping

FRESH STRAWBERRIES
*About 3 cups, halved:
remove stems and hulls*

SUPERFINE GRANULATED
SUGAR *2 to 3 tablespoons
to taste*

KIRSCH (OPTIONAL) *3
tablespoons*

The Pancake Batter

*Use the same ingredients
as above, but* OMIT *the
mustard* ADD:

slices on top, spacing them as evenly as possible.

7. Bake on the middle rack of the pre-heated oven for 18 to 20 minutes. Then reduce the heat to 350 and bake 10 minutes more, or until the pancake is puffed and the edges are golden-brown. Remove and serve at once in the skillet in which it was baked.

TO SERVE: Break the pancake into wedges with a knife and fork. Place on individual warm plates.

THE PUFF PANCAKE WITH FRESH STRAWBERRY TOPPING: 1. Sprinkle the strawberries with 2 or 3 tablespoons of the superfine sugar to taste and then with the kirsch. Toss well and refrigerate. This may be done several hours ahead. Turn frequently.

2. Follow steps 1 through 7 in the recipe for *kielbasa*-topped puff, but omit the mustard, add 2 tablespoons of sugar, and omit the *kielbasa* topping.

3. While the pancake is baking, whip the cream, adding the powdered sugar as you whip, until it forms soft peaks. Spoon into a serving bowl and refrigerate.

4. When the puff is baked, remove it from the oven and spread it evenly with the strawberries and a little of the juice. Bring to the table at once in the skillet in which it was cooked.

TO SERVE: Break into wedges with a knife and fork. Put on individual plates. Pass the

SUGAR 2 *tablespoons*
OMIT *the sausage topping*

The Garnish
HEAVY CREAM *1 cup*
POWDERED SUGAR 2
tablespoons

6 SERVINGS

Must be prepared just
before serving.

You will need a pan that
you can carry to the
table.

————————

The Sauce
APRICOT JAM *1 jar (12
ounces)*
GOLD OR LIGHT RUM ½
cup

The Nockerl
BUTTER 2 *tablespoons*
EGG WHITES 7, *at room
temperature*
SUGAR 6 *tablespoons*
CREAM OF TARTAR *1 tea-
spoon*
EGG YOLKS 7, *at room
temperature*
FLOUR 3 *tablespoons*

whipped cream separately. The contrast
between the hot puff and the cold cream is
superb.

SALZBURGER NOCKERL

Nockerl *are literally dumplings. The name
of this light, frothy, delectable soufflé-like
concoction may be deliberately misleading
to call attention to its origin in the beautiful, proud city of Salzburg.*

Assemble and prepare all ingredients.

THE SAUCE: In a small saucepan, mix the
apricot jam with the ½ cup of rum. Place
over low heat until hot. Reserve and keep
warm.

THE NOCKERL: 1. Preheat the oven to
350 degrees.

2. Put the butter into an ovenproof
serving pan 12 by 8 by 2 inches and place
in the oven to heat.

3. Beat the egg whites until frothy, then
gradually add the sugar and cream of tartar. Beat well until the whites form soft
peaks.

4. In a separate bowl, beat the egg
yolks thoroughly. Add the flour and beat
again until well blended. Add the ⅓ cup
of rum and mix well.

GOLD OR LIGHT RUM ⅓
cup

5. Stir about ¼ cup of the egg whites into the yolk-and-flour mixture to lighten it. Then fold in the balance of the beaten egg whites, blending thoroughly, but only until there are no large globs of egg whites visible.

6. Spread the melted butter in the pan and spoon in the egg mixture. It should stand in soft peaks and mounds. (These are the *Nockerl*.)

7. Bake in the upper third of the preheated oven for 10 to 12 minutes, or until light golden-brown on the outside but soft on the inside. Serve at once.

TO SERVE: Bring the Nockerl to the table, serve individual portions, and pass the warm apricot-rum sauce in a pitcher or a pretty bowl.

NOTE: This recipe can be adjusted for more or fewer people, but we don't recommend that you make it for more than 8.

For fewer than 6 people:

1 egg per person, plus 1 extra egg.

1 tablespoon sugar per egg.

2 teaspoons flour per egg.

Decrease rum and cream of tartar proportionately.

Use a smaller baking pan.

For more than 6 people:

1 egg per person, plus 2 extra eggs.

1 tablespoon sugar per egg.

2 teaspoons flour per egg.

Increase rum and cream of tartar

proportionately.
Use a larger baking pan.

CHEESE BLINTZES WITH STRAWBERRY TOPPING

8 SERVINGS (2 BLINTZES
PER SERVING)

The pancakes may be
made up to 3 days
ahead and refrigerated,
or they may be frozen:
let them come to room
temperature before
separating or they will
tear.

The filling and the sauce
may be made up to a
day ahead.

The blintzes may be
assembled up to 8
hours before serving:
refrigerate and bring
to room temperature
before frying.

They must be fried just
before serving.

The Pancakes
EGGS *3*
MILK *1½ cups*
SALT *½ teaspoon*

*Creamy and bland inside, with a luscious
strawberry sauce and sour cream topping,
these Jewish filled crêpes are rich snacks.*

THE PANCAKES: Assemble all ingredients.

1. Break the eggs into a medium bowl.
Beat with a wire whisk or rotary beater
until well mixed. Add the milk and salt
and combine.

2. Sprinkle the flour slowly into the
mixture, beating vigorously. Beat until
all the lumps are dissolved and the batter
is smooth. Cover and refrigerate, or let
stand at room temperature for 30 minutes. Then blend the batter again. It
should be the consistency of light cream.

3. Place a 7-inch *crêpe* pan or skillet
over moderate heat, and when it is hot,
add about ⅓ teaspoon of butter, rotating
the pan so that the bottom and about ½
inch of the sides are covered with butter.
Lift the pan from the heat and put in 2
tablespoons of the batter, quickly and
simultaneously rotating the pan so the
bottom is covered with batter. Return the
pan to the heat and fry until the top of
the pancake is dry to the touch. *Do not
turn it.* Slide it out of the pan with the
help of a spatula, if necessary, onto a

ALL-PURPOSE FLOUR ¾
  cup, unsifted
BUTTER FOR FRYING
  PANCAKES

The Filling
CREAMED SMALL CURD
  COTTAGE CHEESE 2½
  cups
COMMERCIAL SOUR
  CREAM ¾ cup
VANILLA 1½ teaspoons
GROUND GINGER 1 tea-
  spoon
SUGAR 1 tablespoon

The Sauce
WATER ¾ cup
SUGAR ⅓ cup
CORNSTARCH 1 table-
  spoon
FRESH STRAWBERRIES 2
  baskets (12 ounces each),
  washed, hulled, and
  sliced (two 10-ounce
  packages of frozen
  strawberries, thawed,
  may be substituted if
  necessary)
BUTTER FOR FRYING
  BLINTZES About ⅓ cup

The Topping
COMMERCIAL SOUR
  CREAM About 1½ cups

cookie sheet covered with a dish towel. Stack the pancakes browned side up as you take them from the pan.

4. Continue until you have used all the batter. You should have 16 pancakes. If any stick or there are crumbs remaining in the pan, clean them out before making the next pancake to avoid having that one stick.

5. When cool, they may be covered with the towel and set aside until you are ready to fill them, or they may be refrigerated or frozen. To freeze, wrap them tightly in aluminum foil. Thaw completely before using.

THE FILLING AND THE SAUCE: Assemble and prepare all ingredients.

1. *To make the filling:* combine the cottage cheese, the ¾ cup of sour cream, the vanilla, ginger, and 1 tablespoon of sugar. Mix well. If you wish, you may cover the filling and refrigerate it up to a day ahead.

2. *To make the sauce:* put the water, ⅓ cup of sugar, and the cornstarch into a 1½-quart saucepan and mix until the cornstarch is dissolved.

3. Add the strawberries and bring to a boil over high heat, stirring constantly and well to prevent lumps.

4. When the sauce is clear and thickened, remove it from the heat. It may be refrigerated up to a day ahead and reheated just before serving.

TO ASSEMBLE, SHAPE, AND FRY: 1. For each blintz, place about 2 mounded tablespoons of the filling in the center of the pancake on the *browned* side. Fold the pancake up from the bottom to a little over halfway. Then fold in each side to a little over halfway and, last, fold the top down in the same manner to completely enclose the filling. The packet will be about 2½ inches square. Place on a cookie sheet with the folded side down.

2. Make the rest of the blintzes in the same way. When completed, they may be refrigerated for 6 to 8 hours (from morning to evening, for example). It is best to have them at room temperature before frying so that they will heat more quickly.

3. Just before serving reheat the sauce over low heat. In the meantime heat a large, heavy skillet over moderate heat. Add 2 to 3 tablespoons of butter. When it is sizzling, put in as many blintzes as the pan will hold, *folded side down,* without crowding. Fry each one until golden-brown. Turn and fry on the other side. Remove and keep warm. Fry the rest in the same way, adding more butter if necessary.

TO SERVE: Put 2 blintzes on each hot plate. Spoon 2 or 3 tablespoons of hot strawberry sauce over them and top with a generous tablespoon of sour cream. Serve hot.

BANANAS MAITRE FROM ISOBEL

6 SERVINGS

"One of life's better sweets," says Isobel. She's right.

May be prepared in the kitchen, but for on-stage flair, to the delight of your guests, finish them at the table in a chafing dish or any other table-top heating unit with a pan large enough to hold 6 bananas.

Assemble all ingredients.

UP TO SEVERAL HOURS AHEAD: In a small saucepan, combine the crème de cacao, apricot liqueur, black currant syrup, and strawberry jam. Put over very low heat. Stir and blend until syrupy. Set aside.

Assemble and cook part 1 up to several hours ahead.

Prepare the bananas and finish cooking just before serving.

JUST BEFORE SERVING: 1. Prepare the bananas by cutting off both ends and peeling off only 1 nice, big section of skin, leaving the rest intact in a boatlike shape. Set aside.

2. Reheat the liqueur mixture and put it on a tray, along with separate small bowls of the butter, orange juice, sugar, and cinnamon, and the prepared bananas.

3. Now you can finish cooking in the kitchen, using a skillet or *gratin* dish, or finish at the table. Either way, you must have a pan large enough to hold 6 bananas.

4. If you opt for finishing at the table, put the chafing dish and its blazer pan (the upper section), or any other type table-top cooker—an electric frying pan will do—on the table along with the tray and topping.

5. Melt the butter over low heat. Add

Part 1

CREME DE CACAO 2 *ounces*

APRICOT LIQUEUR 2 *ounces*

BLACK CURRANT SYRUP 2 *ounces*

STRAWBERRY JAM 6 *tablespoons*

Part 2

RIPE BANANAS 6, *firm and fully colored*

SWEET BUTTER *1 table-*
spoon
ORANGE JUICE *½ cup*
SUGAR *1 tablespoon*
GROUND CINNAMON

The Topping
(Optional)
WHIPPED CREAM OR
COMMERCIAL SOUR
CREAM *About 6 table-*
spoons, well chilled
OR VANILLA ICE CREAM
6 tablespoons or more

6 SERVINGS

You will need a 12-inch
skillet.

Make just before serving:
it will take less than
15 minutes.

———————

MELTED BUTTER *¾ cup*
(1½ sticks), 3 table-
spoons for the skillet and
the remainder for the
pancake mixture
ALL-PURPOSE FLOUR *To*
make 1½ cups when
sifted
SUGAR *2 tablespoons*

the orange juice and sugar. Stir and cook
until the sugar is melted. Add the liqueur
mixture and combine.

6. Place the bananas open side up, skin
side down, in the pan. Sprinkle each with
a little cinnamon. Constantly spoon the
syrup over them until they are heated
through. Serve hot.

TO SERVE: Place 1 banana "boat" on each
of 6 warm plates. Spoon some of the sauce
over it and put a dab of topping at each
end. Eat right out of the skin, with a fork
and knife.

EMPEROR'S PANCAKE
(Kaiserschmarren)

A childhood special that our tiny German
grandmother made for us almost on re-
quest. In later years we searched for a
recipe, but no one had heard of it. That
was because we remembered it only as
"shmodda"! Here it is again, giving us
sweet recollections of a grandmother's
fond indulgence.

Assemble and prepare all ingredients.

1. Put 3 tablespoons of butter in a
12-inch skillet and let it warm on the lowest heat while you prepare the batter.

2. Sift the flour, sugar, and salt together into a large bowl.

3. In a separate bowl, combine the
egg yolks, milk, and the remaining butter.
Whip with a rotary or electric beater until

SALT *¼ teaspoon*
EGGS *3, separated*
MILK *1½ cups*

The Topping

FRUIT SAUCE (SEE BELOW)
OR A MIXTURE OF
    CINNAMON CONFEC-
    TIONERS' SUGAR
OR COMMERCIAL SOUR
    CREAM

the mixture is light and frothy.

4. Make a well in the center of the flour and pour the egg-yolk mixture into it. Stir and beat vigorously by hand, until it is well blended and you have a smooth batter.

5. Beat the egg whites until they are stiff but not dry and fold them into the batter.

6. Raise the heat under the skillet to medium-low and, when the butter begins to bubble, pour in the batter all at once.

7. Cook until the pancake is well puffed and the bottom is golden. Then, using a spatula, turn it over in large sections. The .sections will break in pieces; this is as it should be.

8. Continue to cook until it is lightly set, moist in the center, and the underside is gold. Serve immediately.

TO SERVE: Using 2 forks (not a knife), break into smaller sections if necessary and spoon onto individual plates. Pass the fruit sauce, cinnamon-sugar mixture, or sour cream separately. Sometimes we pass the sauce or sugar mixture *and* the sour cream!

FRUIT SAUCE: Melt about 2 cups of a fruit jam or preserve over low heat. Good jams are strawberry, raspberry, cherry, apricot, or blackberry. To gild, add 2 tablespoons of rum or brandy. Serve the sauce warm.

SOPAIPILLAS

28 TO 30 PUFFS

These may be made ahead and rewarmed but are best served right after frying.

ALL-PURPOSE FLOUR 4 *cups*

BAKING POWDER 2 *tea-spoons*

SALT ½ *teaspoon*

SUGAR 3 *tablespoons*

EGGS 2

MILK *1 cup*

SALAD OIL 2 *tablespoons*

OIL, FOR DEEP FRYING

These tender, tasty puffs are wonderful with Mexican Hot Chocolate, page 282. They can be used either as bread with butter, or as dessert, covered with syrup, honey, jam, or confectioners' sugar.

Assemble and prepare all ingredients.

1. Sift the flour together with the baking powder, salt, and sugar.

2. Beat the eggs until light and fluffy, then add the milk and salad oil and blend.

3. Combine the 2 mixtures thoroughly. Let stand for 30 to 60 minutes.

4. Roll out half the dough on a lightly floured board to a thickness of ¼ inch. Cut into rectangles about 2½ by 3 inches. Do the same with the remaining dough.

5. Heat the frying oil to 380 degrees in a frying pan or electric deep fryer. Have enough oil so that it is at least 2 inches deep.

6. Drop in about 4 puffs and turn them as soon as they begin to rise so that they will puff evenly on both sides. Fry them until they are brown, turning again.

7. Drain on paper towels. Serve warm, as suggested in the introduction. If they have been made in advance, rewarm in a 350-degree oven for 10 or 15 minutes.

FLUFFY CHOCOLATE FONDUE

8 SERVINGS

You will need a ceramic
or earthenware pot that
holds about 6 cups, a
table candle warmer or
electric food warmer,
and 8 fondue forks,
wooden skewers, or
hibachi sticks.

The fondue may be made
several hours ahead
and reheated.

The fruit, except for the
bananas, may be
prepared ahead and
refrigerated.

Serve the fondue warm
and the fruit cold.

———————

The Fondue
LIGHT CREAM ½ *cup*
SWEETENED CONDENSED
  MILK *1 can* (*14-ounce
  size*)
MARSHMALLOWS
  8 ounces, cut in quarters
  (*or small marshmallows,
  whole*)
SEMISWEET CHOCOLATE

*This is our own adaptation of a favorite
with everyone who has tried it. We seldom
see it served and wonder why not, since
it is simple to do, may be prepared well
ahead and reheated, and is a truly delicious concoction.*

Assemble and prepare all ingredients except the bananas.

THE FONDUE: Put all the ingredients except the liqueur into the fondue pot. On
the kitchen stove, set over very low heat
and stir gently until the marshmallows,
chocolate, and butterscotch are well
blended into a smooth, thick sauce. It
should be thick enough to cling to the
fruit without dripping after it has been
twirled and cooled for a second or two. If
it is too thick, thin it with a little cream.
You will add the liqueur just before serving. At this point it may be refrigerated,
covered, in the fondue pot.

FOR DIPPING: Put the pineapple and
strawberries into separate bowls and refrigerate until ready to serve.

JUST BEFORE SERVING: 1. Put the fondue pot over very low heat. Stir frequently
until melted and warmed through. Be
careful not to overheat or the fondue may
scorch.

CHIPS 6 *ounces*

BUTTERSCOTCH CHIPS
   6 *ounces*

RUM, COINTREAU, OR
   TRIPLE SEC ¼ *cup*

CREAM FOR THINNING,
   IF NECESSARY

For Dipping

FRESH PINEAPPLE
   *1 medium, peeled, cored,
   and cut in 1-inch-square
   chunks*

STRAWBERRIES *1 quart,
   washed, dried, and hulled*

BANANAS *4 firm, cut in
   1-inch chunks*

2. Add the liqueur and blend well.

3. In the meantime prepare the bananas and drain the pineapple and strawberries.

TO SERVE: Put the fondue pot on the table or buffet over very low heat. Combine the fruits and put into a bowl. Have the forks and skewers handy. Each person can spear a piece of fruit, dip it into the fondue, remove, turn it until the fondue does not drip, and eat it. Keep the flame low and stir the fondue frequently so that it does not burn or stick to the bottom of the pan. The leftover fondue (if such a thing should happen) may be refrigerated and reheated and used the same way later, or as a sauce for ice cream.

CAPPUCCINO

1 SERVING

The "syrup" may be made
ahead.

———————

Per Person

CHOCOLATE DRINK MIX
   (WITHOUT MALT)
   *1 heaping teaspoon: see
   note at end of recipe for
   substitute*

INSTANT COFFEE, REGU-
   LAR OR DECAFFEINATED
   1 rounded teaspoon

A fine substitute for both dessert and coffee, or an evening snack. This is our own version of an Italian drink which is a San Francisco favorite, made there in a machine that is a gleaming collection of chromium pipes and valves, hissing and sizzling.

Assemble and prepare all ingredients.

1. Mix the chocolate drink mix (or substitute), instant coffee, and half the water in a saucepan. Heat, stirring constantly, until blended and dissolved. This "syrup" can be made ahead.

WATER *½ cup*
MILK *⅓ cup*
RUM *I ounce*
WHIPPED CREAM,
    FLAVORED WITH
    VANILLA *I tablespoon*
    (*½ cup of heavy cream
    whipped and flavored
    with vanilla will serve
    8*)

2. Add the rest of the water and the milk. Heat thoroughly but do not boil.

3. Put the rum into a cup or mug. Add the hot mixture. Top with a tablespoon of whipped cream. Be prepared to serve seconds.

NOTE: As a substitute for the chocolate drink mix, use 1 heaping teaspoon of cocoa, plus 1 teaspoon of sugar, and use light cream instead of the milk.

MEXICAN HOT CHOCOLATE

MAKE IT FOR 1 OR MORE

An egg beater or a
    Mexican chocolate
    beater (*molinillo*) is
    necessary.

Must be made fresh.

Per Person
WATER (TRADITIONAL:
    OR MILK IF YOU
    PREFER) *I cup*
MEXICAN CHOCOLATE
    *I tablet, I½ ounces,
    grated*

Perfect with hot, fresh Sopaipillas, page 279, on a chilly evening. If you can't find Mexican chocolate, which is reasonably available, you might try 1½ ounces of semisweet chocolate with 2 or 3 teaspoons of sugar, and cinnamon to taste. Not the same flavor, but similar.

1. Heat the water or milk to a boil and add the grated. chocolate. Simmer gently for 5 minutes.

2. Remove from the heat and beat vigorously with the egg beater or Mexican chocolate beater until frothy.

SERVING SUGGESTIONS: Of course, serve with hot Sopaipillas, page 279. Also good after Moctezuma's Pie, page 208, or Mexican Grilled Cheese with Guacamole, page 262.

Three Party Buffets

A TRAY OF HORS D'OEUVRE

*Another attractive first course too often neglected. Variety here is the
secret of success, so prepare and use as many of the following as you can
manage, at least 8 or 10. Be sure to include different textures and colors
of meat, fish, and vegetables. Estimate the quantities needed for the number of guests you will be serving. Unless you want a lot left over, we
suggest you make half the recipe of your choice of those in this book.*

These can be made several days ahead and refrigerated:

LENTIL SALAD, *page* 69
SPICED RED ONION RINGS, *page* 71
MARINATED CARROTS, *page* 56
ZUCCHINI IN SALSA VERDE, *page* 45
SHRIMP IN MARINADE, *page* 23
MARINATED KIELBASA, *page* 33
PATE DE CAMPAGNE, *page* 144
MARINATED OYSTERS WITH DILL SAUCE, *page* 29

If you are short of time, make only a few of the above and add a selection
of the following, available at your grocery store:

CANNED PATE
OLIVES OF SEVERAL TYPES
SARDINES
ANCHOVIES
SALAMI
MARINATED ARTICHOKE HEARTS
SMOKED SALMON
SMOKED OYSTERS

TO SERVE: Put each item into a bowl or on a small plate and arrange on a
tray. Add crackers or bread and butter as accompaniments, provide a
small, chilled plate for each guest, and let them serve themselves.

A TRAY OF PUPUS

In the Hawaiian Islands, a dinner is almost always preceded by a tray of Pupus, or appetizers—sometimes only 2 or 3, sometimes a grand array. Many or few, they always have the special flavor appeal of the Islands, designed to whet the appetite and delight the palate. The danger is in eating too many—but of course you can increase the amount of Pupus and forget dinner, and no one would miss it. Plan it either way.

Herewith is a selection of Pupus—select any or all. All can be prepared ahead, a few need to be reheated just before serving.

FROM THIS BOOK: For a small group, prepare ½ the recipe.

    HOISIN CHICKEN WINGS, *page 213:* serve at room temperature.

    SHRIMP TOAST, *page 194:* serve warm.

    MARINATED SMOKED SALMON, *page 25:* serve cold.

    STUFFED EGGS, *page 37:* serve only the eggs.

    ANCHOVY CRESCENTS, *page 303:* serve warm.

    ROQUEFORT SHORTBREAD, *page 310:* serve at room temperature.

Buy:

    COCONUT CHIPS

    BANANA CHIPS

More Easy Pupus to Prepare Ahead:

RUMAKI: Cut each chicken liver in a 10-ounce package into 4 pieces. Sauté in 3 tablespoons of butter or margarine for 3 or 4 minutes, until golden but not thoroughly cooked. Cut 16 bacon slices in half. Wrap a piece of liver and a water chestnut in ½ slice of bacon. Skewer with a strong toothpick. Broil 3 to 5 minutes on each side. If you prepare ahead, broil only 2 minutes on each side and finish broiling just before serving. Makes 32.

EXOTIC FRESH PINEAPPLE: Peel and clean 1 fresh pineapple and cut in 1-inch cubes. Skewer each with a pretty toothpick. Put on a small tray with a bowl of Cheddar cheese, grated fine, and a bowl of fresh-grated coconut. To peel a fresh coconut, see page 182. Instruct your guests to dip the pineapple first in the cheese, then in the coconut.

FILLED LICHEES: For 2 cans of lichees, make a filling of 2 packages of cream cheese (3 ounces each), softened with a little cream, and ⅓ cup of macadamia nuts, chopped fine.

TO SERVE YOUR PUPUS: Arrange them in bowls or on plates on 1 or more trays decorated with leaves and flowers. Provide small individual plates and napkins for your guests.

SUGGESTED MAIN COURSE:
Chicken with Long Rice, page 214
OR *Roast Fresh Leg of Pork*

A TAPA BAR

The tapa bar is a unique and most pleasant feature of Madrid night life and one easily adapted to home entertainment. Tapas are snacks, and tapa bars feature an almost endless variety of them, hot and cold. Madrileños spend hours drinking sherry at sidewalk tables, getting up now and then to try a new selection of tapas. We have a large selection of recipes for appropriate tapas for you, both cold and hot. Most may be prepared days ahead, some warmed just before serving. Arrange all on a large buffet table, provide small plates and a good sherry, and let your guests enjoy a "night in Madrid" with you.

Cold Tapas:
SHRIMP IN MARINADE, VERACRUZ STYLE, *page 23*
CEVICHE, *page 14*
TARAMASALATA, *page 31*
ZAKUSKA OF HERRING AND BEETS, *page 17*
BRANDADE OF SALTED COD, *page 9*
ZUCCHINI IN SALSA VERDE, *page 45*
SPICED RED ONION RINGS, *page 71*

MARINATED CARROTS, *page 56*
MARINATED GREEN PEPPERS AND BLACK OLIVES, *page 57*
VEGETABLES A LA GRECQUE, *page 75*

Hot Tapas:

SPINACH CHEESE PUFFS, *page 114*
SWEDISH PANCAKES, *page 123*
CROQUE MONSIEUR, cut into small pieces, *page 248*
BAGNA CAUDA, *page 238*
MYSTERY SAVORY, *page 236*
ANCHOVY CRESCENTS, *page 303*

Additional Tapa Suggestions:

MARINATED OLIVES: Drain either green or ripe olives, reserving the liquid. Add a clove of minced garlic and several hot dried peppers to the liquid, and marinate the olives in the spiced liquid for several days.

FRIED ALMONDS: Fry peeled almonds in a small amount of olive oil, slowly so they do not burn, until golden-brown. Drain on paper towels and salt.

PALITOS ("little sticks"): Load toothpicks or longer skewers with pieces of sausage, ham, cold meats, cheeses, olives, tiny tomatoes.

The Basics

BROTHS, DRESSINGS, SAUCES, BREADS, BATTERS, AND PASTRIES

FULL-FLAVORED BEEF BROTH

3 TO 4 QUARTS

You will need an 8-to-10-
quart kettle and 1 or 2
large roasting pans.

Cheesecloth to line a
colander is helpful but
not essential.

May be stored in the
refrigerator for up to 3
days or frozen.

**FRESH BEEF BRISKET OR
HEEL OF THE ROUND**
2 pounds
BEEF SHANK *2 pounds, cut
in ½-inch slices*
BEEF BONES *2 pounds, cut
in 3-inch chunks*
VEAL KNUCKLE *Split and
cut in 3-inch pieces*
OR VEAL BONES *1 pound,
cut in 3-inch chunks*
ONIONS *2 medium, washed
but not peeled: cut in
chunks*
CARROTS *3 medium, sliced
thick: wash but do not
scrape*
FRESH GARLIC *2 large
cloves, peeled and split*

*It takes time (6 hours or more) and dedi-
cation to make a delicious, full-bodied,
homemade broth, but the results are
worth the effort. The flavor can't be duplicated by shortcuts or canned beef bouillon,
and the time is mostly for simmering the
stock. The reward, however, is not limited
to the resulting broth. A bonus of meat is
left for at least 2 other dishes. See note at
the end of the recipe.*

*Does the vinegar seem a strange in-
gredient? The small amount will completely evaporate and leave no flavor. Its
function is to help dissolve and extract the
gelatinous matter from the bones, thereby
enriching the broth.*

Assemble and prepare all ingredients.

1. Preheat the oven to 475 degrees.
2. Arrange the meat and bones, preferably in a single layer, in 1 or 2 large, shallow roasting pans. Surround them with
the onions, carrots, garlic, and leeks, also
preferably in a single layer. This is a large
amount of meat and vegetables, so you
may have to brown it in 2 batches unless
you have a wide oven. Roast uncovered for
30 to 40 minutes, turning the meat and
vegetables once or twice so that they color
evenly to a deep golden-brown. Watch
them because they burn easily.
3. Transfer to an 8-to-10-quart kettle.
Deglaze the roasting pans by adding 2 or

LEEKS 4, *cut in half: wash well and cut in chunks, retaining a little of the green tops*

HOT WATER

CIDER VINEGAR 3 *tablespoons*

CELERY 3 *stalks with leaves, cut in chunks*

DRIED THYME LEAVES *½ teaspoon, crumbled, or ¼ teaspoon, ground*

BAY LEAF 1, *crushed*

WHOLE CLOVES 3

DRIED HOT CHILE PEPPER (OPTIONAL) 1 *small, crushed*

PEPPERCORNS 6

PARSLEY 8 *sprigs*

SALT 1 *teaspoon*

3 cups of hot water to each pan and bringing it to a boil. Scrape the bottom and sides to dislodge all the nice brown bits and incorporate them in the water. Add this to the kettle and then add enough additional hot water to cover the ingredients by 2 inches.

4. Add the vinegar, set over moderate heat, and bring to a slow simmer. Remove any scum that rises to the top. Cover and simmer gently for 2 hours. Do not allow the liquid to boil at any time. From time to time, remove any additional scum as it forms and wipe the inside edge of the kettle at the liquid level with a damp cloth.

5. At the end of this cooking period, add the celery, thyme, bay leaf, cloves, chile pepper, the peppercorns, parsley, and salt. Push the vegetables well down into the broth. Add more hot water if the liquid does not cover the ingredients by a full 2 inches.

6. Bring the liquid again to a slow simmer, removing any additional scum. Partially cover, leaving an opening of about 1 inch. Continue cooking slowly for 4 hours. Add a little more hot water if the broth evaporates below the level of the ingredients.

7. At the end of the cooking time, taste for flavor. If the broth is not full-bodied and rich, continue simmering 1 to 2 hours longer but no more.

8. Strain the broth through a colander, preferably lined with 4 layers of dampened cheesecloth, into a large bowl. Discard the bones and vegetables but keep the brisket

and bits of meat. They can be used for a delicious meal or two. See below.

9. Remove the fat from the top of the broth with a spoon, or, better and easier, put in the refrigerator, uncovered, until the fat hardens and can be scraped off. Refrigerate or freeze until ready to use.

NOTE: For a delicious cold meat main course, take the brisket that you have removed from the broth and put it in a deep bowl or pan not much larger than the meat. Cover the top of the meat with plastic wrap or waxed paper folded to fit. Now put on top of the paper any heavy items to press the meat down. Canned goods are fine. Put in the refrigerator. Chill overnight or up to 2 days with the weights on top. The resultant meat will slice evenly and neatly. Serve with potato salad and horseradish or mustard sauce, or with a vinaigrette sauce, onion rings, and hard-cooked eggs, or as Cold Meat with Anchovy Sauce, page 142.

The bits and pieces of cold meat may also be made into Salade Russe—a savory mixture of meat, vegetables, pickles, and herbs, tossed with a spicy dressing, page 153.

CHICKEN BROTH

2 TO 2½ QUARTS

Cheesecloth to line a strainer is helpful but not essential.

The vinegar in this recipe, as in the recipe for Full-Flavored Beef Broth, may seem an odd ingredient, but according to the late Adelle Davis, well-known and re-

May be stored in the
refrigerator for up to 3
days, or frozen.

CHICKEN PARTS 4 *pounds*
(*backs, wings, necks,
giblets, and feet, if available*), *well cleaned*
COLD WATER 4 *quarts*
CIDER VINEGAR 3 *table-
spoons*
SALT 2 *teaspoons*
LARGE ONIONS 2, *wash,
cut off root and stem
ends but do not peel: cut
in chunks*
CARROTS 2 *medium: wash
but do not peel: then cut
in chunks*
CELERY 3 *stalks with
leaves: wash and cut in
chunks*
LEEKS 3: *discard the green
tops, cut in half, and
wash very thoroughly,
then cut in chunks*
PARSLEY 4 *sprigs*
WHOLE CLOVES 3
BAY LEAF 1, *crumbled*
DRIED THYME LEAVES
1/4 *teaspoon, crumbled*
PEPPERCORNS 10
BOILING WATER
If necessary
SALT
WHITE PEPPER, GROUND
FRESH

*spected author, lecturer, and nutritionist,
it helps break down the connective tissue
that holds the meat to the bones, thereby
extracting flavor and natural gelatin, and
shortening the cooking time. The taste of
the vinegar will disappear.*

Assemble and prepare all ingredients.

1. Put the chicken parts in a deep kettle. Add the water, vinegar, and salt. Bring
to a boil and skim off any scum that rises.

2. Lower the heat and simmer very
slowly, with the cover slightly askew, for
4 hours. From time to time, take off any
additional scum as it forms and wipe the
inside edge of the kettle at the liquid level
with a damp cloth or paper towel.

3. Add the onions, carrots, celery, leeks,
parsley, cloves, bay leaf, thyme, and peppercorns. Push the vegetables well down
into the broth. If necessary, add a little
boiling water to keep the ingredients covered.

4. Bring to a boil again and remove
any scum. Lower the heat and simmer very
slowly for 2 hours longer, with the cover
slightly askew.

5. Strain the broth through 4 layers of
dampened cheesecloth into a clean pot.
Put the strained broth back on the heat
and reduce it by boiling rapidly, uncovered, until you have 2 to 2½ quarts. Season to taste with salt and pepper.

6. Chill the broth in the refrigerator
and scrape off the fat when it is firm. Refrigerate or freeze.

NOTE: Strip the chicken meat from the

bones and use it for salads, sandwiches, or for any other dish requiring cooked chicken.

AIOLI SAUCE

1 ½ CUPS

A blender is essential.

Must be made 4 hours ahead, but may be made up to 4 days in advance.

Best served at room temperature.

GARLIC 8 *medium cloves, peeled and rough-cut*
LEMON JUICE *1 ½ tablespoons*
EGG YOLKS *3*
SALT *½ teaspoon*
OLIVE OIL *½ cup*
  MIXED WITH:
SALAD OIL *⅔ to 1 cup*
COLD WATER *If necessary*

Aïoli *sauce is a favorite in Provence, France. It probably originally came from the early Greeks—a similar, coarser sauce is still used in Greece. The Greek version, however, includes bread crumbs or potatoes. Ours is simpler, but warn those sad souls who don't like or can't tolerate garlic. It has an intoxicating aroma and so will you!*

Assemble and prepare all ingredients.

1. Put the garlic, lemon juice, egg yolks, and salt into a blender. Cover and blend at high speed for about 1 minute.

2. Continuing to blend at high speed, uncover and add the mixed oils in a slow, steady stream. When the mixture thickens, you may add the oil a little faster, but do not let it stand in puddles in the mixture.

3. If it does not blend, add 1 or 2 tablespoons of cold water, blend, and then start the oil stream again, slowly. Incorporate as much of the oil as you can, but do not add more water.

4. Transfer to a bowl and chill, covered, for at least 4 hours, to mellow. Serve at room temperature.

NOTE: Aïoli Sauce will keep for about 4 days, after which the garlic flavor deteriorates. As far as we are concerned, this is rumor only. It never stays around our houses long enough to deteriorate! In fact, it is so versatile and so good that you too will become addicts.

SUGGESTIONS FOR SERVING: Aïoli Sauce complements:
> Cold cooked shrimp or lobster
> Hot or cold cooked green beans or artichokes
> Hot or cold poached halibut, cod, or other lean fish, served whole as a first course, garnished with raw or whole cooked vegetables.
> Hard-cooked eggs
> Tomatoes
> Cauliflower
> Mushrooms
> Turnips
> Zucchini
> Green peppers
> Endive

BLENDER MAYONNAISE

1¼ CUPS

Keeps well for weeks in the refrigerator.

The egg must be at room temperature.

Do not double the recipe as the mayonnaise is apt to separate: it's better

Assemble all ingredients.
1. Break the egg into a blender. Add the vinegar, mustard, salt, and cayenne pepper. Cover.
2. Blend at medium-high speed for about a minute. Remove the cover and begin adding the oil in a slow, steady stream. The mayonnaise will thicken when you have added about half of the oil. If the oil remains in a little puddle on top, stop the

to make the recipe twice.

WHOLE EGG *1, at room temperature*

WHITE WINE VINEGAR *2 tablespoons*

OR LEMON JUICE AND VINEGAR *1 tablespoon* each

DIJON MUSTARD (OP-TIONAL) *½ teaspoon*

SALT *¼ teaspoon*

CAYENNE PEPPER *3 or 4 dashes*

SALAD OIL, OLIVE OIL, OR A MIXTURE OF BOTH *1 cup*

ABOUT 1 CUP

You will need a blender.

Will keep a week in the refrigerator.

SALAD OIL *½ cup*

EVAPORATED MILK *½ cup*

LEMON JUICE *2 table-spoons*

DRIED DILL WEED *1 table-spoon*

GARLIC *2 cloves, peeled*

(CONTINUED)

blender, mix the oil in with a rubber spatula, and start again, adding more oil until all is incorporated. The mayonnaise should be thick and hold its shape.

3. Taste for seasoning, adding more salt if necessary. Refrigerate.

CREAMY DILL DRESSING

Put all the ingredients into a blender along with a few grinds of the pepper mill. Whirl until creamy and refrigerate. Easy, isn't it?

and rough-cut
DIJON MUSTARD *1 table-*
spoon
SALT *½ teaspoon*
WHITE PEPPER, GROUND
FRESH

ABOUT 1⅓ CUPS

Keeps well for a week in
the refrigerator.

MAYONNAISE, PREFER-
ABLY HOMEMADE
(*page 296*) *1 cup*
CHILI SAUCE *3 table-*
spoons
LEMON JUICE *½ teaspoon*
GREEN BELL PEPPER
To make 1 tablespoon
when chopped fine
CHIVES *To make 1 table-*
spoon when chopped fine
CANNED PIMIENTO
1, chopped fine: first
blot with a paper towel
to dry
HARD-COOKED EGG
1, chopped fine: chop
the yolk and white
separately (do not
combine)
SALT
WHITE PEPPER, GROUND
FRESH

RUSSIAN DRESSING

Good on seafoods, greens, vegetables,
meat, and sandwiches.

Assemble and prepare all ingredients.

1. In a small bowl, put the mayonnaise,
chili sauce, lemon juice, green pepper,
chives, pimiento, and chopped egg yolk.
Mix well.

2. Fold in the egg whites—you want a
little texture. Add salt and pepper to taste.
The mixture will be quite soft. Refrigerate.

MARIE'S MAGIC BASIC PASTRY MIX

Will keep in refrigerator
up to 6 months.

ALL-PURPOSE FLOUR
  *To make 5 cups when
  sifted*
SALT *1 tablespoon*
VEGETABLE SHORTENING
  *2½ cups (about 1
  pound), chilled and cut
  in small chunks*

This is truly a "find" and a convenience, and we hope the recipe will become important to you. Have it on hand in your refrigerator and use it for pies, quiches, tarts, turnovers, or anything else when you want a tender, flaky crust.

Assemble all ingredients.

1. Put the flour, salt, and shortening into a large bowl. Using the tips of your fingers or a pastry blender, rapidly rub the flour and shortening together until the shortening forms little flakes about the size of oatmeal, and is well distributed.

2. Put into a tightly covered container and refrigerate for up to 6 months.

NOTE: When ready to use, stir well and measure out the amount needed, as specified in the recipe.

CRUST FOR A ONE-CRUST PIE OR QUICHE

AN 8- OR 9-INCH CRUST

ALL-PURPOSE FLOUR
  *¼ cup, unsifted: stir
  and spoon into a measure*
ICE WATER *3 tablespoons,
  plus a little more if
  necessary*
MARIE'S MAGIC BASIC

Assemble all ingredients.

1. In a small bowl or cup, mix the flour with the 3 tablespoons of water until smooth.

2. Put the pastry mix into a medium bowl. Make a hole in the center, add the flour and water paste, and blend with your hands or a fork until the pastry forms a ball. If necessary, sprinkle it with 1 table-

PASTRY MIX (*page 299*) *1⅓ cups: stir before measuring*
ADDITIONAL FLOUR FOR ROLLING

spoon more water, adding it where the mix is driest, but use just enough to hold the pastry together. It should be moist but not sticky.

3. Remove from the bowl and, with your hands, form it into a flat smooth ball about 1 inch thick. Sprinkle very lightly with flour, wrap in plastic or waxed paper, and refrigerate for about 20 minutes, or until firm.

4. When ready to bake, put the pastry on a lightly floured board or marble slab. Roll from the center out in all directions (do not push the roller back and forth) to form a circle a little less than ⅛ inch thick and about 3 inches larger in diameter than your pan. You will probably need to sprinkle with a little flour as you roll to be sure that the pastry is free-moving at all times. Lift with a spatula and sprinkle a little underneath, if necessary, but too much flour will toughen the pastry. If the edges crack while rolling, trim off any bulge and use it as a patch. Dampen the cracked area, press the scrap in place, and roll. It should be invisible.

5. Roll the pastry circle lightly onto your rolling pin, hold it over 1 side of the pan and gently unroll. Center the pastry circle and press it gently to fit against the contours of the pan.

6. Using a sharp knife or scissors, trim off any excess, but leave about 1 inch overhanging the edge of the pan. Fold the overhang under even with the rim. Pinch it together to form a high edge. Then flute the edge by placing the index finger of

your right hand on the inside of the pastry, and with your left thumb and index finger, pinch the pastry at that point. Repeat every ¼ or ½ inch around the edge, or simply press against the rim with the prongs of a floured fork.

7. If the pastry is to be baked before filling, prick the bottom and sides all over with the tines of a fork and chill. Bake as directed in the recipe.

CREAM CHEESE PASTRY

A fragile, delicate pastry that has no match for flaky richness.

The following directions are for a stationary electric mixer:

Assemble and prepare all ingredients.

1. Put 1 cup of the flour and the salt into the largest bowl of the mixer. Add the butter and cream cheese chunks.

2. Starting on lowest speed (careful, at first the flour has a tendency to scatter), then on higher speed, mix until just combined.

3. Turn the motor off, add the remaining cup of flour, pushing it down well, turn the motor on lower speed until blended and then on higher speed until it forms a soft dough and there are no visible bits of butter or cream cheese. Don't overdo this or the pastry will be too soft to handle.

4. Remove from the bowl with a rubber spatula. Lightly flour your hands and

FULL RECIPE MAKES
ENOUGH FOR:
32 three-inch squares, or 16 four-inch squares, or 18 four-and-a-half-inch circles, or a 2-crust, 9-inch pie.

A stationary electric mixer is recommended: if the pastry is to be mixed by hand or with a portable electric mixer, see note at end of recipe.

Must be chilled before, and possibly during, shaping.

Will keep several days in the refrigerator or may be frozen unbaked, but must be shaped first.

ALL-PURPOSE FLOUR
*2 cups, unsifted (stir and
spoon into measuring
cup), plus a little more
for rolling.*
SALT *½ teaspoon*
CHILLED BUTTER (NO
SUBSTITUTE) *1 cup
(2 sticks) cut in chunks*
CHILLED CREAM CHEESE
*1 package (8-ounce
size) cut in chunks*

the pastry (it will be quite sticky) and divide the mixture in half. Shape each half into a 1-inch-thick flat ball, rectangle or square, depending on the shape needed.

5. Wrap each half in foil or plastic wrap and refrigerate overnight or up to a week, or put in the freezer for an hour. If it is to be frozen for more than an hour, it is best to shape the pastry first.

6. If using the full recipe, roll only half of the dough at a time. Refrigerate the other half, as it softens quickly. If it softens at any time that you are working with it, refrigerate it until chilled and then continue. Cream cheese pastry is easiest to roll between 2 sheets of waxed paper, but you will need to loosen or change the papers several times to prevent the pastry from wrinkling or sticking and to allow it to be free-moving at all times.

7. Shape and bake according to individual recipe instructions. In general, set the oven at 350 or 375 degrees.

NOTE: If mixing by hand or with a portable electric mixer, cream the butter and cheese until light and fluffy. Mix the salt with the flour and gradually add it to the butter-and-cheese mixture until it is well blended and forms a very smooth dough, with no bits and pieces identifiable.

ANCHOVY CRESCENTS

ABOUT 50 CRESCENTS

May be made up to a day
    ahead, or frozen, baked
    or unbaked.

Serve warm or cold.

CREAM CHEESE PASTRY
    ½ recipe, page 301
FLOUR *For flouring board
    and rolling*
ANCHOVY PASTE *1 tube*
    (*2-ounce size*)

*Tasty morsels, especially good with cold
soups such as our Chilled Cream of Avocado Soup, page 5, or the Bisque of Hearts
of Palm, page 86.*

Assemble and prepare all ingredients.

1. Cut the pastry in half and refrigerate
one half wrapped in waxed paper while
you roll and fill the other half.

2. Flour a pastry board or marble slab
generously. Carefully and quickly roll out
the pastry in a circle or rectangle, as thin as
possible. It must be free-moving at all
times. If it starts to stick, lift it and sprinkle
a little flour underneath. If it cracks or
breaks, pull the torn edges together with
your fingers or patch it with a small piece
of pastry and pat it together.

3. Using a floured 2-inch circular cutter, cut as many circles as you can, pressing
down but not twisting the cutter. Squeeze
a small amount—about ¼ teaspoon—of
anchovy paste onto each circle, placing it
slightly below the center. Then, with a
small spatula, lift the unfilled portion and
fold the circle in half to form a crescent.
Press the edges together with a floured fork
to seal them. Lift each crescent onto a
Teflon or lightly greased baking sheet. Refrigerate while you roll and shape the trimmings to make more crescents. If the pastry gets too soft or sticky, pop it into the
freezer for a few minutes.

4. Continue making crescents with the other half of the pastry in the same manner.

At this point you may:

a. Preheat the oven to 350 degrees and bake the crescents in 1 or 2 batches in the upper third of the oven for about 15 minutes or until they are puffed and a light gold. Serve warm or cold.

b. Bake and freeze them. To serve cold, simply defrost them. To serve warm, defrost and put them in a 300-degree oven for 5 to 7 minutes.

c. Freeze them unbaked and put them frozen into a 400-degree oven for about 15 minutes.

May be refrigerated for up to 10 days, or may be frozen: see note at end of recipe.

MILK *1 cup*
BUTTER *¼ cup, cut in chunks*
SALT *1 teaspoon*
WHITE PEPPER, GROUND FRESH *½ teaspoon*
ALL-PURPOSE FLOUR *1 cup, unsifted*
LARGE EGGS *4*

PATE A CHOUX
(Cream Puff Paste)

One of the most versatile of the pastry doughs—look at the Index for the variety of uses, and try them all.

Assemble and prepare all ingredients.

1. Put the milk, butter, salt, and pepper into a heavy-bottomed saucepan and bring to a boil slowly, to give the butter time to melt. When it has reached a full boil, remove from the heat, add the flour all at once, and blend thoroughly. Continue beating until the paste forms a ball.

2. Return the saucepan to medium heat and continue beating vigorously, flattening the paste against the bottom of the pan,

bringing it against the sides, and flipping it over. Repeat this for 2 or 3 minutes or until a grainy film forms on the bottom of the pan. The object of the flattening and flipping is to dry as much of the paste as possible. Do not let it color.

3. Remove the saucepan from the heat, make a well in the center of the paste, and break in 1 egg. Smash it a little with your spoon and beat it as fast as possible until the egg is thoroughly absorbed. Repeat with each of the other eggs, *1 at a time,* or use an electric mixer. Beat until all is smooth and well blended. The paste should be stiff but not heavy.

4. Shape and use as directed in the individual recipe.

NOTE: If the paste is to be refrigerated before shaping, rub it with butter and cover it tightly with plastic wrap or foil. It may also be frozen. *Do not freeze if making large puffs* or it will not rise to its imperial height. Either way, bring it to room temperature before shaping and baking.

TINY CHEESE PUFFS

MAKES 200 PUFFS

After baking, they may be stored in an airtight container or frozen.

Before serving, warm the puffs to make them crisp.

These are special in or with soups, cold or hot. If they are left around, they'll disappear quickly because they're equally good eaten by the handful, like peanuts or popcorn. We don't know how long they'll keep—ours last only a few days.

Assemble and prepare all ingredients.

OIL FOR BAKING SHEETS

PARMESAN CHEESE
  *To make ½ cup when
  grated fresh*

TABASCO SAUCE *3 shakes*

DIJON MUSTARD *1 tea-
  spoon*

PATE A CHOUX *1 recipe,
  page 304*

1. Preheat the oven to 375 degrees and oil 1 or 2 baking sheets.

2. Beat the cheese, Tabasco sauce, and mustard into the Pâte à Choux paste and mix well.

3. Using a teaspoon and a small spatula or butter knife, form tiny balls about ½ inch in diameter and push them onto the baking sheets.

4. Bake for about 30 minutes or until crisp and golden-brown. If you use 2 sheets, do not bake them at the same time. Keep second sheet at room temperature. Remove from the oven and put on racks to cool.

5. To rewarm, return them to the baking sheets and put them in a 350-degree oven for about 10 minutes.

CREPES

15 TO 20 CREPES

You will need a *crêpe* or omelette pan measuring 6 to 6½ inches in diameter at the bottom.

The batter must rest at room temperature for at least 2 hours before cooking.

The *crêpes* may be made up to 8 hours in advance, cooled, stacked, wrapped in foil, and left at room temperature, or

A stack of crêpes *in the freezer is as comforting to the cook as money in the bank to the miser. We are never without them.*

Assemble all ingredients.

1. Sift the flour, sugar, and salt together into a large mixing bowl.

2. In a small bowl, beat the egg yolks and whole eggs until they are blended but not too foamy. Add the milk and mix well.

3. Make a well in the center of the flour and add the milk-egg mixture. Gradually combine the flour with the eggs; start out using a wire whisk, but you may complete the blending using a rotary beater. Beat until there are no lumps, and all the flour

refrigerated for several days.

Or they may be frozen for a month or more: either way, bring them to room temperature before rolling and filling.

ALL-PURPOSE FLOUR
1 cup, unsifted
SUGAR *1 teaspoon*
SALT *¼ teaspoon*
EGG YOLKS *2, at room temperature*
WHOLE EGGS *2, at room temperature*
MILK *1¾ cups*
BUTTER (**NOT MAR-GARINE**) *To make 2 tablespoons when melted, plus part of a stick to butter the* crêpe *pan*

is incorporated, then stir in the 2 table-spoons of melted butter. The mixture should be about the consistency of light cream and as smooth as silk. Let it rest at room temperature for at least 2 hours.

TO COOK THE CREPES: 1. Place the bowl of batter near the cooking surface and put a 2-tablespoon measure beside it—a coffee measure is ideal, or you may use a ¼-cup measure, half filled.

2. Rub a pastry brush or a bit of waxed paper over a stick of butter and grease the *crêpe* pan well. Place over moderately high heat until it is very hot and just beginning to smoke. Remove the pan from the heat. With the handle toward you, grasp it in your hand and raise it slightly above the stove. Immediately start pouring in the 2-tablespoon measure of batter, starting at the side of the pan opposite the handle. Quickly rotate left and right, pouring the batter downward toward the handle as you go. You want to cover the bottom completely with a thin film of batter. If there are any holes, dab them with a little batter, or if there is any excess batter, pour it back into the bowl.

3. Return the pan to the heat and cook for about a minute or until the Crêpe is almost dry on top, but still shiny and a very light gold underneath.

4. Remove the pan from the heat and loosen the edges. Using a spatula, flip the Crêpe over. Return it to the heat and cook the other side for about 60 seconds, or until it is very light gold underneath. The

second side will be spotty. Remove from the heat and place on a cloth or paper towel *spotty side up*. This is the side that will be inside when you roll the Crêpe.

5. Butter the pan lightly again, heat it just to smoking, and repeat the whole procedure, stirring the batter each time you take a measure, until you have used all the batter. The first 1 or 2 may not be just right, but the rest should turn out perfectly. Stack the Crêpes on top of one another as they are cooked.

6. If they are to be used within 8 hours, cover lightly with foil and let stand at room temperature, or they may be wrapped tightly in foil, refrigerated for several days, and brought to room temperature. They may be frozen a month or more. If frozen, defrost thoroughly before filling and rolling.

CHEESE FLOWERS

ABOUT 120 ONE-INCH
  FLOWERS OR 60 TWO-
  INCH FLOWERS

You will need a cookie press with a flower disk and 1 or 2 large baking sheets.

May be stored in an airtight container for several days.

They freeze well and take just minutes to thaw.

Why not make the full recipe? They're so good that you will always want to have them on hand when unexpected guests arrive for a drink.

Assemble and prepare all ingredients.
  1. Preheat the oven to 300 degrees.
  2. Put the cheese, margarine, and Tabasco sauce into a large bowl, or directly onto a pastry board or marble slab. Using the heel of your hand, smear together and knead until well blended. (It is almost impossible to incorporate the cheese smoothly with a beater.)

SHARP CHEDDAR CHEESE
*1 pound, grated and
softened to room tem-
perature (overnight is
best)*

MARGARINE OR BUTTER
*1½ sticks (¾ cup),
softened to room tem-
perature*

TABASCO SAUCE *6 dashes*

ALL-PURPOSE FLOUR
*2 cups, unsifted: spoon
into cup*

BAKING POWDER *1½ tea-
spoons*

SALT *½ teaspoon*

CAYENNE PEPPER *1 tea-
spoon*

3. Sift together the flour, baking powder, salt, and cayenne pepper. Add it to the
cheese-and-butter mixture and blend thoroughly. This is best done by hand because
it makes a stiff dough.

4. Attach a flower disk to a cookie press
and fill the cylinder with part of the dough.
Refrigerate the rest. If you prefer small
flowers, use a disk with a small cutout and
press the flowers less than 1 inch in diameter. For 2-inch flowers, use a larger flower
form and press out the dough to form flowers about 1½ inches in diameter. They
will expand as they bake.

5. Hold the press in an upright posi-
tion over an unbuttered or Teflon baking
sheet. Press the flowers out, spacing them
about 1 inch apart. When you have formed
a flower, lift the press directly upward. If
you have difficulty detaching the flowers
from the bottom of the press, chill the cylinder and dough for about 15 minutes.
Continue until all the dough is used.

6. If using 2 baking sheets, stagger
them on the upper and middle racks of the
oven. Bake for 10 minutes at 300 degrees.
Lower the heat to 225 degrees, opening
the oven door to reduce the heat quickly,
and bake for about 20 minutes more. If
the flowers are baking too rapidly, leave
the oven door open while they continue to
bake. Do not let them brown. Burned
cheese just doesn't taste good!

7. Remove immediately from the baking sheets and cool on a rack. Store in an
airtight container or freeze.

ROQUEFORT SHORTBREAD

You will need 2 large
  baking sheets.

Will keep well for about
  a week in an airtight
  container.

May be baked and frozen:
  let stand at room tem-
  perature for about 30
  minutes before serving.

Rice flour is available in
  health-food stores and
  many supermarkets.

**BUTTER, NOT MAR-
  GARINE** *1 cup, slightly
  softened*
**ROQUEFORT OR BLUE
  CHEESE** *1 cup, at room
  temperature: the cream-
  iest, most pungent available and the more blue
  veins the better*
ALL-PURPOSE FLOUR
  *2 cups when sifted, plus
  a little extra for flouring
  the board*
RICE FLOUR *¾ cup, plus a*

A perfect accompaniment for many of our first courses—soups and salads particularly. They have a delicate flavor, melt in the mouth, and are habit-forming.

Assemble all ingredients.

1. Using a fork, mash the butter and Roquefort cheese together in a bowl until smooth, creamy, and well blended, but don't overwork it or let the butter become oily.

2. Sift the 2 cups of all-purpose flour with the ¾ cup of rice flour and gradually work it into the butter-Roquefort mixture. The dough should be smooth and pliable, and hold together.

3. Divide the dough in 2 parts. Refrigerate 1 part while you shape the other.

4. Place the dough on a lightly floured board or marble slab. (Use a little of each of the flours.)

5. Using your fingers and the heel of your hand, pat the dough into a circle or oblong ¼ inch thick. If it starts to stick at the bottom, lift it and sprinkle underneath with a little more flour.

6. Using a floured cutter, cut in 1¼ inch rounds. Use a spatula to transfer them to 1 or 2 unbuttered or Teflon baking sheets, placing them ½ inch apart. Refrigerate along with the trimmings.

7. Pat out the remaining half of the dough and repeat steps 4 through 6.

little extra for flouring the board (rice flour is preferable, but if you cannot obtain it, substitute ½ cup of all-purpose flour plus 2 tablespoons of cornstarch)

8. Knead all the trimmings together briefly, pat to the same thickness, and cut out as many rounds as you can.

9. Chill in the refrigerator for 30 minutes, or in the freezer for 15 minutes before baking.

WHEN READY TO BAKE: 1. Preheat the oven to 375 degrees.

2. Prick each wafer in 2 places with a floured fork. Place on the middle rack of the oven. If you don't have a double oven, it's best to bake them in 2 batches. Bake at 375 degrees for 5 minutes, then lower the temperature to 300 degrees and continue baking for about 7 minutes more, or until the bottoms are pale gold and the tops are very delicately colored. Watch them constantly. They burn easily.

3. Remove from the oven and cool on the baking sheet. They will firm up a little as they cool. When cold, store in an airtight container or freeze.

MARINATED SODA CRACKERS

36 CRACKERS
You will need 1 or 2 large baking sheets and 1 or 2 flat, shallow pans.

May be made up to a week ahead.

Serve warm or cold.

Hal Sands, creator of 8 mouth-watering varieties of commercial chutney, gave us this unusual recipe. A master in the kitchen and a superb host, he also, as a U.S. Air Force officer, originated a vegetable farm near Cairo during World War II that fed 35,000 ears of sweet corn daily to U.S. airmen of nearby airfields!

Assemble and prepare all ingredients.

SODA CRACKERS *36, about*
  2 inches square
CANNED BEEF BROTH
  1¾ cup (1 can, 13¾-
  ounce size): add a little
  water, if necessary, to
  make the correct amount
MELTED BUTTER *About ⅓*
  cup, plus extra for butter-
  ing baking sheets
SEASONINGS *Choose one*
  or several of the
  following:
  CELERY SEEDS
  POPPY SEEDS
  CARAWAY SEEDS
  SESAME SEEDS
  POWDERED GARLIC
  DRIED DILL WEED
  DEHYDRATED ONION
    FLAKES COMBINED
    WITH DRIED SUMMER
    SAVORY LEAVES *Soak*
    onions in water to
    soften: drain before
    mixing with a little of
    the summer savory

1. Preheat the oven to 250 degrees and butter 1 or 2 large baking sheets.

2. In 1 or 2 large, flat, shallow pans with a raised edge, place the crackers side by side in a single layer about ½ inch apart. They will swell as they marinate.

3. Pour the beef broth over them, distributing it evenly, to wet each cracker thoroughly. Let them soak 5 minutes or until they absorb all the liquid that they will take.

4. Using a wide, flexible spatula, carefully transfer them, 1 at a time, to the prepared baking sheets, placing them about ½ inch apart. If they crack a little, just press the cracked edges together.

5. Sprinkle each cracker with ½ teaspoon of the melted butter, spreading it with the back of the spoon so that the edges are well coated.

6. Sprinkle each evenly with 1 or 2 generous pinches of the seasoning of your choice. Place them on the middle rack of the oven (or middle and upper racks, if using 2 sheets), for about 1½ hours or until they are dry and crisp. Watch them so that they do not brown too deeply. Transfer to a rack to cool.

7. When cool, put them into a well-sealed cookie jar or plastic box. They will keep up to a week.

TO SERVE: Reheat in a very low oven, or serve cold.

BENNE (SESAME) SEED WAFERS

75 TO 100 WAFERS
May be made a day or so in
   advance, then warmed
   and crisped before
   serving.

Or may be frozen, baked,
   or unbaked: if unbaked,
   it is not necessary to
   thaw them before bak-
   ing, but allow a little
   more oven time.

Serve warm.

———————

ALL-PURPOSE FLOUR
   *⅓ cup, unsifted, plus a
   little more for rolling*
ICE WATER *5 tablespoons,
   plus 1 tablespoon more
   if necessary*
MARIE'S MAGIC BASIC
   PASTRY MIX (*page
   299*) *2 cups, stir before
   measuring*
BENNE (SESAME) SEEDS
   1 cup
CAYENNE PEPPER *⅛ tea-
   spoon*
COARSE SALT

*Adapted from an old Charleston "receipt."
This recipe will make more wafers than
you will probably need for 1 party. But
they freeze so beautifully you might as
well make the full recipe and have some
on hand for another time. They are delicious served alone or with cocktails or
beer and a cheese spread.*

Assemble and prepare all ingredients.

1. In a small cup, mix the ⅓ cup of
flour with 5 tablespoons of the water to
form a smooth paste.

2. Put the Basic Pastry Mix into a large
bowl. Make a hole in the center and add
the flour-and-water paste. Blend with the
fingers or a fork until the pastry can be
formed into a ball. If necessary, sprinkle
up to 1 tablespoon more ice water on the
driest parts, but no more. It should hold
together and be pliable but not sticky.

3. Add the benne seeds and sprinkle
with the cayenne. Using the heel of one
hand, and a kneading motion, work in all
the seeds, distributing them as evenly as
possible. It will take a little time and the
pastry will become quite thick. Don't be
impatient. If the pastry starts to get soft,
chill it in the refrigerator for 15 minutes
before continuing.

4. Put on a lightly floured board or
marble slab and cut in half. Cover and refrigerate 1 part while you roll and cut the
other.

5. Shape half of the dough into a flat ball. Lightly flour the top and roll into a rough-shaped circle, ⅛ inch or less thick. The pastry will be quite stiff, and you may have to press fairly hard. Be sure it is free-moving at all times. If necessary, lift and sprinkle underneath with a little flour.

6. Using a cutter 2½ inches in diameter, cut in rounds. You may have to press hard and turn the cutter a couple of times to cut through the seeds. Save the scraps.

7. Place the rounds about ½ inch apart on an ungreased baking sheet and refrigerate.

8. Repeat the rolling and cutting with the remaining half. If you don't have 2 baking sheets, put the rounds on a large plate in a single layer. A second layer may be put on top of the first if waxed paper is put in between. Refrigerate.

9. Gather the scraps and add them to the scraps from the first cutting. Form into a ball and roll, cut, and refrigerate similarly. At this point the wafers may be frozen if desired.

WHEN READY TO BAKE: 1. Preheat the oven to 300 degrees. Place 1 or 2 baking sheets of wafers at a time on the middle rack of the oven. Bake from 15 to 20 minutes (a little more if frozen), or until they just start to color. Do not let them brown.

2. Remove them from the oven and, while hot, sprinkle them with a little coarse salt. Put on a rack to cool while you bake the remaining wafers. They may be stored, tightly covered, for a day or so, or frozen.

JUST BEFORE SERVING: Put in a very slow oven to warm and crisp.

POPPY SEED CRACKETS

ABOUT 80 CRACKETS

After baking, may be stored in an airtight container for up to a week, or may be frozen.

Serve warm or at room temperature.

***

ALL-PURPOSE FLOUR
To make 2¼ cups when sifted, plus a little extra for flouring the board
WHEAT GERM *⅔ cup*
SALT *1 teaspoon*
WHOLE POPPY SEEDS
2 tablespoons
BUTTER OR MARGARINE
1 cup (2 sticks), softened to room temperature
CREAMED COTTAGE
CHEESE *1 cup*

Lilo, our German housekeeper in Stuttgart, who was a happy, giggly 50, always served "crackets" because she couldn't say "crackers." So now we do, too—a "cracket" sounds more appropriately crisp somehow.

Assemble all ingredients.

1. In a large bowl, combine the 2¼ cups of flour, the wheat germ, salt, and poppy seeds. Stir well to blend.

2. Add the butter and cottage cheese. Using a pastry blender or 2 knives, scissors-fashion, cut together until well combined. Little bits of cottage cheese will show.

3. Divide the pastry in 2 parts and form each into a flattened ball, about 1 inch thick. Wrap each in waxed paper and refrigerate for about 1 hour.

4. Lightly flour a pastry board or marble slab. Taking 1 of the balls, give it several whacks with a rolling pin to get a circle started. Roll to a little less than ⅛ inch thick.

5. Using a 2½-inch cookie cutter, cut in circles and place them on 1 or 2 ungreased baking sheets, about ½ inch apart. Press the trimmings together and roll and cut as many as you can. Prick each cracket all over with a fork and refrigerate while you roll and cut the remaining half of the pastry in the same manner.

6. When ready to bake, preheat the oven to 425 degrees. Place on the middle rack of the oven. Bake, 1 batch at a time unless you have a double oven, for 15 minutes, or until lightly browned. Remove from the oven and cool on racks.

7. The crackets may be stored in an airtight container for up to a week, or may be frozen. Before serving, rewarm in a 250-degree oven for a few minutes to crisp. Serve them with cheese as a snack.

HERB BREAD

24 SLICES

May be prepared hours ahead.

Bake just before serving.

Serve hot.

_____

BUTTER *1 cup (2 sticks), softened to room temperature*

BASIL, PREFERABLY FRESH *To make ⅓ cup chopped, if fresh, or, if dried, 2 tablespoons, crumbled*

PARSLEY *To make ¾ cup when minced*

CHIVES *To make ¾ cup when snipped*

FRENCH BREAD 2 *loaves,*

Assemble and prepare all ingredients.

1. Put the butter, basil, parsley, and chives into a small bowl. Mash and mix to blend thoroughly.

2. Spread each cut side of the bread with a quarter of the mixture. Reserve, lightly covered, for several hours or bake at once.

TO BAKE AND SERVE: 1. Just before serving, preheat the oven to 450 degrees.

2. Put the bread on a baking sheet and bake it on the middle rack for 10 minutes or until it is heated through.

3. Cut each half loaf into 6 slices and serve at once.

*each cut in half length-
wise*

12 LOAVES, 8 INCHES IN
DIAMETER

Serve within a day of
making, or freeze.

ACTIVE YEAST 2 *packages*
WATER ½ *cup warmed to
105 to 115 degrees*
SUGAR ¼ *teaspoon*
ALL-PURPOSE FLOUR
  *6 cups, plus 1 to 1½
  cups more for kneading
  and rolling*
OLIVE OIL 3 *tablespoons,
  plus a little more for
  oiling the bowl*
SALT 1 *tablespoon*
WARM WATER 2 *cups*
CORN MEAL FOR BAKING
  SHEETS

PITTA BREAD

*Just once, make your own. It is fun and
satisfying and the bread is really delicious.
If we aren't right,* next *time buy it!*

Assemble and prepare all ingredients.

1. In a small bowl, mix the yeast, ½
cup of warm water, and the sugar. Stir until the yeast is thoroughly dissolved. Set
aside.

2. Put the 6 cups of flour into a large
bowl and add the 3 tablespoons of olive
oil, the salt, and the 2 cups of warm water.
Beat well and vigorously with a wooden
spoon or with the dough hook of an electric mixer.

3. Add the yeast mixture and again
beat very well. The dough will be soft
and sticky.

4. Turn it out onto a well-floured
board and knead for about 10 minutes,
adding more of the remaining flour until
the dough is no longer sticky, and is
smooth, satiny, and elastic.

5. Oil a large bowl and put the dough
into it, turning to oil it all over. Cover
with a towel, put it in a warm place, and
let it rise until doubled in volume or until
a dent remains in the dough when it is
lightly pressed to the depth of ½ inch.
This will take about 1½ to 2 hours.

6. Turn the dough out onto a floured

board, knead it a little to flatten it, and form it into a ball. Cover with a towel and let it rest for 10 minutes.

7. Cut the dough into quarters and each quarter into 3 equal parts. Form each piece into a ball. Cover with a towel and let them rest 10 minutes more.

8. Sprinkle the board lightly with flour. Roll each ball into a circle 6 inches in diameter and ¼ inch thick. Cover and let rise at room temperature for 30 minutes.

9. In the meantime preheat the oven to 500 degrees and prepare 1 or 2 baking sheets by sprinkling 1 tablespoon of corn meal on each.

10. Put 2 circles of dough on each sheet. Put 1 sheet on the lowest rack of the oven and bake *without opening the door* for 5 minutes. Reserve the other sheet. The bread will puff up like small balloons. Then transfer them to the top rack and continue baking for 3 minutes or so more, or until they are very lightly brown on top but not hard. Remove from the baking sheet and put them on a rack to cool.

11. Repeat with the second baking sheet. When the first sheet is cold (this is important; put it under cold water for quicker cooling), prepare it with another tablespoon of corn meal and put 2 more circles on it.

12. Repeat until all are baked. They will flatten as they cool, but when cut will form pockets to be filled with good things, page 166.

NOTE: The bread may be used immediately or may be set aside in plastic bags to keep it soft for up to 1 day; or it may be frozen. To serve warm, reheat in sealed foil in a 350-degree oven for 10 to 15 minutes.

ABOUT PHYLLO PASTRY SHEETS

Phyllo pastry sheets are those incredibly flaky, tissue-thin sheets of dough that are so delightful to bite into when buttered, filled with good things, and baked. Everyone loves them.

They can be bought fresh at most Greek or Mediterranean grocery stores, and in some specialty food shops. Frozen, they can be stored indefinitely. They are available in 1-pound and ½-pound packages. The 1-pound package contains 20 to 24 sheets. either 12 by 18 inches, or 17 by 14 inches, depending upon the manufacturer. If frozen, remove from the outer carton but not from the plastic bag; put in the refrigerator and defrost slowly for a day or overnight before using.

Using *phyllo* sheets is easy if you remember 2 things:

1. Use just 1 sheet at a time and keep the sheets not being used covered, first with waxed paper and then with a damp kitchen towel. They will dry out at the wink of an eye as soon as they hit the air.

2. The other absolute *must* is butter and plenty of it. Melt it and brush it generously on each sheet as you use it, covering the entire surface. We use a 2- or 3-inch paintbrush—very handy.

PANIC PARAGRAPH: If some of the sheets won't separate, use 2 or 3 layers and extra butter. The resulting pastry won't be as flaky, but it will taste just as good. Don't be upset if a sheet tears, it will probably be covered up with the next sheet or turn, or it can be patched with a piece of *phyllo,* cut oversized to fit, and fastened on with butter. Don't be afraid to patch and don't throw any away. It's all delicious.

RADISH ROSES

Choose very firm radishes and wash them well. Holding the root end up, and using a small, sharp knife, cut off the root. Then, starting from this point, make 4 or 5 slices to two thirds the length of the radish, cutting the red part away from the white part so as to form petals. Trim off most of the green stem. Put in ice water for at least an hour, or until ready to serve. Drain before serving.

GUACAMOLE

2 CUPS

May be made several hours in advance if tightly covered.

Serve cold.

—————

FIRM, RIPE AVOCADO
1 large or 3 small (each about 4 inches long) to make about 1⅔ cups when cut in dice: see text for preparation
ONION *To make ½ cup when chopped fine*
GARLIC SALT *¼ teaspoon*
FRESH LEMON JUICE
½ to 1 tablespoon
TABASCO SAUCE *3 or 4 dashes*
DIJON MUSTARD *1 teaspoon*

Assemble and prepare all ingredients.

1. Peel the avocado, cut in half, remove the seed and reserve it. Discard any dark bits or fibers clinging to the flesh. Slice the flesh into pieces about 1 inch square. Then mash roughly with a fork, but leave it lumpy. The texture is far more pleasant, as well as authentic, if the avocado is not mashed smooth.

2. Add the onion, garlic salt, lemon juice—the lesser amount first—Tabasco sauce, mustard, and mayonnaise. Mix thoroughly and gently and taste. We like the flavor a little bit tangy and use the full amount of lemon juice, but season it to your own liking.

3. Add the chopped tomato and salt to taste and mix lightly with a fork. Bury the avocado seed in the center of the mixture. We haven't been able to find out why, but our Mexican friends insist that the seed adds flavor or something!

4. If not to be served immediately,

MAYONNAISE, PREFER-
ABLY HOMEMADE
(*page 296*) *1 table-
spoon*

FIRM, RIPE TOMATO
*1, about 3 inches in
diameter, to make ¾
cup when coarse-
chopped: first core, peel,
and cut in half crosswise,
then gently squeeze and
shake to remove the
seeds and juice*

SALT

prevent the Guacamole from darkening by covering it tightly with plastic wrap. Press the wrap against the surface of the Guacamole so that none is exposed to the air. Refrigerate until ready to use.

Appendix A

*First-Course Recipes That May Be
Used as Late-Evening Snacks*

Brandade of Salted Cod
Caviar Pie
Cheese Pie with Phyllo Pastry
Cold Poached Fish with Aïoli Sauce
Crabmeat Mornay
Crêpes with Crabmeat and Avocado
Fettuccine con Pesto
Gazpacho

Gnocchi Mornay
Jane's Cream of Chicken Soup
Lentil Salad
Spiced Red Onion Rings (in sand-
wiches)
Tabbouleh
A Tray of Pupus

Appendix B

Late-Evening Snack Recipes That May Be Used as First Courses

Artichoke Frittata
Bagna Cauda
Baked Sardines with Walnuts
Black Bean Soup with Rum
Blue Cheese Pie
Chicken-Curry Deem Sum
Chilled Cheddar Cheese Cream
Croque Monsieur
Don Felipe's Tarascan Soup
German Onion Pie (Zwiebelku-
  chen)
Hard-Cooked Eggs in Tapénade
Hoisin Chicken Wings

Lake Chapala Fish Market Pâté
MacDougall's Scotch Eggs
Mexican Grilled Cheese with Gua-
  camole
Mystery Savory
Pâté de Campagne
Provincial Onion Soup
Quiche Provençale
Royal Cheese Mousse
Shrimp Toast
Stuffed Eggs in Soubise Sauce
Stuffed Lettuce Leaves
A Tapa Bar

Appendix C

Recipes That May Be Used as Main Courses for a Late or Hearty Breakfast

Artichoke Frittata
Baked Eggs and Sausages with Cheddar Cakes
Cheese Pie with Phyllo Pastry
Chicken Livers on Croûtes
Crabmeat Mornay
Crêpes with Crabmeat and Avocado
Farmer's Breakfast (Bauernfrühstück)
Gateau de Six Omelettes
German Onion Pie (Zwiebelkuchen)
Ham and Bananas in Crêpes

Hangtown Fry
Joe's Special
Kedgeree
MacDougall's Scotch Eggs
Oven Puff Pancake
Quiche Provençale
Scandinavian Fish Pudding with Shrimp Sauce
Souffléed Toasts
Steamed Shrimp Rolls
Stuffed Eggs in Soubise Sauce
Stuffed Eggs on Pâté

Appendix D

Recipes That May Be Used as Main Courses for a Luncheon or Light Supper

Artichoke Frittata
Baked Sardines with Walnuts
Brazilian Sardine Pudding
Cheese in Captivity
Cheese Pie with Phyllo Pastry
Chicken Livers on Croûtes
Chicken Salad in Puffs
Chupe—a Seafood Casserole
Cold Meat with Anchovy Sauce
Cold Poached Fish with Aïoli Sauce
Cold Swedish Salmon Mousse
Crabmeat Mornay
Crabmeat Tostadas
Crêpes with Crabmeat and Avocado
Croque Monsieur
Curried Egg Mousse with Curried Toast
Fettuccine con Pesto
Gateau de Six Omelettes

German Onion Pie (Zwiebelkuchen)
Gnocchi Mornay
A Greek Salad
Hangtown Fry
Ham and Bananas in Crêpes
Jambalaya
Joe's Special
Kedgeree
Lake Chapala Fish Market Pâté
Moctezuma's Pie
Nevin's Fondue
Oven Puff Pancakes
Oyster Loaf with Ish's Beer Batter
Pâté de Campagne
Peggy's Salad
Pitta Bread with a Choice of Fillings
Provincial Onion Soup
Pupusas

Quiche Provençale
Reuben Sandwiches
Roulade of Sole
Salade Russe
Scallops Florentine
Scandinavian Fish Pudding with Shrimp Sauce
Shrimp in Marinade, Veracruz Style
Shrimp on a Velvet Cloud
Skewered Bread and Cheese (Spiedini alla Romano)
Souffléed Toasts
Spring Torte
Steak Tartare
Steamed Shrimp Rolls
Stuffed Eggs in Soubise Sauce
Stuffed Eggs on Pâté
Stuffed Pasta Shells
Stuffed Shrimp
Swedish Pancakes with a Choice of Fillings
Tomato and Avocado Pie

Appendix E

Recipes That May Be Used as Main Courses for a Dinner

"Bones"
Brazilian Sardine Pudding
Chicken and Long Rice
Chupe—a Seafood Casserole
Cold Meat with Anchovy Sauce
Cold Poached Fish with Aïoli Sauce
Crabmeat Mornay
Crêpes with Crabmeat and Avocado
Fettucine con Pesto
A Greek Salad
Ham and Bananas in Crêpes

Jambalaya
Kedgeree
Moctezuma's Pie
Pitta Bread with Beef-on-Skewers
    Filling
Roulade of Sole
Salade Russe
Scandinavian Fish Pudding with
    Shrimp Sauce
Stuffed Pasta Shells
Stuffed Shrimp

Recipes That May Be Used as Cocktail Party Fare

Anchovy Crescents
Antipasto Misto
Bagna Cauda
Benne Seed Wafers
Blue Cheese Pie, with crackers
Brandade of Salted Cod, with toast points
Cafe Mystique, as a "nightcap"
Caviar Pie, with toast rounds
Ceviche
Cheddar Cakes
Cheese Flowers
Chicken-Curry Deem Sum, made in bite-size pieces
Croque Monsieur, cut in small pieces
Guacamole, with corn chips or fried tortillas
Hoisin Chicken Wings

Marinated Carrots
Marinated Green Peppers and Black Olives
Marinated Kielbasa
Marinated Oysters in Dill Sauce
Marinated Soda Crackers
Mexican Grilled Cheese with Guacamole
Mystery Savory, with toast points
Nevin's Fondue
Onions Monaco
Pâté de Campagne, cut in small pieces
Pissaladière, cut in quarters
Poppy Seed Crackets
Ropa Vieja, with tortillas
Roquefort Shortbread
Royal Cheese Mousse, with bread rounds

Shrimp in Marinade, Veracruz Style

Shrimp Toast, each triangle cut in half

Spiced Red Onion Rings, with buttered French bread

Steak Tartare, with bread or toast

Stuffed Lettuce Leaves

Swedish Pancakes with a Choice of Fillings

A Tapa Bar

Taramasalata, with crackers

Tiny Cheese Puffs

A Tray of Pupus

Vegetables à la Grecque

Index

Charlotte Getleson McNamara, an art director by profession, has been associated in that capacity with many publications, including *Bride's* magazine, *True Story,* and *Glamour.* Now retired and living in Chapala, Mexico, she devotes her life to cooking, a long-time passion, entertaining, and collecting cookbooks—2400 to date.

Lenore Price Howell, who spent more than twenty years as a member of the Women's Army Corps, has lived, traveled, cooked, and collected recipes around the United States and throughout the world. Since her retirement with the rank of lieutenant colonel, she and her husband have divided their time between San Diego, California, and Mexico.